DEATH AND DYING - WHO DECIDES?

The President's Commission for the Study of Ethical Problems in Medicine and Biomedical and Behavioral Research was the source of the first major government study on death. Two portions of the Commission's report, *Defining Death* and *Deciding to Forego Life-Sustaining Treatment* (1981, WDC) set the standards for medical and bioethical decisions.

The U.S. Department of Health and Human Services is the primary source of health statistics. The agency publishes the annual *Health United States: 1991* (1992, WDC); and its Centers for Disease Control publishes health data in both the *Monthly Vital Statistics Report* and the *Morbidity and Mortality Weekly Reports*. The Health Care Financing Administration, an agency of the of Health and Human Services, in its quarterly *Health Care Financing Review* reports on the nation's health care expenses. The United States Bureau of the Census publishes demographic information.

The Hastings Center's bimonthly magazine, the *Hastings Center Report* is an excellent source of nonpartisan research in medical bioethics. The Park Ridge Center (Chicago, IL) has examined faith and ethics in their 1991 publication, *Active Euthanasia, Religion, and the Public Debate*. Information Plus thanks them for their kind permission to reproduce quotes.

The Hemlock Society, the National Right to Life Committee, the National Hospice Association, and the National Conference of Catholic Bishops all publish position papers on the right to die and euthanasia. Choice in Dying (formerly Concern for Dying and the Society for the Right to Die) supplies information on living wills and advance directives.

The *Journal of the American Medical Association* (Chicago IL) and the *New England Journal of Medicine* (Boston, MA) frequently publish articles that deal with life support, medical ethics, and medical care expenses. The Brookings Institution and the Rand Corporation have both investigated the expense of medical care. The Brookings Institution (WDC) has published *Serious and Unstable Condition: Financing America's Health Care* (Henry Aaron, 1991) and *Rationing America's Medical Care: The Oregon Plan and Beyond* (Martin A. Strosberg, et al. eds., 1992). The Rand Corporation of Santa Monica, CA has released a monograph, "Will We Need to Ration Effective Health Care?" (Robert Brook and Kathleen Lohr, 1991).

Humana Press of New Jersey was most helpful in making available an advance copy of David Cundiff's forthcoming book, *Euthanasia is Not the Answer*. For a sociological history of death, Philippe Ariès' *The Hour of Our Death* (1981, NY: Knopf) is invaluable.

Information Plus would like to thank the Children's Defense Fund, *The Boston Globe*, and the Health Insurance Association of America for permission to reproduce tables. As always, we are grateful to the Roper Organization (the National Opinion Research Center of the University of Chicago, IL) and the Gallup Organization (Princeton, NJ) for their kind permission to reproduce tables from their opinion polls.

INFORMATION PLUS
WYLIE, TEXAS 75098

EDITORS:
ALISON LANDES, B.A.
CORNELIA B. CESSNA, B.S., M.A.
CAROL D. FOSTER, B.A., M.L.S.

CHAPTER I

DEATH — HOW AND WHEN DO WE DIE?: A HISTORY

It is not a question of dying earlier or later, but of dying well or ill.
And dying well means escape from the danger of living ill. Seneca

Death is sometimes a punishment, often a gift, to many it has been a favor. Seneca

Men die but once, and the opportunity
Of a noble death is not an everyday fortune:
It is a gift which noble spirits pray for.
Charles Lamb

There is a remedy for everything but death, which will be sure to lay
us out flat some time or other. Cervantes

Everyone is born and everyone dies — it is what all of mankind has in common — and yet how each person dies is unique to that person. Over the centuries attitudes towards death have changed, largely in response to changes in religious philosophy and medical care.

THE MIDDLE AGES*

In the early Middle Ages, death came for many, not as a surprise, but as an expected, even welcomed event. Warnings of approaching death were common for a dying man in the tenth century. (Today these premonitions would probably be interpreted as medical indications.) An inscription from 1151 tells how a religious man "saw death standing beside him and knew that he was about to die." He made his will, confessed his sins, went to church to receive the sacrament, and died there.

Even soldiers dying on the field of battle had warning. In the *Chanson de Roland*, a medieval epic poem, Oliver confessed his sins out loud and no sooner did he finish that "his heart failed, and he fell on the ground. The count died without further delay." There was no reason to delay because death, according to Christian theology, gave access to eternal life, while birth into the harsh physical world of the Middle Ages was seen as the real death. When Sir Galahad, in the poems of the *Round Table*, had his vision of the Holy Grail he cried out, "Lord, I thank you for granting my desire! I see now the beginning and end of all things. And now, I beseech you to allow me to pass from this terrestrial life to the celestial one."

In the later Middle Ages, men were not afraid that their lives were ending, but they were afraid of the final judgement brought by the hour of death.

---

* Much of the historical information in this chapter is based on, *The Hour of Our Death*, by French historian, Philippe Ariès (1981, New York: Alfred A. Knopf).

Death was a public spectacle with family and friends gathered around the death-bed. It was believed, at the moment of death, that the spectators were joined by the supernatural beings representing heaven and hell. Philippe Ariès cites an analysis of the art of the period by Alberto Tenenti which found "around his [the dying Christian's] bed a relentless struggle is being waged between the hordes of hell on the one side and the legions of heaven on the other." Death was the final ordeal described in this manner by the Italian monk, Savonarola, "Man, the devil plays chess with you, and he does his utmost to capture and checkmate you at this point. Hold yourself in readiness, therefore, and think well on this point, because if you win here, you will win all the rest, but if you lose, all that you have done before will be worthless."

THE RENAISSANCE

In the Renaissance, attitudes towards death changed again. How one lived one's life determined one's death and after-life. It was no longer possible to bargain between the forces of heaven and hell at the death-bed. Life had to be lived as though death might come at any moment. If a person lived his or her life well, a sudden death was a blessing, sending that person to eternal bliss; if one lived one's life badly, redemption at the last moment would no longer be possible. This was a significant change from the forewarned death of the Middle Ages. Religious teachings, which placed the emphasis on living life in preparation for death, made the actual moment of death much less important than the person's manner of life.

By the end of the seventeenth century, doctors, rather than the clergy, became the spokesmen for the dead. A quasi-scientific approach to death and the dead body prevailed. Doctors and the public began to believe that the dead body continued to live in some way as long as the flesh was preserved. A murdered body reportedly would bleed profusely if the murderer was brought into the presence of the body; bodies moved after death, including pressing the hand of a loved one; and bodies cried out from their graves. In 1708, Christian Friedrich Garmann, a German Lutheran doctor, in *De miraculis mortuorum* (Concerning the miracles of the dead), chronicled the reports of bodies responding after death.

THE EIGHTEENTH AND NINETEENTH CENTURIES

In the Baroque period (1600 to 1750) the fascination with death took on a macabre and sexual aspect. People were fascinated by tortured martyrs and the erotic sufferings of the damned. Death became a form of sexual release, leading, in the eighteenth century, to necrophilia (loving dead bodies). Lovers had their dead disinterred for one last embrace. In one "true" story reported by a surgeon in a book published in 1740, a young man made love to the corpse of a woman he loved. The dead girl came back to life after the man left and gave birth to his child nine months later. The doctor's interpretation was that the sexual act brought the young woman back to life.

The boundaries between life and death became more and more blurred, and by the nineteenth century there was a spreading panic of being buried alive. This was a fear that had long existed, reaching its zenith in the Victorian era. In 1740, Jean-Jacques Winslow proposed in *The Uncertainty of the Signs of Death and the Danger of Precipitate Internments* that putrefaction was the only sure sign of death. Wills frequently specified a list of precautions including instructions not to bury the body right away, or to post a guard to watch it overnight, or that the body not be touched. A will written in 1690 stated, "that I be left for twice twenty-four hours in the same bed in which I shall die, and buried in the same clothes without being touched or handled in any way."

The uncertainty about death was aggravated by the attitude of the medical profession. A medical dictionary from the early nineteenth century stated that it was not seemly for a doctor to associate with a dead person. If the doctor could not save a man's life, the doctor would rather leave the house, leav-

3

ing the determination of death to individuals who had no knowledge of human anatomy. In Germany the first "funeral homes" were actually repositories where bodies could be kept under observation until the onset of decomposition. The arms of the bodies were attached to bells which rang at any unexpected movement. These homes were called "shelters for doubtful life."

THE ROMANTIC DEATH

In the mid-nineteenth century, death became romantic. People frequently slipped into death with the "attractively" flushed cheeks of consumption. Doctors cared for patients, but there was no expectation of a cure. Death was inevitable, bringing with it the eternal repose from illness and the reunion of the dying person with all those who had already passed on. The Brontë family's devastation by tuberculosis prompted both Emily and Charlotte to incorporate this vision of romantic death into their writing. In *Wuthering Heights*, Emily Brontë described Edgar Linton's death:

> He died blissfully . . . Kissing her [his daughter, Catherine's] cheek , he murmured — 'I am going to her [his wife] and you, darling child, shall come to us'; and never stirred or spoke again, but continued that rapt, radiant gaze, till his pulse imperceptibly stopped, and his soul departed. None could have noticed the exact minute of his death, it was so entirely without a struggle.

THE AMERICAN ATTITUDE

In the United States the early record of death was recorded in letters to family members left behind as the settlers moved Westward. A brother was informed of his mother's triumphant death, "I feel gratified to inform you that she left the wourld in the triumfs of faith, in her dying moments Jesse and myself Sung a Cupple of favorite hyms and She slapt her hands and shouted give glory to god and retained her senses while she had breath. Which gave us all a great deel of Satisfaction to See her happy." Educated Americans subscribed to the romantic view of death, and books were published with such titles as *Agnes and the Key of Her Little Coffin* (1870), *Stepping Heaven-ward* (1869), and *The Empty Crib* (1873). Mark Twain mocked this obsession with death in *Huckleberry Finn*. His character, Miss Grangerford, who was destined to die young, thought only of death. She passed the time writing poetry and painting pictures based on the subject and collected obituaries. "She could write about anything you choose to give her to write about, just so it was sadful. Every time a man died, or a woman died, or a child died, she would be on hand with her 'tribute' before he was cold." Huck offered his own tribute to her at her death, "Everybody was sorry she died . . . But I reckoned that with her disposition, she was having a better time in the graveyard."

Death was so common for newborn American settlers that they often were not named for their first year and their baptism was delayed. Lists of family members from oldest to youngest ended with "anonymous" or "unnamed" for the children who were under a year of age. High infant death rates were common in all traditional societies, not just in the United States. Until modern medicine led parents to expect that all their children would survive, parents did not make strong emotional attachments to newborn infants because so many of them would die in their first years of life.

SPIRITUALISM

The church taught that the soul was separate from the body and that the soul was eternal. People reasoned that if the soul lived on, it could perhaps communicate with those who were still living. Many people took the concept seriously and made scientific studies of the phenomenon. In 1852, Edward White Benson, who became Anglican archbishop of Westminster, started the Ghost Society to analyze supranormal phenomena.

Dying persons were reported to be especially close to those who had already passed on and could hear the dead calling to them. Today, those who have had near-death experiences also report hearing or seeing close family members who speak to them from the "other side."

THE TWENTIETH CENTURY

Attitudes towards death changed rapidly in the twentieth century as a result of the tremendous advances in medicine. Hiding the approaching death for as long as possible from the patient, which many think of as contemporary behavior, actually began in the second half of the nineteenth century. Doctors and families thought it was too stressful for the patient to know there was no hope. The family no longer gathered by the bedside for fear of alarming the patient, and the priest was not summoned to perform the last rites until the patient had lost consciousness or had already died. The clergy protested administering to cadavers, causing Vatican II to change the traditional name of "Extreme Unction" (anointing with oil) to the "anointing of the sick" so that the priest could come at any time during a serious illness. Families sacrificed final words of farewell and love because any conversation dealing with impending death were banned. Philippe Ariès (author of *The Hour of Our Death*) compared the death of Tolstoi's Ivan Ilyich (*The Death of Ivan Ilyich*) in 1880, "This lie [hiding impending death from Ivan] that degraded the formidable and solemn act of his death," and the death of a priest in intensive care in France almost a century later, "They are cheating me out of my own death!"

Hospital Death

The mid-twentieth century brought death out of the home and into the hospital, further removing the dying person from his family and spirituality. The image of the dying person became a patient in a sterile hospital room with tubes attached to virtually every orifice of the body. Death was no longer a naturally occurring separation of the soul from the body. It had come under the control of the doctor who could manipulate the time and length of dying with medical technology.

The medical profession, however, saw death as a failure, and doctors frequently chose to avoid dealing with a patient who would soon die. As a result, patients were, and still are, often heavily medicated, permitting them to slip away, unknowing, the complete opposite of the medieval period when men and women prepared themselves, made their peace, and then welcomed death. By 1985, an estimated 80 percent of those who died, did so in a hospital or a nursing home under the care of strangers. These strangers have been taught that their job is to fend off death, furthermore, they often perform their duties under the growing fear that if every effort is not made to postpone death, they have failed and they will be sued for malpractice or for a "mercy killing."

In 1969, Elizabeth Kübler-Ross published *On Death and Dying*, a book which had a profound influence on bringing some dignity and openness to the subject of death. Today death is often discussed with seriously ill or aging patients, physicians and other health care workers are receiving training to deal with death, and hospice care is taking death out of the hospital and bringing it back to the home or to less sterile surroundings. Reports of near-death experiences have also helped to alleviate some of the fear of the unknown. Persons who have been declared dead and then revived through medical intervention frequently report having had a mystical experience of seeing a white light and feeling an overwhelming, enveloping peace they had never known before.

As people take death back into their own control, will they demand the right to die when they feel they are ready? The right to die is becoming an increasingly controversial issue. As more people insist that the right to die is a personal liberty, either to be exercised by the individual or surrogates who claim that right for mentally incompetent patients and seriously ill newborns, those who feel strongly about preserving life at all costs rally together to fight planned suicides, disconnecting life support systems and other efforts to end lives.

CHAPTER II

DEFINING DEATH

Traditionally, death occurred when a person permanently ceased breathing and his or her heart stopped beating. This is no longer the case, however, because since World War II (1945) technology has permitted doctors to artificially maintain these bodily functions, sometimes for years, without any hope that the person will spontaneously regain consciousness or control. The traditional "beating heart" can no longer serve as a standard of life when, for example, technology permits a person to be alive (albeit only briefly) with no heart in his or her body during a transplant operation or when a person with no brain activity can have a machine forcing air into the lungs, which in turn, permits the heart to continue pumping.

In 1980, the President's Commission for the Study of Ethical Problems in Medicine and Biomedical and Behavioral Research was asked through Public Law 95-622 to study the definition of death and the medical and legal implications of that definition. The results of the study were published in *Defining Death: Medical, Legal and Ethical Issues in the Determination of Death* (1981, WDC: Government Printing Office).

THE ROLE OF THE BRAIN

The Commission based its report on the brain's role in determining life. Today, physicians better understand the functioning of the brain and its role in sustaining life. As a result, the definition of death has shifted away from heart/lung activity to a measure of brain activity in both the upper brain, the cerebrum, which controls thought, feeling, and conscious behavior, and the brain stem, the portion of the brain that controls automatic behavior such as breathing, yawning, and sleeping. (See Figure 2.1.)

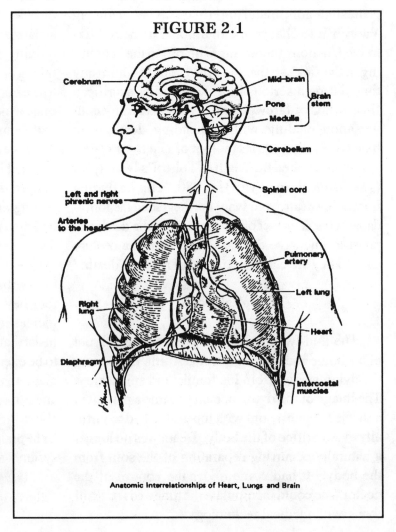

FIGURE 2.1

Anatomic Interrelationships of Heart, Lungs and Brain

The Heart-Lung Connection

The interaction of the heart, lungs, and brain are required for life; machines can support some of the necessary activity to technically keep a patient alive when the body itself has failed. Respiration is controlled by the brain stem, sending messages to the intercostal (between the ribs) muscles, causing the lungs to fill with air. This in turn provides the heart with necessary oxygen. An undamaged heart can continue to beat without brain activity as long as respiration is maintained. There is still no way, however, to maintain a non-functioning heart except for a very short time with a heart-lung machine which is used during surgery. Therefore, when a heart stops supplying oxygen to the brain, death will inevitably follow.

The Brain

Damage to the brain can inflict a wide variety of disabilities. When the total brain loses all function, consciousness is lost and life can be maintained by the brain stem only with the help of intensive medical intervention. Maintaining respiration is effective only for a few days, however, after which the heart will stop. Children can be maintained in this condition for several weeks. Less severe damage to the brain can affect only the upper brain, destroying all thinking processes, but leaving the brain stem intact. When this occurs the patient is in what is called a "persistent vegetative state" (PVS). PVS patients may make involuntary movements such as rolling their eyes or yawning and they may be capable of breathing without a respirator, however, they have no awareness of self or their environment. Karen Ann Quinlan was the most well-known example of someone in a persistent vegetative state. With constant nursing care, a patient can remain in this state for years — the longest survivor lasted 37 years in this condition.

The Commission differentiated between the cessation of the whole brain and patients who still have a functioning brain stem. Patients with intact brain stems breathe, metabolize, maintain temperature and blood pressure. They yawn, sigh, track light with their eyes, and react to pain. To state it simply to a layman, a patient with a functioning brain stem would not be considered dead.

Although patients in a persistent vegetative state appear alive, they have raised questions about what it means to be alive. PVS patients are clearly not dead, and yet they live in a twilight state with no human interaction, a state from which they will never emerge. Is the high emotional and financial cost of maintaining someone with no consciousness worthwhile? Do we have the right to withhold nutrition from someone in this condition so that he or she will die? (See Chapter IV.)

THE WHOLE BRAIN DEFINITION

The Harvard Criteria

In 1968, the Ad Hoc Committee of the Harvard Medical School published a landmark report ("A Definition of Irreversible Coma," vol. 205, *The Journal of the American Medical Association*) which "define[d] irreversible coma as a new criterion for death." The Harvard criteria included unreceptivity and unresponsitivity, no movements or breathing, and no reflexes — a condition they called "irreversible coma." Although no one who fits the above description has ever regained brain function despite being maintained on a respirator, the definition was criticized on several grounds. First, the phrase "irreversible coma" was misleading since "coma" is a condition of a living person and a body without any brain function is dead and thus beyond coma; second, the criteria did not take into account that the spinal cord reflexes can return after the brain has ceased functioning; third, "unreceptivity" cannot be tested in an unresponsive body; and fourth, the criteria given to ensure that the patient was not in a coma due to apnea (temporary cessation of respiration) or drug intoxication were not precise enough.

The President's Commission Definition

The President's Commission for the Study of Ethical Problems in Medicine and Biomedical and

Behavioral Research modified the Harvard criteria and defined death as "the cessation of the vital function of the entire brain — and not merely a portion thereof, such as those responsible for cognitive functions — as the only proper neurologic basis for declaring death." The Commission determined that it was important to define brain death as including the whole brain for several reasons. Aside from legal liability, it is vital that physicians do all possible on the slight chance that a comatose patient might recover consciousness; that a definition of death be established to regulate organ donations; and in order to set standards in the face of the increasingly pressing problems of the allocation of scarce medical and financial resources that are expended on patients in a vegetative state that might be better spent on patients with reversible conditions. (See Chapter VIII.)

In the Commission's whole brain definition of death, the brain is the key to life rather than either heartbeat or respiration. A person's heart and lungs are not basic to life in and of themselves, but rather because "the irreversible cessation of their functions shows that the brain had ceased functioning." The brain is the regulator and integrator of the whole body and when it no longer functions, the person is unquestionably dead.

PERSONHOOD

As machines prolong life and nutrition can maintain PVS patients for years, more people are choosing to define death as a reflection of what life is. They understand that technology can measure total brain death; but if only the upper brain is dead, is a machine-maintained existence considered life? This is a personal judgment, one that cannot necessarily be regulated by medicine or legal statutes. Dr. John Fletcher, an ethicist at the University of Virginia, thinks that "the death of the higher brain is the death of what makes us human." He has put a clause in his living will (a directive for the cessation of medical care in the event of certain

physical conditions — see Chapter VI) that if he ever lapses into a persistent vegetative state and loses his ability to use his mind, he wants to be declared dead so that his organs can be donated to others. Dr. Fletcher is not alone in desiring a change in the definition of death. There are 5,000 to 10,000 people a year who enter a persistent vegetative state* — for many, a state worse than death.

Doctors believe recovery is not possible after a certain amount of time in a persistent vegetative state. After three months, the chances are minuscule, and after six months to a year, virtually nonexistent. There are no recorded cases of a patient regaining any functions after two years in a vegetative state. Dr. Cranford, a neurologist, points out that despite the hopeless situation, it is very difficult to label a person in a vegetative state as dead. "It is pretty horrifying and psychologically jarring, to say the least, to look at someone whose eyes are open and say they are dead." (The question of when and whether to forego life-sustaining treatment is further discussed in Chapters III and IV.)

The President's Commission did not accept the reasoning that the loss of consciousness equalled death and, in agreement with the American Bar Association, the American Medical Association, and the National Conference of Commissioners on Uniform State Laws, proposed the following model statute to define death:

> An individual who has sustained either (1) irreversible cessation of circulatory and respiratory functions, or (2) irreversible cessation of all functions of the entire brain, including the brain stem, is dead. A determination of death must be made in accordance with accepted medical standards.

---

*The estimates of how many people are in a persistent vegetative state vary from 5,000 to 25,000 patients, depending on the source.

In addition, the Commission provided a statement of currently accepted medical standards. The criteria that physicians should use in determining that death has occurred should

1. Eliminate errors in classifying a living individual as dead,
2. Allow as few errors as possible in classifying a dead body as alive,
3. Allow a determination to be made without unreasonable delay,
4. Be adaptable to a variety of clinical situations, and
5. Be explicit and accessible to verification.

The criteria (without the medical details) included:

A. An individual with irreversible cessation of circulatory and respiratory functions is dead.

1. Cessation is recognized by an appropriate clinical examination.

B. An individual with irreversible cessation of all function of the entire brain, including the brain stem, is dead.

1. Cessation is recognized when evaluation discloses finding of a and b:
   a. cerebral functions are absent, and
   b. brain stem functions are absent.

2. Irreversibility is recognized when evaluation discloses findings of a and b and c:
   a. The cause of coma is established and is sufficient to account for the loss of brain functions, and
   b. the possibility of recovery of any brain functions is excluded, and
   c. the cessation of all brain functions persists for an appropriate period of observation and/or trial of therapy.

The guidelines concluded with additional warnings about the complicating conditions which can mimic death, including drug and metabolic intoxication, hypothermia (when the body's core temperature drops below 32.2° C), children's brains which have increased resistance to damage than do adults, and patients in shock.

CHAPTER III

THE RIGHT TO DIE:
MORAL CONSIDERATIONS

There is a time to live and a time to die. Ecclesiastes 3:2

Nobly to die were better than to save one's life. Æschylus

*Just as I choose a ship to sail in or a house to live in, so I
choose a death for my passage from life. . . . Nowhere should
we indulge the soul more than in dying. . . . A man's life
should satisfy other people as well, his death only himself,
and whatever sort he likes best.* Seneca

Whether or not hopelessly ill patients (or their representatives) have a right to choose the manner of their death is an increasingly controversial issue. At one extreme, the Hemlock Society advocates assisted suicide if life becomes more painful than death. At the other end, vitalists believe in preserving all life and equate mercy killing with Nazi death policies.

In ancient Greece it was common practice to abandon or kill infants who were, as Plutarch observed, "ill suited from birth for health and vigor." In *The Republic,* Plato recommended suicide as a remedy for unbearable pain. Among the ancient Greeks and Romans, voluntary euthanasia, especially for the aged and the ill, was sanctioned by, among others, Pythagoras, Seneca, Cicero, and Pliny the Younger. In Indian society it was once customary to drown old people in the Ganges River and, in ancient Sardinia, sons killed their elderly fathers.

RELIGIOUS TEACHINGS

Judaism, Islam, and Christianity support the sanctity of life and generally do not support euthanasia (mercy killing). Life is bestowed by God and only God has the right to take it away. Prolonging the life of someone who is near death, however, is a more complicated issue, and fine distinctions have been drawn by all three religions.

Catholicism

In the fifth century, Augustine held that life and its suffering were divinely ordained by God. Suffering was viewed as something Christians could value because God used suffering as path to spiritual maturity and the very fact that Christians suffered proved that they were children of God. The relief to be offered was not removal of the suffering but consolation that transformed the suffering into a positive force in the person's life. In the thirteenth century, St. Thomas Aquinas argued that shortening a person's life was a sin because it denied that person the right to repent.

In Catholicism, the body and soul cannot be separated. When a bodily need is served, the total person benefits and, by extension, so does Jesus. "I was hungry and you fed me, I was thirsty and you gave me drink. . . I assure you, as often as you did it for one of the least of my brothers, you did it to me" (Matthew 25:35, 40). The lesson here is that no individual can stop caring for an ill person, nor does that individual have the right to end a person's life because it would be the symbolic killing of Christ.

From as early as the sixteenth century, Catholicism has not said, however, that life must be maintained above all else. The Church's theology holds that man has an obligation to promote and preserve life in order to grow spiritually and serve God. St. Thomas Aquinas pointed out that the test for whether the pursuit of life is useful is whether it serves the goals of knowing, loving, and serving God. When a person has become so ill that these ends are no longer attainable, it may no longer be necessary to submit to burdensome treatment.

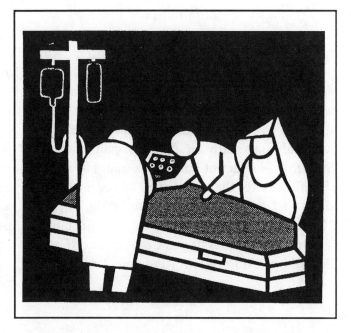

Ordinary and Extraordinary

Traditionally, Catholicism differentiated between "ordinary" and "extraordinary" means of prolonging life. These terms referred to the condition of the patient rather than the medical care. Even the most basic remedy, if it offered no hope of benefit to the patient was considered "extraordinary" and therefore, morally optional. A treatment was "ordinary" if it offered a reasonable hope of improved medical status or quality of life. There are three questions to ask to determine if a means of preserving life should be pursued:

1. Is this means physiologically possible for the patient?

2. Will this means substantially prolong life or relieve useless pain?

3. Will this means, as a means, not significantly add to the burdens of the patient?

If the answer to any of these questions is "no," then the treatment is not obligatory. On the other hand, it does not mean that measures that prolong life should not be used. A seriously ill patient may want to be kept alive for a period of time for personal reasons, perhaps in order to see an absent relative before dying. Catholic moralists warn, however, that these decisions apply only to the *last phase* of terminal illness and not just to the terminally ill.

Irreversible Comas

What is to be done in the case of an irreversibly unconscious patient? Many Catholic theologians today counsel that this patient does not have to be maintained by artificial means, including artificial feeding and hydration (providing water). This is not based on a judgment of the "quality of life" of the comatose patient. Rather, it is based on the judgment that this patient cannot interact and can no longer have a conscious relationship with man or God and is, therefore, in the process of dying.

Kevin O'Rourke, a Dominican priest acknowledged as a theologian who expresses official Catholic teaching, has stated that cognitive-affective function (the ability to understand and influence one's environment) is basic to life. Physiological (the inherent or essential processes of an organism) life, which can be prolonged long after cognitive-affective functioning has been lost, is not a sufficient reason for prolonging life. Furthermore, for a Christian, the purpose of life is the spiritual goal of loving God, and any artificial means that make this useless or burdensome are optional.

Euthanasia

The Catholic Church is very clear that, while prolonging death is not necessary, euthanasia is never permitted. "It is an attack on human life which no one has a right to make or request. . . . It should also be recognized that an apparent plea for death may really be a plea for help and love. Suffering is a fact of human life, and has special significance for the Christian as an opportunity to share in Christ's redemptive suffering," (from "Guidelines for Legislation on Life Sustaining Treatment" by the National Conference of Catholic Bishops Committee for Pro-Life Activities).

Vitalists

Not all Catholics agree with the opinion that life supports can be discontinued. A conservative group of Catholics side with the Right to Life movement in advocating a vitalist position that almost never permits withholding life-sustaining food and water from a patient. William May, et al. in *Issues in Law and Medicine* ("Feeding and Hydrating the Permanently Unconscious and Other Vulnerable Persons," 1987), wrote, "remaining alive is never rightly regarded as a burden . . . in the ordinary circumstances of life in our society today, it is not morally right, nor ought it be legally permissible to withhold or withdraw nutrition and hydration provided by artificial means to the permanently unconscious or other categories of seriously debilitated but nonterminal patients."

Protestant Denominations

There are many Protestant groups in the United States, and their views on euthanasia vary. Many feel that active euthanasia is not acceptable, although prolonging life by extraordinary methods is not necessary. Among those religions who support this view are Seventh Day Adventists, Episcopalians, Jehovah's Witnesses, Church of the Latter Day Saints (Mormon), Mennonites, and some Methodists. The United Methodist Church's General Council adopted a statement in 1980 on "Death with Dignity." It read, in part, "We assert the right of every person to die in dignity, with loving personal care and without efforts to prolong terminal illnesses merely because the technology is available to do so."

There are also many Protestants who support helping a terminal person to die (active euthanasia). Some Methodists approve of euthanasia, although all support alternatives, such as hospice care, as a preferable alternative. Presbyterians advocate the writing of a living will which includes permission for euthanasia if the patient becomes incurable and incompetent. For Presbyterians, the role of the Church is to be an example of care, protection, and nurture while preserving and enhancing human dignity; not to impose values or beliefs.

Unitarians are perhaps the most liberal when it comes to the right to die. ". . . human life has inherent dignity, which may be compromised when life is extended beyond the will or ability of a person to sustain that dignity. . . ." Furthermore, "Unitarian Universalists advocate the right to self-determination in dying, and the release from civil or criminal penalties of those who, under proper safeguards, act to honor the right of terminally ill patients to select the time of their own deaths. . . ."

The United Church of Christ supports the right of persons to chose their own destiny, and "Christian understanding and compassion are appropriate with regard to suicide and euthanasia." The Church is wary of being too concerned with biological life as opposed to spiritual life. It is not the intentional will of God that persons must be tested, and equal regard for both body and spirit is necessary. "Overregard for the body, without proper concern for the needs of the person, or the human spirit, can become a kind of biological idolatry."

Vitalist Protestants

Some other Protestant sects strongly oppose any form of euthanasia. Southern Baptists reject any form of terminating life including designating food and water as "extraordinary care" which can

12

therefore be discontinued (see Chapters IV and VII). Christian Scientists also reject any methods of terminating life as they reject medical intervention in general, because, for Christian Scientists, their faith rests in Jesus' power to cure diseases that are considered incurable.

The Lutheran Church has a strong position on the sacredness of all human life. A resolution adopted in 1977 specifically focused on euthanasia. It stated, in part, "That the Synod [a gathering of church officials] affirm[s] that human life is sacred and finds meaning and purpose in seeking and following God's will, not in self-centered pleasure, a concern for convenience, or a desire for comfort." Furthermore, "the Synod affirm[s] the positive benefits of suffering, so that God's children may be comforted in Christ Jesus and have their sight focused more firmly on eternal values."

The Jewish Point of View

In contemporary United States there are three main branches of Judaism — the Orthodox tradition is the most conservative and observant form of the religion, while Conservative and Reform Judaism are progressively more flexible and more likely to adapt religious teachings to modern life. Orthodox Jews do not believe that Judaism is a religion of personal convenience, and the laws cannot (nor do they need to) be altered to reflect changes in society. The Orthodox remain firm in their vitalist views that life is a gift from God and only God has the right to take it back. It is in the struggle for life that man achieves dignity. In response to the question, "Whose life is it anyway?" the Orthodox Jew would respond, "It is not yours."

Judah HaNasi

No matter how strong and clear Jewish law may be on a subject, there are always fine points to be negotiated. Despite a strong vitalist position, the Talmud, the elaboration of Jewish law beyond the Bible, makes a distinction between the life of the ill person and the person who is truly dying. There is a name for the final stages of death; *goses*, literally,

the death-rattle is in the patient's throat. The Talmud relates a story about life support for a man who is *goses*. The famous rabbi, Judah HaNasi, was dying and all the rabbis gathered to fast and pray for his life. In traditional Judaism, prayer is as powerful as medicine, and the prayers prevented the angels from taking the Rabbi. Judah's handmaiden had pity on the Rabbi's suffering, and she went up to the roof to pray for her master. At first she prayed that the mortals would keep him alive, but then she remembered his suffering and prayed that the angels would prevail. The handmaid picked up a clay pitcher and threw it to the ground. When it shattered, the rabbis were momentarily distracted from their prayer, giving Judah's soul a chance to depart. The Talmud approved this solution to the dilemma because it in no way hastened the Rabbi's death but it removed an external impediment.

More Liberal Judaism

Reform and Conservative Jews are generally more open to accepting the termination of life supports than are Orthodox Jews. Although death cannot be hastened, one may allow death to come unhindered. Conservative Rabbi Seymour Siegel has said, "We must not forget in our loyalty to tradition the welfare of the suffering patient who, when the giver of life has proclaimed the end of his earthly existence, should be allowed to die in spite of our machines."

What Are the Limits?

If a hindrance to natural death that is extraneous or outside the patient can be removed, does this include a respirator and feeding tubes or only factors strictly outside the body such as the prayers for Rabbi Judah? Rabbis do not agree. Some feel that the withdrawal of any influence which artificially delays the death of a patient is permitted. Others insist that this is only the case when the patient is *goses*, while others broadly state that prolonging life is required, but prolonging death is not. However, a Jewish scholar elaborates, "human life is not regarded as a goal to be preserved for

TABLE 3.1
Trends in Death Rates (1920–1989)

Death rates and causes	1920	1940	1960	1980	1987	1988	1989
Death rates (per 100,000 population)	1,298.9	1,076.4	954.7	874.1	872.4	883	868.1
Major causes of death							
Pneumonia and influenza	207.3	70.3	37.3	23.2	28.4	31.5	30.3
Diseases of the heart	159.6	292.5	369.0	335.9	312.4	312.2	296.3
Tuberculosis	113.1	45.9	6.1	*	*	0.8	0.7
Cerebrovascular diseases	93.0	90.9	108.0	75.0	61.6	61.1	59.4
Malignant neoplasms	83.4	120.3	149.2	182.4	195.9	198.6	200.3
Accidents	71.0	73.6	52.3	46.9	39.0	39.7	38.2
Infant mortality (per 1,000 live births)	NA	47.0	26.0	12.5	10.1	9.9	9.7
Maternal mortality (per 100,000 live births)	NA	376.0	37.1	6.9	6.6	0.1	0.1

*Not listed as a major cause of death.

Source: Reprinted from the *Sourcebook of Health Insurance Data 1991*

the sake of other values, but as an absolute basic good. Neither technological complexity nor financial expense should be spared where prolongation of *life* or *potential cure* is deemed possible" (emphasis added).

The Islamic View of Life and Death

Islam views death as a stage in human existence. When life as we know it comes to end, human existence moves to another level which precedes Judgment Day and eternal life. The Qur'an states (2:28), "How do you disbelieve in God seeing you were dead and He gave you life and then He shall cause you to die, then He shall give you life, then unto Him you shall be returned." In the Islamic tradition, if you have lived a righteous life, heaven awaits you — only those who have lived a life of sin need to fear death.

Islamic scriptures prohibit suicide. Life is a gift from God and the prophet Muhammad says, ". . . whoso takes poison and thus kills himself, his poison will be in his hand; he will be tasting it in Hell, always abiding therein. . . . " The patient, therefore, does not have the right to choose death, nor does the family. A patient's suffering is not a valid reason for terminating life-sustaining measures, and families are prohibited from praying for death to end a patient's suffering. Islam, however, warns against letting the means to prolong life become the objective. In a case of brain death,

treatments are not going to bring back recovery; prolonging futile treatment contradicts the principle of *Saddu al Dhara'a*, that is, preventing the means from becoming an end, and is therefore immoral. Furthermore, Islam feels that if an action hurts society, it should not be done. In medicine this means that, because artificial methods for maintaining severely brain-damaged patients require a great deal of time from the medical staff and family and have a high financial cost, the treatment is not in the public interest and can be stopped.

The Islamic Court

To determine whether life support can be terminated, the case should be brought before an Islamic court. Medical professionals (two or more) should clarify the condition of the patient and his or her chances of recovery. The court must also take into account the financial and emotional burden placed on the family since the family's support is essential in treating these patients. The court must not be swayed, however, by emotional appeals by the family to end life simply to end suffering. The court must also balance the demands imposed on the Islamic state and the burdens of extending a patient's life has on the financial resources of that state. The primary duty of the Islamic court is to ensure the safety and welfare of the entire Islamic state above that of an individual. Use of the Islamic court avoids the delays of the United States court system and the media involvement which can cloud the issue. A decision by the Islamic court is final.

CAUSES OF DEATH

Over the past century, the leading causes of death have changed. At the turn of the century, influenza and pneumonia were the most common causes of death, both sudden and swift. Today, heart disease, cancer, and cerebrovascular disease (strokes) are the main killers. In 1920, 207 out of every 100,000 persons died of pneumonia and influenza. In 1987, only 28 out of every 100,000 died of these two illnesses. Deaths from cancer have gone from 83 out of 100,000 in 1920 to 200 out of 100,000 in 1989, while heart disease deaths went from 160 to 296 per 100,000 persons (Table 3.1). Today's top killers are diseases that generally occur in older age and are often progressive over several years. In 1990, approximately one-third of deaths were caused by heart disease, and nearly a quarter were due to malignancies (Table 3.2). In part because of the change in the causes of death and in medical technology, over the past fifty years, the drive to sustain life has often come into conflict with that ancient objective of medicine — the relief of suffering.

TABLE 3.2

Estimated deaths, death rates, and percent of total deaths for the 15 leading causes of death: United States, 1990

[Data are provisional, estimated from a 10-percent sample of deaths. Rates per 100,000 population. Figures may differ from those previously published. Due to rounding, figures may not add to totals. See table 8 for category numbers of causes of death.

Rank	Cause of death (Ninth Revision, International Classification of Diseases, 1975)	Number	Death rate	Percent of total deaths
. . .	All causes	2,162,000	861.9	100.0
1	Diseases of heart	725,010	289.0	33.5
2	Malignant neoplasms, including neoplasms of lymphatic and hematopoietic tissues	506,000	201.7	23.4
3	Cerebrovascular diseases	145,340	57.9	6.7
4	Accidents and adverse effects	93,550	37.3	4.3
. . .	Motor vehicle accidents	47,880	19.1	2.2
. . .	All other accidents and adverse effects	45,680	18.2	2.1
5	Chronic obstructive pulmonary diseases and allied conditions	88,980	35.5	4.1
6	Pneumonia and influenza	78,640	31.3	3.6
7	Diabetes mellitus	48,840	19.5	2.3
8	Suicide	30,780	12.3	1.4
9	Homicide and legal intervention	25,700	10.2	1.2
10	Chronic liver disease and cirrhosis	25,600	10.2	1.2
11	Human immunodeficiency virus infection	24,120	9.6	1.1
12	Nephritis, nephrotic syndrome, and nephrosis	20,860	8.3	1.0
13	Septicemia	19,750	7.9	0.9
14	Certain conditions originating in the perinatal period	17,520	7.0	0.8
15	Atherosclerosis	16,490	6.6	0.8
. . .	All other causes	295,100	117.6	13.6

Source: *Monthly Vital Statistics Report*, Vol. 39, No. 13, National Center for Health Statistics, (WDC, 1991)

THE HIPPOCRATIC OATH

Physicians pledge an oath (medical schools, however, no longer administer the oath at commencement exercises) that originated with Hippocrates which represents their code of ethics. Hippocrates (460 - 377 B.C.) gave Greek medicine its scientific spirit and ethical ideals, separating it from religion, superstition, and magic. The Hippocratic Oath set forth three main principles for doctors: do not breach the confidences of patients, do not have sexual relations with patients, and do not give poison. In part the Oath states,

I will follow that method of treatment which, according to my ability and judgment, I consider for the benefit of my patients, and abstain from whatever is deleterious and mischievous. I will give no deadly medicine to anyone if asked, nor suggest any such counsel . . . With purity and with holiness I will pass my life and practice my art.

The Declaration of Geneva, adopted by the General Assembly of the World Medical Association in 1948, was an adaptation of Hippocrates' Oath which reads in part,

I will practice my profession with conscience and dignity; the health of my patient will be my first consideration. . . . I will not permit consideration of religion, nationality, race, party politics, or social standing to intervene between my duty and my patient; I will maintain the utmost respect for human life from the time of conception; even under threat, I will not use my medical knowledge contrary to the laws of humanity.

The oath, on the one hand, prohibits giving poison (euthanasia), but on the other, vows to give treatments that benefit patients and to abstain from anything deleterious, a requirement that can be interpreted as a call not to prolong dying with needless treatment.

EUTHANASIA

Euthanasia, also known as mercy killing, is the practice of ending life in order to give release from incurable suffering or disease. The word comes from the Greek for an "easy death." Euthanasia, technically, refers to helping patients end their own life and does not apply to stopping life-sustaining treatments that are preventing death from occurring. The difference is often blurred, however, especially by those who oppose any action that hastens death. This chapter is focused on whether or not to forego life supports. For a full discussion of euthanasia see Chapter V.

CONTROL OVER DEATH

Patients today realize that the time and manner of their death is substantially under the control of the medical profession, and they must balance their interests between too quick a death or too prolonged and needlessly painful a demise. Although what is considered "too short" or "too long" varies for each patient and the individual circumstances, the President's Commission for the Study of Ethical Problems in Medicine and Biomedical and Behavioral Research (see also Chapter II for their definition of death) set forth what they considered appropriate guidelines.

In the early 1980s, the President's Commission felt obliged to study the question of foregoing life sustaining treatment, although it was not part of the original legislative mandate. During the hearings for the study on the definition of death, it became clear that many people were troubled about what the proper care should be for patients who were hopelessly ill. The study's conclusions were published in *Deciding to Forego Life-Sustaining Treatment* (1983, WDC: Government Printing Office).

The Commission warned against what it termed, "meaningless code words" like "death with dignity." Death is often messy, and the ideal of a peaceful, aesthetically pleasing death is not always possible. "Terminal illness" can also be a misused term because predicting death is accurate only in the last few hours, not the final months or weeks. Medicare has defined "terminally ill" as patients who have six months or fewer to live. However, a study of patients with advanced cancer found that only 16 percent of the doctors' estimates of remaining life were accurate within one month (plus or minus) of death (Yates, et al., 1982, "A Comparative Study of Home Nursing Care of Patients with Advanced Cancer," proceedings of the Third National Conference on Human Values of Cancer, New York: American Cancer Society). Generally the doctors underestimated their patients' ability to survive.

The Slippery Slope

In the debate on whether or not to prolong life, vitalists frequently argue that it is wrong to make any exceptions because they will lead to a relaxation of standards beyond moral bounds. The Commission warned against falling into this "slippery slope" trap. The slippery slope theory argues against taking a first step along a path that might lead to unintended harm because no specific stopping point exists. For example, if it is acceptable to end a life under circumstance "A," why is it not also acceptable to do it under circumstance "B," and who will determine where to draw the line? On the other hand, all problems have a range of possible answers, and if the first step is never taken, no distinctions can be drawn and social policy cannot be made. Nevertheless, in the case of human life, the Commission advocated being especially cautious.

Decision Making

Most patients whose conditions require life-sustaining treatment want it and benefit from it. For some patients, however, treatment is more burdensome than beneficial and will not sustain life for a long enough time to be worthwhile. To choose to refuse treatment is usually a difficult decision and must be based on each individual's values and goals. Not all patients are capable of making an informed decision. A patient must be mentally stable, have developed personal values, have an ability to communicate and understand information adequately, and have an ability to reason and consider the choices.

Patients and their families are dependent on the information they receive from caregivers and must be aware of the influence and power that medical professionals have. Ill persons often become helpless and needy, allowing the physician to shape the outcome of a patient's treatment through the doctor's own values and the information he or she provides. Three surveys taken between 1953 and 1961 found that 69 to 90 percent of physicians did not inform their patients of a cancer diagnosis, claiming that the truth would be too much for the patients to bear.

Today this attitude is considered patronizing and has mostly vanished in the United States. A 1978 survey found that 97 percent of physicians preferred to inform their patients of a cancer diagnosis. The Commission's survey of doctors and patients (1982, "Views of Informed Consent and Decisionmaking: Parallel Surveys of Physicians and the Public," WDC: Louis Harris and Assoc.) found that 96 percent of the public would want to know of a cancer diagnosis and 86 percent said they wanted a realistic prognosis.

Traditional Moral Distinctions

The competent patient bases a decision to treat or not to treat on how much time it will add to his or her life, the nature of that life, whether it will permit a goal to be achieved (seeing the birth of a grandchild, for instance), the suffering involved, the financial cost, and personal values. Bioethical discussions of the issue often see the factors in terms of opposites: acting or not acting, beginning or stopping therapy, giving pain medication that might hasten death versus pain medication that will kill, and "ordinary" and "extraordinary" care. The President's Commission published their conclu-

sions on these distinctions in order to offer guidance to public policy makers who, in erring on the side of caution, might prevent patients and providers from choosing certain valid options.

• Although not all decisions to omit treatment and allow death to occur are acceptable, such a choice, when made by a patient or surrogate, is usually morally acceptable and in compliance with the law on homicide; conversely, active steps to end life, such as by administering a poison, are likely to be serious moral and legal wrongs. Nonetheless, the mere difference between acts and omissions — which is often hard to draw in any case — never by itself determines what is morally acceptable. Rather, the acceptability of particular actions or omissions turns on other morally significant considerations, such as the balance of harms and benefits likely to be achieved, the duties owed by others to a dying person, the risks imposed on others in acting or refraining, and the certainty of outcome.

• The distinction between failing to initiate and stopping therapy — that is, withholding versus withdrawing treatment — is not itself of moral importance. A justification that is adequate for not commencing a treatment is also sufficient for ceasing it. Moreover, erecting a higher requirement for cessation might unjustifiably discourage vigorous initial attempts to treat seriously ill patients that sometimes succeed.

• A distinction is sometimes drawn between giving a pain-relieving medication that will probably have the unintended consequence of hastening a patient's death and giving a poison in order to relieve a patient's suffering by killing the patient. The first is generally acceptable while the latter is against the law. Actions that lead to death must be justified by benefits to the patient that are expected to exceed the negative consequences and ordinarily must be within the person's socially accepted authority.

• Whether care is "ordinary" or "extraordinary" should not determine whether a patient must accept or may decline it. The terms have come to be used in conflicting and confusing ways, reflecting variously such aspects as the usualness, complexity, invasiveness, artificiality, expense, or availability of care. If used in their historic sense, however — to signify whether the burdens a treatment imposes on a patient are or are not disproportionate to its benefits — the terms denote useful concepts. To avoid misunderstanding, public discussion should focus on the underlying reasons for or against a therapy rather than on a simple categorization as "ordinary" or "extraordinary."

The terms "extraordinary" and "ordinary" have their roots in religion and were used to define what treatments were obligatory and which were optional. Originally the terms were applied to the patient and not the treatment — what would be ordinary care for one patient and will help that patient recover from an acute problem can be extraordinary for a patient who is beyond medical hope. Unfortunately the terms have been used to apply to specific medical treatments such as the use of respirators. For a doctor, using a respirator is an everyday occurrence; for a family of a seriously ill patient, seeing a hole made in the patient's trachea and having a tube inserted so that a machine can do the patient's breathing is extraordinary. The Commission concluded that the terms have become so misunderstood that in order to make it more clear, medical treatments should be discussed in terms of the benefits and burdens of the care.

SURROGATE DECISIONMAKERS

Children, mentally confused patients, and comatose patients lack the ability to make decisions and need others to express their needs. Family members or close friends are generally the best advocates for an incompetent patient. The Commission warned against interference of the courts in the relationship between the doctor and family. "Since the protected sphere of privacy and autonomy is required for the flourishing of this interpersonal union, institutions and the state should be reluctant to intrude, particularly regarding matters that are personal and on which there is a wide range of opinion in society."

Nancy Cruzan

As the Supreme Court has become more conservative and those with vitalists positions have become increasingly influential, families' judgments are sometimes being questioned, and surrogates who wish to terminate treatments are, in some hospitals, being overruled. The Supreme Court ruling in *Cruzan* (58 LW 4917, see also Chapter VII) questioned the validity of the surrogate's right to decide for incompetent patients. Nancy Cruzan had lain in a persistent vegetative state since a car accident in 1983. Her parents asked to discontinue nutrition in order to let her die, a request the hospital refused to honor unless so ordered by the court. The case reached the Supreme Court in 1990. The Court refused the Cruzan's request ruling that although the Fourteenth Amendment guaranteed the right to refuse medical treatment, Nancy had not made clear enough her wishes not to be maintained on life support. The Supreme Court upheld a standard of requiring clear, written evidence from the patient in the form of a living will or an advance directive as proof of intention before life supports could be terminated. Nancy had done neither — her parents had only the reports of casual conversations in which she had clearly expressed the desire to never be kept alive as a "vegetable." In December 1990, the Missouri court reversed the decision when new evidence of Nancy's wishes came to light, and Nancy's feeding tube was withdrawn, leading to her death.

Differing Opinions

Opponents to the Supreme Court decision claim that the Court is jeopardizing the entire surrogate tradition. Most people do not have a living will, and if that standard is upheld, the opinion of a surrogate would become meaningless. People's feelings about death are generally not expressed in legal contracts, but in emotional statements made in conversation. When the courts refuse to acknowledge these feelings, they are ignoring the human consequences of those wishes, and they are treating the patient as little more than words that were or were not written. Furthermore, when the majority opinion wrote in the state court decision in *Cruzan v. Harmon* (Mo.760 S.W.2d, 408), the court "choose[s] to err on the side of life, respecting the rights of incompetent persons who may wish to live despite a severely diminished quality of life," they deny not only the wishes of the patient, but they cast doubt on the loving relationships of a family to act in the best interests of the patient.

In *Cruzan*, the Court distinguished between the initiation of treatment and its discontinuation. The insertion of Nancy's gastrostomy tube was invasive, but continued feedings were not, therefore they were permissible. In making treatment withdrawal nearly impossible (behavior sanctioned under certain circumstances by all major religions and medical associations), the court will make it harder for families to agree to initiate treatment if they know that if it fails, it can not be discontinued. Opponents find that this logic is neither rational nor compassionate in futile cases.

Those who side with the High Court argue that because Nancy could not foresee her present circumstances and make an informed decision, any comments that she made in conversation do not necessarily apply and must be discounted. Since she can no longer express her present desires, it is safer to continue life than not. When nature has deprived a patient of the capacity to choose, the Constitutional right of privacy cannot be assigned to someone else. A patient's autonomy cannot be passed on to a stand-in in the same way that a person's right to vote cannot be passed on to another.

Vitalists are adamantly opposed to making decisions based on the quality of a person's life. The New York Court of Appeals has agreed with this, stating that "no person or court should substitute its judgment as to what would be an acceptable quality of life for another" (*Delio v. Westchester County Medical Center*, 516 N.Y.S. 2d 677). For those who believe in the overriding sanctity of life, the Court did not make a decision just for Nancy, but for the approximately 10,000 people in a persistent vegetative state, the 1.5 million with severe dementia, and (on the slippery slope) the 7.5 million mentally retarded persons.

CHAPTER IV

THE RIGHT TO DIE:
MEDICAL CONDITIONS

PERMANENTLY UNCONSCIOUS PATIENTS

A person's consciousness has two dimensions: arousal and cognitive awareness of arousal. Arousal is a vegetative state that is controlled by the brain stem, while self-awareness and adaptability is controlled by the upper brain. Persons with overwhelming damage to the cerebral cortex pass into a chronic state of unconsciousness. When this state lasts for more than a few weeks, the condition is termed persistent vegetative state (PVS). Although there is no accurate count of how many cases of PVS exist in the United States, estimates put the number at approximately 15,000 to 25,000 persons.*

PVS patients are characterized by chronic wakefulness without awareness. They open their eyes and dart glances around the room, they smile, and make unintelligible noises or screams. On examination, these movements and responses are random and not purposeful responses to stimulus. Whether or not a PVS patient will regain consciousness depends on how old the patient is, the type of brain injury, and how long the coma has persisted. Patients under 40 years of age have a better chance of regaining responsiveness as do patients who have suffered brain trauma or hemorrhage than do those who have suffered a loss of oxygen to the brain (asphyxial injuries).

With the exception of children (there is not enough data to be specific), few patients who have suffered asphyxial injuries recover after one month, and virtually none recover after three months. If a patient does regain some awareness, recovery will not be complete and there will be severe disabilities. It is possible for patients under 40 years old who have suffered head injuries to show some measure of cognition by three to six months, and decisions to terminate treatment should be delayed until after that time. In "Persistent Vegetative State and the Decision to Withdraw or Withhold Life Support," the Council on Scientific Affairs and Council on Ethical and Judicial Affairs of the American Medical Association (1990, vol. 263, no. 3, *Journal of the American Medical Association*, Chicago, IL), calculated that if the handful of reported recoveries of patients with PVS were divided by the number of total estimated cases, the odds of recovery would be less than one in one thousand.

Nonetheless, miracle recoveries do occur. In a 1991 issue of "Life at Risk" (a newsletter opposing euthanasia), the National Conference of Catholic Bishops cited three persons who regained consciousness. The longest comatose period occurred in a 17 year-old who had suffered head injuries and regained the ability to walk and talk after seven months of coma. The other two were comatose for three months and 19 days, respectively.

---

*The estimates of how many people are in persistent vegetative state vary from 5,000 to 25,000 patients, depending on the source.

The Council on Scientific Affairs and Council on Ethical and Judicial Affairs (hereafter referred to as the Council) suspects that some of the "miracle recoveries" are actually cases of "locked-in syndrome" that have been misdiagnosed. A locked-in patient suffers an interruption of the neural impulses from the brain to the body. Paralysis is the cause of unresponsiveness, not coma. Some of these patients can communicate through eye-blinks, but some have lost partial to total awareness. Positron emission tomography (a relatively new technology which measures the positive antiparticle of an electron, not available at all hospitals) can distinguish between a locked-in patient and PVS, while the standard diagnostic tool, an electroencephalogram (EEG — a measure of electrical brain activity), is not always reliable.

Care for PVS Patients

Patients in a persistent vegetative state (PVS) have raised questions about where these patients exist in the continuum between life and death, the reliability of the diagnosis of permanent coma, and what care should be given to a PVS patient. (See Chapter II for a discussion of whether or not being permanently comatose constitutes being alive or not.)

For the family of a permanently unconscious patient, the uncertainty is very stressful. The natural desire to care for the patient in the hope that he or she will awaken is often supported by medical professionals who have been trained to preserve life. In addition, society as a whole has an interest in promoting the value of human life as a standard of behavior, as do patients who are less seriously ill who may benefit from vigorous care and research on brain damage. On the other hand, comatose patients require intensive care, absorbing scarce resources of time and money which many feel could be put to better use caring for patients with a greater hope of recovery.

Comatose patients sometimes need to be supported with respirators, and all require artificial feeding either through tubes inserted through the nose and into the stomach (nasogastric), or a tube inserted directly into the stomach (gastrostomy), or through intravenous feedings. Families usually initially want a patient to be fed, but if the coma persists and there appears to be no hope of recovery, whether to remove the feeding tube or not becomes a difficult issue. To choose to starve someone to death is not an easy decision, even though doctors state that someone without upper brain activity cannot feel hunger or pain. The Council has stated that "it is not unethical to discontinue all means of life prolonging medical treatment" for patients in irreversible comas, including hydration and nutrition.

PVS and Exile

Lawrence Schneiderman, Director of Medical Ethics at the University of California, San Diego, in, "Exile and PVS" (May-June 1990, *Hastings Center Report*, Briarcliff Manor, N.Y.) writes that PVS should actually be labelled a "persistent medicative state" and wonders why doctors permit so many patients to continue in this condition. Aside from the possibilities of financial self-interest and fear of litigation (being sued), Schneiderman thinks doctors fear they will choose death when it is inappropriate, betraying their Hippocratic oath to preserve life. While doctors agree that a dying patient should be given as much pain medication as necessary to keep the patient comfortable even if it does hasten death, PVS patients are not necessarily dying and they do not feel pain, so what is the justification in hastening their death?

Schneiderman sees the PVS patient as isolated, in effect, in exile, from humanity. Man is a social animal whose connection with family and community defines his or her humanity. In ancient Greece and Rome, exile or death were the punishments for capital crimes. Early Christians used banishment and burning at the stake as the punishment for heresy, equating exile with the most painful death. Shakespeare described banishment as "solemn shades of endless night," an apt description of PVS. According to Schneiderman,

> ... in deliberately prescribing treatments that prolong the lives of patients in a vegetative state, we are causing the *persistent* vegetative state; thus we are unwittingly yet cruelly resurrecting the archaic practice of banishment. Under the name of beneficence, we are ironically condemning them to an existence long recognized by society as equal to, if not worse than, death.

Helen Wanglie

The National Right to Life Committee is deeply troubled by the growing acceptance of turning off life support measures for unconscious but not terminally ill patients. For vitalists, the case of Helen Wanglie is a perfect example of what society has to fear in accepting the premise that an unaware life equals no life. Helen Wanglie broke her hip at age 86 and in the course of treatment suffered respiratory failure. She was placed on a respirator from which she could not be weaned. Six months later she experienced cardio-pulmonary arrest which the doctors felt had left her with severe and irreversible brain damage. The hospital ethics committee recommended that life sustaining treatment be discontinued, but her family refused. Despite understanding that Helen was now in a persistent vegetative state and that her prognosis (her likelihood of recovery) was very bad, her husband agreed to an order not to resuscitate, but not to discontinue life sustaining treatment. Mr. Wanglie felt that only God can take life and the doctors should not play God.

Who Decides?

The hospital staff opposed continued treatment for the patient, but no other facility would accept Helen in her condition. Her medical expenses (covered by insurance) had already reached $800,000. Helen's own wishes were not clear. Initially her husband had said that her views were unknown, but when the hospital went to court, Mr. Wanglie indicated that his wife had always stated that "she did not want anything done to shorten or prematurely take her life." The medical director informed Mr. Wanglie, "We do not believe that the hospital is obliged to provide inappropriate medical treatment that cannot advance a patient's personal interest." The Society of Critical Care Medicine agreed with this position, expressing the mainstream consensus of critical care doctors:

> Treatments that offer no benefit and serve to prolong the dying process should not be employed. In light of a hopeless prognosis, the indefinite maintenance of patients reliably diagnosed as being in a persistent vegetative state (PVS) raises serious ethical concerns both for the dignity of the patient and for the diversion of limited medical and nursing resources from alternative application that could offer medical and nursing benefits to others.

Supporters of ending life support in a case like Helen Wanglie's point out that if the court were to decide in the Wanglies' favor, the court would be establishing an unqualified right to biologic existence, erasing a long tradition of case law supporting conscientious objection to health care (refusing health care on religious grounds). On the other hand, it would also give patients a right to demand health care for reasons other than medical necessity, a potential disaster for health insurance claims.

Do Not Turn Off the Life Support

Supporters of Mr. Wanglie's position argue that cost should not be a factor in deciding to maintain Mrs. Wanglie's respirator. Also, the judgment that her medical treatment is "inappropriate" is itself inappropriate. The question is not whether the respirator will sustain her life, the question is whether or not her life is worth maintaining. This is not a medical question, but a question of values. For doctors to make this decision is presumptuous and ethically inappropriate. To argue that a PVS patient is unable to enjoy any quality of life and should be allowed a "death with dignity" is logically flawed. If the patient is totally unaware, how can he or she benefit from death or be aware of its dignity? The patient's wishes are a better measure of the dignity that should be accorded to him or her. The court decided in favor of continuing the life support.

DO NOT RESUSCITATE

When a patient is terminally ill the question of whether or not to resuscitate (to mechanically force the heart and lungs to function) becomes crucial. Should the doctor perform cardio-pulmonary resuscitation (CPR) and should the decision be discussed with the patient beforehand? The President's Commission concluded that, when possible, a patient's interests should be heeded, although, if it is not possible, then sustaining life must take precedence. Doctors and ethicists, however, frequently differ on this question. Historically, doctors felt that patients could not handle discussions of death and that "Such explanations to the patient. . . are thoughtless to the point of being cruel, unless the patient inquires, which he is extremely unlikely to do" (Steven S. Spencer, 1979, " 'Code or No Code': A Non Legal Opinion," vol. 300, *New England Journal of Medicine*). In 1977, William Ketterer, an attorney for the National Institutes of Health, claimed CPR is different from normal medical treatments because it is an emergency response that if not undertaken will surely allow the patient to die. The patient, being uncon-

scious, cannot agree or refuse treatment, and there is no option for alternative treatment.

Doctors have long considered decisions on resuscitation to be within their domain and based them on their professional expertise. Doctors in hospitals have used secret notations to indicate to the staff whether or not to revive a person in cardiac arrest, and have written "no code" (that is, not to call for assistance to perform CPR) orders in pencil (to be erased after death) on patient records without ever discussing it with the patient or the family. Today, as patients demand more rights of self-determination, this is considered less and less acceptable.

Depending on one's attitude toward prolonging life, some complain that CPR is not being used often enough, while others feel it is overused. Right-to-life advocates protest that too many patients are being "no-coded" to avoid maintaining expensive medical care for terminal patients. Others feel that terminally ill patients are being unnecessarily abused by futile CPR attempts because doctors are afraid of being sued.

Over the past few years, some doctors have become concerned that patient self-determination has led to too many attempts at futile resuscitation. Frequently patients and families express the desire that everything possible be done, requiring hospitals to perform CPR on hopeless patients. Many thousands of patients endure brutal, rib-cracking pounding, large tubes inserted into their lungs, and powerful electric shocks in order to live for perhaps a few more days or not at all. CPR was originally intended to save the lives of basically healthy persons who suffered sudden cardiac failures from accidents such as a drowning. Today, almost no one dies in a hospital without undergoing CPR at some point.

The Patient's Rights

Patients' rights now encourage the patient to have the final say in whether or not they want to be resuscitated. For the hospital, if the patient, or his or her surrogate, has not made a clear choice, the choice must be to attempt resuscitation. If a patient dies suddenly without documentation of DNR ("do not resuscitate") and without CPR, someone will be held accountable. One solution for doctors in a situation when a terminal patient's wishes are not known is the "Hollywood code." Doctors and nurses pull the curtains around the patient's bed and pretend to perform CPR. Advocates of patient's rights claim that excessive CPR could be avoided if doctors would take the time to communicate with their patients and truthfully explain the situation rather than simply thrusting documentation forms at the patient.

Consent

Giles R. Scofield, in "Is Consent Useful When Resuscitation Isn't?" (Nov-Dec 1991, *The Hastings Center Report*, Briarcliff Manor, NY), believes consent is essential. He points out that cardiopulmonary resuscitation has transformed medicine and society's expectations about mortality. CPR defies death by restarting the human heart — the common symbol of life. It has quickly become the standing order against death, not just a tool to be used in an emergency, and presumed consent has become the rule. Doctors have always made private treatment decisions based on their education and experience, and whether or not to use CPR became their responsibility.

Some physicians, while they accept DNR orders (for example whether or not to start a respirator) from their patients, feel that CPR should not be included because it is an emergency measure that traditionally is performed with "presumed consent." Doctors feel that they have the expertise that allows them to determine when CPR is futile. Furthermore, asking the patient to decide is stressful and unnecessary if there is no hope. Scofield points out that these arguments consider only the physician's perspective and ignores the patient's desires to be treated or not.

For Scofield, physicians who claim to be able to recognize that a patient's condition is futile (there is no hope for recovery) is presumptuous. Futility is a judgment, a way of interpreting facts. Furthermore, when the doctor makes a unilateral judgment, he denies the autonomy of the patient. Although the patient may be past being able to express his or her wishes, that does not suddenly permit the doctor to choose what is right without respecting the patient's values. In Scofield's opinion, consent is linked to: "respecting human dignity; promoting rational decisionmaking; encouraging professional self-scrutiny; avoiding deceit and coercion; and educating the public." The patient has personal values, religious beliefs, and plans for dealing with death that she brings to the situation, and consent is an individual decision to which the patient has a right.

Respect for the Patient

Scofield asserts that when doctors view resuscitation as a "presumed consent" because of its emergency nature, they are protecting the autonomy of the medical profession.

> Medicine's professional autonomy — its right to be let alone — rests on a belief in professional expertise that causes individuals and society to surrender to medical authority. . . . Among the most powerful sources of our faith in medicine is the belief that it can "do something" about death. Resuscitation, which transformed our view of medicine and death, symbolizes medicine's power and lies at the crux of its authority.

By not discussing consent with the patient, the doctor is erecting a wall of silence around patients, isolating them "from the human community before death actually takes them from the world. It offers social death and exclusion at the one moment when we most need the consolation of our fellow men and women."

TABLE 4.1

Infant mortality rates, by age and for 10 selected causes of death: United States, 1987–90

Provisional data for 1987–90 are estimated from a 10-percent sample of deaths. Rates per 100,000 live births.

Age and cause of death (Ninth Revision, International Classification of Diseases, 1975)	1990 (prov.)	1989 (prov.)	1988 (prov.)	1988 (final)	1987 (final)
Total, under 1 year.	908.0	973.3	992.9	995.3	1,008.2
Under 28 days	574.7	625.0	641.7	631.5	646.5
28 days to 11 months	333.3	348.3	351.5	363.7	361.8
Certain gastrointestinal diseases 008–009,535,555–558	5.0	5.8	4.4	4.8	5.3
Pneumonia and influenza 480–487	14.1	12.5	14.4	16.4	17.7
Congenital anomalies 740–759	205.2	204.7	207.2	208.2	207.0
Disorders relating to short gestation and unspecified low birth weight 765	95.1	100.1	90.9	83.6	88.0
Birth trauma 767	4.1	4.3	4.6	5.5	6.5
Intrauterine hypoxia and birth asphyxia 768	18.8	19.5	20.3	19.9	20.8
Respiratory distress syndrome 769	59.1	86.6	80.4	81.4	86.2
Other conditions originating in the perinatal period 760–764,766,770–779	232.2	248.0	273.2	271.0	272.9
Sudden infant death syndrome 798.0	129.0	126.4	117.4	140.1	137.3
All other causes . . . . Residual	145.4	165.6	179.7	164.5	166.5

Source: *Monthly Vital Statistics Report*, Vol. 39, No. 13, National Center for Health Statistics, (WDC, 1991)

SERIOUSLY ILL NEWBORNS

The issue of seriously ill newborns is especially hard to discuss in an abstract, theoretical manner. Parents faced with a critically ill infant must make difficult decisions about treatment with no guarantees of the outcome. Between 1970 and 1980 tremendous advances in the field of neonatology (medical care for newborns) were achieved, and the death rate during the first 28 days of life was almost halved (neonatal mortality dropped 57 percent in the years between 1930 and 1970 and 24 percent in the ten years between 1970 and 1980), a gain made mainly in the increased survival of babies with low birth weights. Today babies weighing less than 1000 grams (2.2 pounds) have a good chance of survival compared to fewer than 10 percent of the infants who survived 30 years ago. Ironically, the increased chances of an infant's survival have made the decision of whether or not to treat more difficult than ever. Although an infant may survive, he or she may be left with severe disabilities that will impose a heavy financial and emotional burden on the family and raise questions of the quality of the child's life. In some cases painful and invasive treatments are pursued with no apparent benefit to the child. There is no sure way at the outset to predict which infants will survive and which will not, and if they do, how normal a life they will achieve.

Provisional numbers for 1990 for causes of death in children under one year old reveal that the most common cause is conditions arising during the perinatal period (the late fetal period and the first seven days of life) which include maternal and delivery complications and infections. There were 232 deaths per 100,000 live births in this general category. The second most common cause of death was congenital defects such as anencephalus, spina bifida, abnormalities of different organs, and Down's syndrome (205 per 100,000 live births). Disorders connected to low birth weight and premature delivery caused 95 deaths for every 100,000 live births. (See Table 4.1.)

A study in *Morbidity and Mortality Weekly Reports* of postneonatal (28 to 364 days of age) mortality from 1980 to 1987 (Solomon Iyasu, et al., July 1991, "Surveillance of Postneonatal Mortality, United States, 1980-1987," Waltham MA: *New England Journal of Medicine*) found that the mortality rates from birth defects had the greatest decline — in white babies it dropped from 66.7 per

TABLE 4.2

Postneonatal mortality rates* for birth defects as underlying cause of death, by type of defect and race, United States, 1980-1981 and 1986-1987.

Type of birth defect	White 1980-1981 Rate	%†	White 1986-1987 Rate	%†	% Change per year	Black 1980-1981 Rate	%†	Black 1986-1987 Rate	%†	% Change per year
Cardiovascular	37.2	55.8	29.6	55.4	-3.7	40.3	52.0	37.4	52.7	-1.4
Central nervous system	10.0	15.0	6.5	12.1	-7.2	12.4	16.0	8.0	11.3	-6.3
Chromosomal	7.1	10.6	7.4	13.9	+1.2	8.3	10.7	10.8	15.3	+3.7
Musculoskeletal	2.2	3.3	1.5	2.8	-5.5	2.4	3.1	2.4	3.4	-1.2
Respiratory	1.6	2.4	1.9	3.5	+4.9	2.9	3.7	3.0	4.2	+1.4
Gastrointestinal	3.9	5.9	1.9	3.6	-11.9	5.1	6.6	3.1	4.4	-9.2
Other	4.6	6.9	4.6	8.6	+0.6	6.2	8.0	6.2	8.7	-0.3
Total	66.7	100.0	53.4	100.0	-3.4	77.6	100.0	70.9	100.0	-1.6

*Per 100,000 live births.
†Percentages may not add up to 100 because of rounding.

Source: *Morbidity and Mortality Weekly Report*, "Special Focus on Reproductive Health Surveillance," Centers for Disease Control, (Atlanta, GA, 1991)

100,000 births in 1980-1981 to 53.4 in 1986-1987, while in black infants the rates fell from 77.6 to 70.9 per 100,000 in the same time period. Central nervous system defects (spina bifida, etc.) had the second greatest decline, dropping from 10 to 6.5 per 100,000 white infants and 12.4 to 8.0 per 100,000 black infants. (See Table 4.2.)

The study did find that conditions like low birth weight, which originated in the perinatal period were causing more deaths which were not occurring until the postneonatal period. The postneonatal mortality for these conditions increased about 13 percent for both black and white babies. Other than "ill-defined conditions," "perinatal conditions" was the only cause of death to show an increase between 1980 and 1987. (See Table 4.3.) As medical technology improves, seriously ill newborns are being kept alive for longer periods, delaying their deaths into the postneonatal time period.

Low Birth Weight Babies

Approximately 7 percent of all live births are to low birth weight (LBW) babies (less than 2,500 grams or 5.5 pounds), while 1.3 percent are to very low birth weight babies under 1,500 grams (a little more than three pounds). (See Table 4.4.) The consequences of LBW are sometimes as damaging to the infant as the ill effects of prematurity. LBW babies are threatened by hyaline membrane disease (an inability of the lungs to function) and require oxygen from a mechanical ventilator. The disease

TABLE 4.3

Postneonatal mortality rates,* by race and cause of death, United States, 1980 and 1987

Cause of death	White 1980 Rate	%†	White 1987 Rate	%†	%† change per year	Black 1980 Rate	%†	Black 1987 Rate	%†	%† change per year
Sudden infant death syndrome (SIDS)	118.9	33.8	113.0	36.1	-0.4	257.1	35.6	205.9	33.5	-2.7
Congenital anomalies	68.0	19.4	53.8	17.2	-3.4	79.5	10.9	71.9	11.7	-1.6
Infections	42.3	12.0	31.7	10.1	-4.2	120.2	16.5	86.2	14.0	-4.3
Injuries	31.1	8.9	25.3	8.1	-3.1	66.5	9.1	55.0	9.0	-1.9
Perinatal conditions	19.6	5.6	22.1	7.1	+2.2	48.5	6.7	55.0	9.0	+2.7
Ill-defined conditions	9.2	2.6	15.0	4.8	+4.6	27.3	3.7	40.5	6.6	+3.9
Others	62.2	17.7	51.9	16.6	-1.9	129.9	17.8	99.4	16.2	-2.7
Total	351.7	100.0	312.9	100.0	-1.6	729.3	100.0	614.3	100.0	-2.0

*Per 100,000 live births.
†Percentages may not add up to 100 because of rounding.

Source: *Morbidity and Mortality Weekly Report*, "Special Focus on Reproductive Health Surveillance," Centers for Disease Control, (Atlanta, GA, 1991)

TABLE 4.4

Low birth weight live births, according to race and Hispanic origin of mother: United States, 1970 and 1980–89

[Data are based on the National Vital Statistics System]

Race, and Hispanic origin of mother	1970	1980	1981	1982	1983	1984	1985	1986	1987	1988	1989
					Total number of live births[1]						
All mothers	3,731,386	3,612,258	3,629,238	3,680,537	3,638,933	3,669,141	3,760,561	3,756,547	3,809,394	3,909,510	4,040,958
White	3,109,956	2,936,351	2,947,679	2,984,817	2,946,468	2,967,100	3,037,913	3,019,175	3,043,828	3,102,083	3,192,355
Black	561,992	568,080	564,955	568,506	562,624	568,138	581,824	592,910	611,173	638,562	673,124
American Indian or Alaskan Native	22,264	29,389	29,688	32,436	32,881	33,256	34,037	34,169	35,322	37,088	39,478
Asian or Pacific Islander	27,706	74,355	84,553	93,193	95,713	98,926	104,606	107,797	116,560	129,035	133,075
Chinese	7,044	11,671	12,628	12,552	13,193	14,725	16,405	16,701	17,818	21,322	20,982
Japanese	7,744	7,482	7,589	7,211	7,190	7,625	8,035	7,938	8,054	8,658	8,689
Filipino	8,066	13,968	15,040	15,419	16,413	18,680	20,058	21,237	22,134	23,207	24,585
Other Asian or Pacific Islander[2]	4,852	41,234	49,296	58,011	58,917	57,896	60,108	61,921	68,554	75,848	78,819
Hispanic origin[3,4]	---	307,163	321,954	337,390	336,833	346,986	372,814	389,048	406,153	449,604	532,249
Mexican American	---	215,439	222,143	227,558	221,788	225,767	242,976	246,174	251,189	271,170	327,233
Puerto Rican	---	33,671	33,376	34,108	33,856	34,219	35,147	36,588	38,139	46,232	56,229
Cuban	---	7,163	8,369	9,603	9,709	9,477	10,024	9,924	9,987	10,189	10,842
Central and South American	---	21,268	24,380	28,958	31,043	36,401	40,985	45,026	50,350	57,610	72,443
Other and unknown Hispanic	---	29,622	33,686	37,163	40,437	41,122	43,682	51,336	56,488	64,403	65,502
Non-Hispanic white[3]	---	1,245,221	1,258,739	1,363,237	1,358,303	1,361,814	1,394,729	1,388,251	1,399,129	1,664,239	2,526,367
Non-Hispanic black[3]	---	299,646	298,938	321,508	321,787	325,754	336,029	342,179	355,644	434,843	611,269
Low birth weight (less than 2,500 grams)					Percent of live births						
All mothers	7.93	6.84	6.81	6.75	6.82	6.72	6.75	6.81	6.90	6.93	7.05
White	6.85	5.72	5.69	5.64	5.69	5.61	5.65	5.66	5.70	5.67	5.72
Black	13.90	12.69	12.72	12.61	12.82	12.58	12.65	12.77	12.98	13.26	13.51
American Indian or Alaskan Native	7.97	6.44	6.27	6.06	6.17	6.15	5.86	5.94	6.15	6.00	6.26
Asian or Pacific Islander	8.77	6.68	6.74	6.74	6.57	6.57	6.16	6.47	6.41	6.31	6.51
Chinese	6.67	5.21	5.55	5.26	5.07	5.05	4.98	4.85	5.02	4.63	4.89
Japanese	9.03	6.60	6.22	6.09	6.05	5.91	6.21	6.03	6.49	6.69	6.67
Filipino	10.02	7.40	7.50	7.15	7.28	7.78	6.95	7.42	7.30	7.15	7.35
Other Asian or Pacific Islander[2]	9.36	6.87	6.89	7.03	6.77	6.65	6.22	6.64	6.47	6.48	6.66
Hispanic origin[3,4]	---	6.12	6.12	6.23	6.29	6.15	6.16	6.13	6.24	6.17	6.18
Mexican American	---	5.62	5.61	5.72	5.77	5.68	5.77	5.62	5.74	5.60	5.60
Puerto Rican	---	8.95	9.01	9.11	8.90	8.88	8.69	9.22	9.30	9.42	9.50
Cuban	---	5.62	5.83	5.76	5.65	5.86	6.02	5.46	5.89	5.94	5.77
Central and South American	---	5.76	5.73	5.61	6.20	5.81	5.68	5.69	5.74	5.58	5.81
Other and unknown Hispanic	---	6.96	7.00	7.30	7.23	6.89	6.83	6.87	6.91	6.85	6.74
Non–Hispanic white[3]	---	5.67	5.63	5.62	5.64	5.53	5.60	5.58	5.63	5.62	5.62
Non–Hispanic black[3]	---	12.71	12.79	12.60	12.83	12.54	12.61	12.85	13.10	13.28	13.61
Very low birth weight (less than 1,500 grams)											
All mothers	1.17	1.15	1.16	1.18	1.19	1.19	1.21	1.21	1.24	1.24	1.28
White	.95	.90	.91	.92	.93	.93	.94	.93	.94	.93	.95
Black	2.40	2.48	2.52	2.56	2.60	2.60	2.71	2.73	2.79	2.86	2.95
American Indian or Alaskan Native	.98	.92	.89	1.06	1.07	1.02	1.01	.99	1.13	1.00	1.00
Asian or Pacific Islander	1.17	.92	.93	.91	.88	.93	.85	.86	.83	.84	.90
Chinese	.80	.66	.68	.70	.77	.70	.57	.63	.65	.57	.61
Japanese	1.48	.94	.75	.94	.63	.81	.84	.86	.80	.92	.86
Filipino	1.08	.99	1.03	.89	.98	.97	.86	.87	.94	.91	1.12
Other Asian or Pacific Islander[2]	1.37	.97	.99	.95	.90	.98	.92	.92	.84	.89	.91

See footnotes at end of table.

(Continued)

TABLE 4.4 (Continued)

**Low birth weight live births, according to race and Hispanic origin of mother:
United States, 1970 and 1980–89**

[Data are based on the National Vital Statistics System]

Race, and Hispanic origin of mother	1970	1980	1981	1982	1983	1984	1985	1986	1987	1988	1989
Very low birth weight (less than 1,500 grams)—Con.					Percent of live births						
Hispanic origin[3,4] . . .`.	- - -	.98	.98	.99	1.03	1.01	1.01	1.02	1.06	1.01	1.05
Mexican American .	- - -	.92	.92	.93	.96	.93	.97	.94	.96	.89	.94
Puerto Rican	- - -	1.29	1.43	1.54	1.46	1.49	1.30	1.47	1.63	1.61	1.71
Cuban	- - -	1.02	1.17	.90	.97	1.04	1.18	1.09	.97	1.17	1.13
Central and South American	- - -	.99	.93	.83	.99	1.04	1.01	1.04	1.02	.97	1.05
Other and unknown Hispanic	- - -	1.01	.93	1.03	1.08	1.05	.96	1.08	1.15	1.11	1.04
Non–Hispanic white[3] . .	- - -	.86	.87	.89	.90	.88	.90	.89	.91	.89	.93
Non–Hispanic black[3] . .	- - -	2.46	2.50	2.53	2.57	2.56	2.66	2.68	2.73	2.82	2.97

[1]Includes live births with unknown birth weight.
[2]Includes Hawaiians and part Hawaiians.
[3]Data shown only for States with an Hispanic-origin item on their birth certificates.
[4]Includes mothers of all races.

NOTES: The race groups, white and black, include persons of both Hispanic and non-Hispanic origin. Conversely, persons of Hispanic origin may be of any race.

SOURCE: National Center for Health Statistics: Data computed by the Division of Analysis from data compiled by the Division of Vital Statistics.

can cause complications such as pulmonary and cerebral bleeding, usually resulting in brain damage. The respirator, however, sometimes requires a long-term tracheostomy, the insertion of a tube in the baby's neck which prevents the baby from making any sounds, a physical and psychological burden for the infant. Treatment can also lead to blindness and lung damage. LBW babies require special feeding, usually intravenously because they are unable to swallow or suck and their intestines are unable to absorb nutrients. It is difficult to provide enough nutrition for the infant without overwhelming the kidneys and the heart with the excessive fluids.

Neural Tube Defects

Approximately 4 percent of babies are born with congenital abnormalities. Some abnormalities are genetic, like Tay Sachs disease (an always fatal illness that generally affects children with Eastern European Jewish heritage), or chromosomal, like Down's syndrome, causing mental retardation. Some are caused by drugs or viral infections received by the baby during pregnancy, and some are unknown, probably a complex interaction of genetic and environmental factors. Two types of abnormalities have been especially prominent in discussions of the ethics of neonatal care: neural tube defects (NTDs) and permanent handi-

caps combined with surgically correctable, life-threatening factors (for example, Down's syndrome combined with a defective heart). Defects involving the neural tube (the embryonic version of the spinal cord) mainly cause anencephaly, a condition in which most, or all, of the brain is missing; or spina bifida in which the development of the brain and spinal cord is abnormal, causing physical and mental impairments that can vary widely in severity and may involve many organ systems. Controversy over NTD babies includes how aggressively to treat a baby with spina bifida and what kind of life the child will be able to achieve.

Approximately four out of every 10,000 live births is to a baby with spina bifada, but not anencephaly. A little more than one out of every 10,000 live births is to an anencephalic baby (Table 4.5).

Recently, controversy developed when a Florida couple discovered that they were going to give birth to an anencephalic child. The mother chose to carry the baby to term (late abortions in the United States are performed almost exclusively on women who are carrying babies like this who have no chance of surviving) so that the baby's organs could be used to transplant and save other seriously ill infants. The baby, Theresa Ann, was born with a fully formed face and body, but the top of her

TABLE 4.5

By 1990, the incidence of the two major forms of neural tube defects, anencephaly and spina bifida without anencephaly, should be reduced to 0.60 per 1,000 live births. (In 1979, the rate was 0.90 per 1,000.) (Baseline and objective revised from those originally published.)

| Year | Incidence rate of major neural tube defects | | |
	Total	Anencephaly	Spina bifida without anencephaly
1979	0.90	...	...
1980	0.85	0.33	0.52
1981	0.86	0.35	0.51
1982	0.81	0.33	0.48
1983	0.77	0.30	0.47
1984	0.76	0.26	0.50
1985	0.72	0.27	0.45
1986	0.71	0.26	0.45
1987	0.63	0.20	0.43
1988	0.68	0.31	0.37
1989	0.57	0.17	0.40
1990	0.53	0.11	0.42
1990 objective	0.60	...	...

SOURCE: Data from National Center for Environmental Health and Injury Control, Division of Birth Defects and Developmental Disabilities.

skull was missing, leaving a partially formed brain stem exposed.

Babies like Theresa Ann can feel nothing. Her parents wanted her short life to have a purpose by providing other seriously ill children a chance for life through transplants. For many people, though, using Theresa Ann for organ transplants raises the alarm of "organ harvesting." Some doctors fear that in changing the definition of death to upper brain inactivity (Theresa Ann was born with some brain stem activity), the public could lose trust in the organ donor program and would begin to fear that organs will be removed from persons who are not yet dead.

Dr. John Fletcher, director of the University of Virginia's Center for Biomedical Ethics, disagrees. "There's a refusal to accept the reality of death at work in this. And an overvitalistic understanding of personhood, dependent on biological functions." Dr. Fletcher feels that anencephaly is a unique condition and should be the exception to brain death policy. These infants will not survive for long, and there is no question of them ever gaining any consciousness because the upper brain does not exist. "Slippery slope" proponents fear, however, that exceptions for anencephalic babies will slide over to other NTD infants, and judgments will then be made as to the value of life of spina bifida babies.

Down's Syndrome

Children with Down's syndrome are often born with correctable life-threatening defects like heart abnormalities or gastrointestinal blockages. In the past these babies would have died, but today surgery is able to correct the problems. If parents choose not to treat these defects, they will likely be overruled by the hospital and the baby's fate may end up being decided in court. Unlike a generation ago, when Down's syndrome children were usually institutionalized, today they are usually raised at home. Raising these children with special needs is a challenge, a challenge many parents are willing to meet. Others, however, believe it would be better for the child or themselves if the child died in infancy. Many people, including advocates of the disabled and right-to-lifers, are strongly opposed to this attitude and equate it with the Nazi euthanasia policies which promoted killing the disabled. Unfortunately, the families of the disabled frequently receive inadequate financial and medical help in raising their children. If the family cannot cope, often the only option is to place the child for adoption.

To Treat or Not

In 1982, the Judicial Council of the American Medical Association (Dr. John H. Burkhart, "Opinion of the Judicial Council of the American Medical Association," Chicago: AMA) observed that, "In desperate situations involving newborns, the advice and judgement of the physician should be readily available, but the decision whether to exert maximal efforts to sustain life should be the choice of the parents. . . . Unless there is convincing evidence to the contrary, parental authority should be respected." The President's Commission supported this position, but cautioned that communication between the doctor and the family is not always adequate; that professionals, as well as parents, do not always understand the bases of a decision to treat or not treat; and actions are sometimes taken without informed approval from the family.

The Commission concluded that doctors do not always understand why they choose a path of treatment for a patient. Diana Crane, in "The Sanctity of Social Life: Physicians' Treatment of Critically Ill Patients" (1975, New York: Russell Sage Foundation), found that doctors said they would treat an anencephalic infant, but they could give no reason why other than it was unthinkable not to treat a baby. The doctors reported that babies were put on a respirator simply because the staff could not agree not to do so. Furthermore, the doctors reported that, "Consultation with the family is used in part as a method of ensuring that they will accept the decision and not take legal action against the physician later. It is not considered appropriate for the family to make the final decision."

Many of the therapies undertaken to save the lives of babies will leave the survivors with permanent handicaps either from the underlying defect (a heart abnormality for a Down's syndrome child) or from the treatment itself (blindness from the extended use of a respirator). Should these handicaps be considered in the decision whether or not to treat the infant? The Commission decided that "such permanent handicaps justify a decision not to provide life-sustaining treatment only when they are so severe that continued existence would not be a net benefit to the infant." This strict standard means that the child's life would have to be worse

than death to justify not treating the infant. The Commission pointed out that physical and mental handicaps that an adult would find too burdensome for their child as to offer no benefits arise from the parents' hopes and aspirations for their child. The Commission's standard did not consider the effect an impaired child will have on his or her family and siblings and emphasizes setting realistic goals for an impaired child. The Commission stressed that many severely impaired persons create meaningful lives despite their handicaps.

The Baby Doe Rules

In 1982, an infant was born with Down's syndrome and other complications. Among them, the baby's stomach was connected to the trachea rather than the esophagus, resulting in bile which was eating away the esophagus and even the lungs. The parents and the doctor agreed not to perform surgery, which meant that the child could not be fed and would starve to death. Other physicians in the hospital were disturbed by the decision, and the hospital insisted on taking the case to court. The judge refused to order surgery, as did the higher state court. The baby died before the case could be brought to the Supreme Court. Right-to-life advocates were distressed by the decision and felt more should have been done to protect the baby's life. The case received nationwide attention, attracting the attention of the Reagan Administration.

The White House ordered the Department of Health and Human Services (HHS) to inform all hospitals receiving federal funding that failing to provide nourishment or necessary medical treatment to a "handicapped" newborn would be a violation of Section 504 of the 1973 Rehabilitation Act (PL 93-112). The notice stated,

No otherwise qualified handicapped individual. . . shall, solely by reason of his handicap, be excluded from the participation in, be denied the benefits of, or be subjected to discrimination under any program or activity receiving Federal financial assistance. . . .Under section 504 it is unlawful for a recipient of Federal financial assistance to withhold from a handicapped infant nutritional sustenance or medical or surgical treatment required to correct a life-threatening condition if:

1. the withholding is based on the fact that the infant is handicapped; and

2. the handicap does not render the treatment or nutritional sustenance medically contradindicated.

For example, a recipient may not lawfully decline to treat an operable life-threatening condition in an infant, or refrain from feeding the infant, simply because the infant is believed to be mentally retarded.

In addition, the Reagan administration issued regulations that all hospital delivery rooms and nurseries post warning signs that "Discriminatory Failure to Feed and Care for Handicapped Infants in this Facility Is Prohibited by Federal Law." The signs listed a toll free hotline to take anonymous reports of mistreatment.

In the first three weeks the hotline received more than 500 calls reporting mistreatment from all over the country. When government inspection teams went to verify the claims, they found they were unfounded — some of the babies in question were being treated and others were beyond hope. The American Academy of Pediatrics, the Children's Hospital National Medical Center, and the National Association of Children's Hospitals went to court to have the rules overturned. Judge Gerhard Gesell agreed, saying, in part, that the Administration had failed to show that the regulations would actually improve the medical care of those it claimed to protect. The HHS responded with new regulations that made clear that it did not intend to compel the use of futile treatments in hopeless cases. On October 9, 1984, President Reagan signed the Child Abuse Amendments of 1984 (PL 98-457), a compromise between the demands of the American Academy of Pediatrics and right-to-life organizations. It forbade doctors from withholding nourishment or medically indicated treatments unless the infant were comatose, the treatment would prolong dying, or the treatment would be "futile in terms of the survival of the infant." The quality of the infant's life was not to be considered and the hotline was to be shut down.

The President's Commission understood that the decision to disregard quality of life in deciding whether or not to treat infants often left a legacy of continuing care for the child's lifetime. Unfortunately, the families of these children often feel abandoned by the government and the medical profession once the child is released from the hospital. In an essay included in *Who Speaks for the Child* (Gaylin and Macklin, eds., 1982, New York: Plenum Press), Joseph Goldstein expressed the opinion,

As long as the state offers institutions that provide little more than storage space . . . for medical science's achievements, the law must err on the side of its strong presumption in favor of parental autonomy and family integrity. Thus for the state to do other than *either assume* full responsibility for the treatment, care, and nurture of such children *or honor* the parent's decision to consent to or refuse authorization for treatment would be but to pay cruel and oppressive lip service to notions of human dignity and the right to life.

Many parents who have brought home severely disabled children express their deep love for their babies, but feel bitter at the lack of help they receive from the government and even right-to-life groups who work passionately to save the infants, but are not involved in the living and raising of these children.

The Expense of Home Care

While some families raising a seriously disabled child receive financial support either from private insurance (most private insurance, however, only covers hospitalizations) or from Medicaid, most families get very little, if any, financial help. Medicaid is available to those whose income falls below the poverty level (in 1992 it was $13,950 per year for a family of four), and as of October 1, 1991 it was also available to the medically needy in 41 states. The medically needy are eligible if they earn no more that 133.3 percent of the poverty level for their family size. They are entitled to medical help only, not food stamps or any other government support.

In 1981, the federal government permitted the states to use Medicaid for home care services under the model waiver system included in the Omnibus Budget Reconciliation Act (PL 97-35). Minnesota's model waiver act was approved in 1985 permitting up to 50 children to receive financial support based only on the child's income, not the parents'. Barbara Leonard, et al., in "Providing Access to Home Care for Disabled Children: Minnesota's Medicaid Model Waiver Program," (September-October 1989, *Public Health Reports*, U.S. Department of Health and Human Services), found that the average monthly charges for a ventilator-dependent person ranged from $15,000 to $51,517 in the hospital compared to $389 to $7,425 for home care. Monthly home care costs for technology-dependent persons ranged from $300 to $20,000 with an average of $8,000.

Prior to the 1980s seriously ill children were often institutionalized. Today home care is the rule. The model waiver program was designed to help families cover the high cost of home care, but, in two years in Minnesota, only 24 families qualified for the program. While there are other state programs to help defray medical expenses, the funding limit is generally much lower. Furthermore, there are no realistic options for the children other than either hospitalization or home care. Because studies have shown that home care is less expensive, professionals responsible for public funding are obliged to encourage home care no matter what the circumstances (cases of child abuse and neglect are not uncommon) and to limit hospi-

talization. The authors recommended that professionals should not always consider home care to be the placement of choice.

Baby Andrew

The issues discussed in this chapter are not simply matters of theory and debate. They involve human beings who are confused and searching for the right choices while they are under great stress, anxiety, and pain. The story of baby Andrew (Robert and Peggy Stinson, 1979, *The Long Dying of Baby Andrew*, Boston: Little, Brown and Co.) took place early in the development of neonatology. His parents were the victims of medical technology that was still not fully understood and a hospital that had not yet developed a reasoned ethical stand on terminating life support. Today these problems have been better resolved, however, the events of Andrew's life are still relevant to the experience of parents of seriously ill newborns.

Andrew was born in December 1976, almost 16 weeks premature and weighing one pound, 12 ounces. Not many years earlier, a baby this size would have been called a miscarriage and would have died in the delivery room. Andrew began to show signs of fighting for life long enough for the pediatrician to insert a breathing tube down his tiny throat. Ultimately, Andrew survived six tortured months while his parents, Peggy and Robert, suffered severe emotional stress which almost caused them to divorce.

Although the Stinsons were Andrew's parents, they soon lost all control over his care. The neonatal department of the hospital where Andrew was treated was headed by doctors who opposed the Stinson's request to let Andrew die and judged them to be "bad parents" for expressing this desire. Medical records obtained after Andrew's death reveal that the doctors concealed information, made decisions without informing the parents, and deliberately misled them. Andrew had been worse at almost every stage of his deterioration than anyone had told his parents. Andrew, by the time of his death, had suffered cerebral bleeding, lungs that were permanently scarred by the respirator, eyes that were going blind, and a brain that had stopped growing and was seriously damaged. Robert Stinson wrote in his journal,

What they never understood was that one *can* care deeply enough about a child like Andrew to want his misery ended. Allowing Andrew to die naturally was what we wanted *for* him, not just to him. I thought often. . . about his massive pain. . . . As often as I wanted to gather him into my arms I wanted him to be allowed to die. What is the name for that?

Kristen: A Miracle Baby

In 1988, Kristen was born prematurely at one pound, six ounces. Her feet were the size of paper clips and her hands, the size of an adult thumb nail. Her doctor determined that she was barely alive, but saw no point in trying to maintain her life — she was simply too premature to survive. Within two hours of her birth, with no medical intervention, Kristen began to breathe. The pediatrician told Kristen's parents that she had not died, but that she had almost surely no chance of being normal; she would probably be blind, deaf, and brain damaged. He encouraged them to let her die, but instead, they chose to transfer her to a hospital with better facilities and take their chances.

Over 100 days later, Kristen came home from the hospital, weighing four pounds. Four years later, Kristen appears to have defied the doctor's predictions and is a normal, healthy child. Ironically, doctors theorize that neglecting her those first few hours actually saved her life. Her body's temperature had dropped in a primitive, physical response that allowed her to survive without sufficient oxygen and protected her organs from damage. But Kristen's survival still remains a mystery and a miracle of the will to survive.

CHAPTER V

EUTHANASIA

O Death the Healer, scorn thou not, I pray,
To come to me: of cureless ills thou art
The one physician. Pain lays not its touch
Upon a corpse. Æschylus

No greater good can man attain than to alleviate
another's pain. Alexander Pope

BACKGROUND

Euthanasia, from "good death" in Greek, was common in ancient Greek and Roman societies. Unhealthy infants and the elderly were regularly left to die. In modern times the rise of euthanasia reappeared in England in the 1930s. In 1936, the Voluntary Euthanasia Society proposed legislation to allow the terminally ill to seek euthanasia. It was voted down by Parliament.

When the Nazis gained power in Germany, in the 30s, they turned to a book published in 1920, *The Permission to Destroy Life Unworthy of Life* by professors Hoche and Binding. The book proposed safeguards and criteria for who should be permitted to seek euthanasia. The authors also stated that patients with brain damage, or who were mentally retarded, or had a severe psychiatric illness were "mentally dead," and their death was therefore a useful act. The Nazis distorted the concept in using it as an excuse to justify the mass extermination of all "undesirables" — Jews, Gypsies, homosexuals, and "impaired" children and adults. When the death camps were liberated and the truth of the Holocaust was revealed , the very idea of euthanasia became an abomination. Today, the link is sometimes made between limiting health care for the seriously disabled and Nazi policies,

although, for the majority of those who question whether they would choose to continue their lives under certain circumstances, euthanasia has no connection to Nazi philosophy.

In the mid-1970s the case of Karen Ann Quinlan brought the issue back into the public eye. Quinlan fell into a coma after taking a mixture of alcohol and tranquilizers. Her parents went to court (see Chapter VII) to have the life support turned off; the New Jersey Superior Court agreed. Quinlan lived without the respirator for another nine years.

DEFINITIONS

Today, although the distinction is not always made, most discussions of euthanasia emphasize the difference between suicide (physician assisted or not) and the termination of life support. In the former case, the patient is not necessarily terminally ill, but has decided that, for whatever reason, life is no longer worth living, and the person actively seeks death through such means as a drug overdose. Within the debate on euthanasia there is also a distinction between physician assisted suicide, in which a doctor provides medications and instructions for the patient to commit suicide and active euthanasia when the doctor actually injects the lethal dose. Stopping life support is considered passive euthanasia — the physician finds that the patient is no longer able to survive without the support of mechanical means, and when that support (respirator, gastrostomy tube) is withdrawn, the patient will soon die.

Ironically, both proponents of active euthanasia and vitalists try to link the two concepts together — one side, to make it more acceptable to the public, while the other side emphasizes the dangers of permitting any kind of help in dying. The difference though, recognized by the courts and medical associations, is that the patient is killed by active euthanasia, while allowing someone to die permits the disease, aging, or injury process to take over.

THE NATIONAL HEMLOCK SOCIETY

The National Hemlock Society is the most well known organization advocating active euthanasia. Started in 1980 by Derek Humphry, the Society was the outgrowth of Humphry's experience in helping his cancer-ridden wife take her life and his subsequent book about her suicide, *Jean's Way*. The organization's goals are to inform terminally ill people of how to take their own lives and to make autoeuthansia legal through the passage of a Death with Dignity Act. The Hemlock Society supports rational suicide, not emotional suicide (taking one's life because of depression or mental illness) and points out that, while suicide is no longer against the law, aiding someone to commit suicide is in 27 states. (See Table 5.1.)

In a letter prepared for the "pro" side of a debate, "Can There be Rational Suicide?" held at a conference run by the Center for Applied Biomedical Ethics (1986), the Hemlock Society justified suicide on the following grounds:

1. Advanced terminal illness that is causing unbearable suffering to the individual.
2. Grave physical handicap, which is so restricting that the individual cannot, even after due consideration and training, tolerate such a limited existence.

TABLE 5.1

States in Which Assisted Suicide is a Crime, 1991

Alaska	Nebraska
Arizona	New Mexico
Arkansas	New Hampshire
California	New Jersey
Colorado	New York
Connecticut	North Dakota
Delaware	Oklahoma
Florida	Oregon
Hawaii	Pennsylvania
Kansas	South Dakota
Maine	Texas
Minnesota	Washington
Mississippi	Wisconsin
Montana	

Source: Based on data from Choice in Dying, December 1991

The first position is the most common reason for expressing the desire to die, while the second is rather rare.

The Society offered guidelines for autoeuthanasia:

1. The person is a mature adult.
2. The person has clearly made a considered decision.
3. The self-deliverance has not been made at the first knowledge of the life-threatening illness, and reasonable medical help has been sought.
4. The treating physician has been informed, and his or her response has been taken into account.
5. The person has made a will disposing of his or her worldly effects.
6. The person has made plans to exit this life that do not involve others in criminal liability.
7. The person leaves a note saying exactly why he or she is committing suicide.

The Hemlock Society believes in living wills and/or durable powers of attorney (see Chapter VI) because they indicate that the person has considered his or her death under calm, rational conditions. (See Appendix I.)

The reaction to Humphry's second book, *Final Exit* (1991, Secaucus N.J.:Carol Publishing), exposed the public interest in the right to die. This suicide manual, which teaches how to use pills and plastic bags to achieve death, was on the *New York Times* best-seller list the first week it was published. Arthur Caplan, bioethicist at the University of Minnesota, observed, "It is the loudest statement of protest of how medicine is dealing with terminal illness and dying."

Critics of autoeuthanasia claim that suicide is not necessary for patients who seek to die and that they would be better off with hospice care. The Hemlock Society feels that the hospice movement does the best that it can in a difficult situation, but that not everyone wants a "beneficent lingering." Hospice is the answer for some patients, but not all. (See below for more on hospice treatment.)

Humphry believes that euthanasia is the most important issue facing Americans. Although the debate is frequently compared to the abortion controversy, Humphry insists that it is far more significant. Not everyone contemplates an abortion, but everyone dies. "With abortion, people are moralizing about other people's lives to a large extent. But in the death-with-dignity movement, we're talking about your own life."*

THE RIGHT TO LIFE

The National Right to Life Committee (NRL) opposes any action that hastens death, regardless of the patient's condition. David O'Steen, Executive Director National Right to Life, in "Euthanasia: Modern America's Rendezvous With Death," (1991, WDC: NRL, Education Trust Fund) presents the slippery slope argument, linking what vitalists see as the immorality of denying nutrition and hydration (liquids) to terminal or permanently comatose patients to assisted suicide. They condemn the practice claiming that, with court approval, incompetent patients are being killed against their will for the convenience or financial gain of the family. (See Appendix II.)

The NRL blames the public acceptance of euthanasia on the media for a campaign of "disinformation."

> . . . "right-to-die" has joined "right-to-choose" as a synonym for "right-to-kill." This is part of the pretense that decisions by third parties to starve incompetent patients, who cannot speak for themselves, are really decisions of the patient. This mind-boggling bit of semantic nonsense is aided by the legal pretense of the courts that these third party judgements are really "substituted judgements" that patients would make themselves if they were able.

The legal basis of "substituted judgement," (see Chapter VII) which permits doctors to stop

---

* Derek Humphry, a charismatic speaker, has brought the concept of controlling one's death out into the open, however, he has been widely attacked, even by some in his own organization. The Hemlock Society was dealt a blow when Humphry's second wife, who co-authored *Jean's Way* with him, recently took her own life. Suffering with cancer, Ann Wickett reported that Humphry left her three weeks after her cancer surgery and divorced her. She questioned the compassion of an organization that turned against her and regretted having helped her own parents to commit suicide. She took a overdose of drugs, leaving a suicide note for Humphry which said, in part, "Ever since I was diagnosed as having cancer, you have done everything conceivable to precipitate my death. I was not alone in recognizing what you were doing. What you did — desertion and abandonment and subsequent harassment of a dying woman — is so unspeakable there are no words to describe the horror of it." This conflict has cast a shadow on the purity of Humphry's motives and behavior.

giving food and fluids to the patient has created a "right-to-die" which the NRL feels threatens the right to life of all incompetent patients.

> A competent patient can now choose euthanasia by lethal injection as part of his "right to die." Since the right to die is just as basic a right for incompetent patients, they, too must have the option of choosing euthanasia by lethal injection. However, since incompetent patients cannot make their "decision" known, a decision can be made on their behalf by a court or third party recognized by a court, to give them a lethal injection, either by employing "substituted judgement" or by concluding that death is in the patient's "best interests."

Religious Opinions

The Roman Catholic Church officially believes that while treatment can be denied, there is a difference between active and passive euthanasia. The church condemns the former and permits the latter under certain circumstances. Their "Statement on Euthanasia" (1991, Administrative Committee, National Conference of Catholic Bishops) explains,

> we are not morally obligated to use all available medical procedures in every set of circumstances. But that tradition clearly and strongly affirms that as a responsible steward of life one must never directly intend to cause one's own death, or the death of an innocent victim, by action or omission.

The Committee for Pro-Life Activities of the National Conference of Catholic Bishops published a statement in 1992 which acknowledged the split in the Catholic Church over whether or not it was morally acceptable to withdraw life support. The bishop's committee has come down on the side of maintaining life support. They fear the slippery slope that will be broached if there is any accepted minimization of human life. If the permanently comatose are permitted to die, other categories of mentally impaired patients could soon follow. Catholic hospitals have, for the most part, taken this vitalist position and do not differentiate between active and passive euthanasia and resist withdrawing treatment from any patient.

The Catholic Church is not alone in its condemnation of euthanasia. Southern Baptists and Orthodox Jews also oppose any form of mercy killing. More liberal branches of Protestant churches, however, do support limited forms of euthanasia. The United Church of Christ, some Methodists, and Unitarians support the patient's right to self-determination (see Chapter III).

MEDICAL AND BIOETHICAL OPINIONS

Support for Euthanasia

It is very difficult to determine doctors' attitudes towards active euthanasia. Publicly, most physicians will support the Hippocratic Oath's injunction not to kill, while privately or in anonymous polls, many will advocate helping a hopelessly ill patient to die. Some will admit to having done it. In a survey (prepared by the San Francisco Medical Society) of San Francisco area physicians taken shortly before the vote on the "Humane and Dignified Death Initiative" (an initiative voted down by California voters in 1988 which would have legalized euthanasia), 70 percent of doctors supported the rights of patients to active euthanasia, 23 opposed the bill, while 7 percent were unsure. If the initiative were to pass, 45 percent said they would participate in euthanasia and 35 percent said they would not. The Hemlock Society produced a survey in which 79 California doctors admitted in anonymous questionnaires that they had already actively taken the lives of terminal patients. Twenty-nine said they had done so three times or more. (These polls were published in "The California Humane and Dignified Death Initiative" by Allan Parachini and published in a *Hastings Center Report*, "Mercy, Murder, & Morality: Perspectives on Euthanasia," Jan/Feb 1989.)

Arthur Caplan, ethicist at the University of Minnesota, maintains that more than a dozen doctors have confided in him about their roles in assisting patients to die. They came to him because they felt public policy and medical care did not accurately reflect patients' needs. The doctors claimed they wanted the stories known so that the issue would enter public discussion, but, if questioned, indicated they would deny any involvement. Joel Feinberg, professor of philosophy and law at the University of Arizona, thinks doctors are deceiving themselves. "A doctor discontinuing a treatment often thinks he isn't morally responsible but thinks that he is when he gives a lethal injection. That is superstitious — he's responsible either way." As to whether euthanasia could lead to abuses, he feels that keeping someone alive for an additional six months of pain and suffering is also an abuse.

Opposition to Euthanasia

Those who oppose euthanasia fear that the difference between physicians' public and private points of view is one of the reasons why doctors should not be given the legal right to mercy killing. A physician's behavior cannot be adequately regulated — it is all too easy for a doctor to write on a patient's death certificate that the patient died from respiratory failure rather than an intentional overdose of pain killers. Leon Kass, M.D., bioethicist and professor at the University of Chicago, in "Why Doctors Must Not Kill" (August 9, 1991, *Commonweal* [a Catholic publication], N.Y.), sees several problems with legalizing euthanasia. In part, he fears the basic trust between doctor and patient will be eroded and that sometimes doctors might not be able to treat a patient with the utmost care when the physician knows that the possibility of legally killing the patient exists. Kass points out that doctors are human beings with fallibilities, and they can become annoyed with patients who are difficult or patients who do not respond well to treatment. Doctors, among themselves, commonly refer to terminal patients as "gorks," "vegetables," and other uncomplimentary names.

It is foolish, Kass writes, to think that because only those who ask for euthanasia would be put to death, those who do not really want to die are not at risk. Doctors' experience has taught them that pleas for death are more often an anxious plea for help, stemming from fear of rejection or abandonment or fear of pain.

Dying people are all too easily reduced ahead of time to "thinghood" by those who cannot bear to deal with the suffering or disability of those they love. Withdrawal of contact, affection, and care is the greatest single cause of the dehumanization of dying. Not the alleged humaness of an elixir of death, but the humaness of connected living-while-dying is what medicine — and the rest of us — most owe the dying. The treatment of choice is company and care.

David Orentlicher, MD, JD, Ethics and Health Policy Counsel of the American Medical Association agrees with Kass. Orentlicher is concerned that the trust between a physician and the patient is eroded by the possibility of euthanasia. Furthermore, he worries that some hopelessly ill patients will not be able to freely resist a recommendation from the doctor that suicide is appropriate. Patients feel their lives have become worthless, that they are a bother to all who must care for them, and they do not wish to be an emotional and financial burden on their families. In this mental state, if a doctor were to urge euthanasia, many patients would agree.

In her article, "Holding the Line on Euthanasia" ("Mercy, Murder, & Morality," see above), Susan Wolf, an associate at the Hastings Center, presents a different argument against active euthanasia. She is concerned that if active euthanasia becomes legal, the progress that has been made in terminating care for the terminally ill will be lost. First, the prohibition against active euthanasia has allowed the law, for the most part, to stay out of decisions to stop treatment. The courts have permitted nonlegalistic processes to decide what is best for the patient, relying on physicians to do no harm. Second, maintenance of the prohibition has allowed the courts to be flexible in their determination of the right to end life-sustaining treatment, even for non-terminal patients. Third, the prohibition has forced doctors and health care providers to pay attention to the dying and treat their symptoms of pain and distress until the end. Fourth, knowing that a life cannot be taken creates a safer atmosphere for the highly emotional discussion of when to terminate treatment.

HOSPICE CARE

Hospice, also known as palliative (to relieve without curing) care, is not yet available as an option to many who are terminally ill. To help a patient die with attention, pain medication, relief of symptoms, but not with aggressive medical techniques and treatments, is still relatively rare. In other countries (England, for example) hospice care is better developed, and more doctors are involved not only in providing palliative care for their patients, but also in training other doctors in the specialty.

The National Hospice Organization (NHO) defines their philosophy:

> Hospice affirms life. Hospice exists to provide support and care for persons in the last phases of incurable disease so that they might live as fully and comfortably as possible. Hospice recognizes dying as a normal process whether or not resulting from disease. Hospice neither hastens nor postpones death. Hospice exists in the hope and belief that, through appropriate care and the promotion of a caring community sensitive to their needs, patients and families may be free to attain a degree of mental and spiritual preparation for death that is satisfactory to them.

Hospice care includes physical, psychological, social, and spiritual treatment, concentrating on controlling symptoms of the disease (mainly to ease pain) and psychological counseling for the whole family. Hospice patients may be at home or, if their symptoms cannot be managed at home, in a hospice center. Hospice workers believe that dying is a natural process. "Where cure is not possible, care is still needed." Hospice treats the patient and her family, not the disease. Euthanasia is rejected by hospice workers as unnecessary if a patient's illness is managed with care.

In November 1990, the NHO passed a resolution opposing active euthanasia and physician assisted euthanasia. (See Appendix III.) The NHO questions whether, "the choice of euthanasia is fully informed and truly voluntary. The choice between euthanasia and a painful, suffering death presented by euthanasia proponents is far different from the choice between euthanasia and a peaceful, comfortable death supported by appropriate hospice care." Hospice care's goal is to provide families with a peaceful time to come to terms with death. The National Hospice Organization claims to have restored public trust in the health care system, something they believe euthanasia cannot do. In addition, hospice providers are concerned that legalizing euthanasia would "abort ongoing efforts to enhance the quantity and quality of palliative care."

The NHO seeks to expand and educate the public about the option. Alternatives to home care, such as clinics and hospice care within a hospital setting, must be developed as well as care for those who are not terminal, but who would benefit from the hospice approach to illness. Hospice workers believe that the growing interest in euthanasia makes it even more urgent that they educate the public about an alternative that allows terminal patients to live and die as comfortably as possible.

Medicare Coverage

Hospice care is usually less expensive than conventional hospital care because the family provides much of the care and expensive technology is not used. Hospice care is covered under most private insurance plans and under Medicare. Medicare covers:

- Nursing services on an intermittent basis
- Physician services
- Drugs for pain relief and symptom management
- Physical, occupational, and speech therapy
- Home health aide and homemaker services
- Medical supplies and appliances
- Short-term inpatient care, including respite care
- Medical social services
- Spiritual, dietary and other counseling
- Continuous care during a crisis

Not all the costs, however, are covered by insurance, and hospice is dependent on volunteers and donations. There are approximately 1,800 hospices in all fifty states serving more than 200,000 terminal patients a year.

Hospice care is often not easy for the patient's family. Medication and care must be delivered on a 24-hour basis including bathing and changing a bed-bound patient who was once perhaps a totally different person from what she is now. But, hospice workers claim that for most families, the effort is more than repaid by knowing that they have enabled their loved one to have the death he wanted and to be able to be there until the end.

Hospice and the Medical Establishment

The American medical system is not structured to support hospice care. Doctors are trained to use all available technology partly because keeping someone alive is their job and partly because research and conquering new frontiers in medical science is a laudable goal. On the other hand, both doctors and hospitals can benefit financially by pushing expensive treatments. A hospital and a doctor can make more money by subjecting a patient to questionable treatments than they can by helping a patient die by giving that patient the time to listen to the patient express anxiety and fear and

sufficient morphine to alleviate pain. Patients who return to the hospital when their terminal illness is out of control must receive active treatment to justify their stay. These treatments may include hyperalimentation (tube feedings that provide all the necessary nutrients to sustain life) that their bodies cannot absorb or doses of expensive antibiotics which will have no benefit. Additional radiation or chemotherapy may be administered when it has already been found to be ineffective. If a hospital offered good palliative care it would take in far less revenue than its competitors and would soon be out of business. (See Chapter VIII for the expenses of medical care.)

WHY PATIENTS ASK FOR DEATH

David Cundiff, MD, in a soon to be published book, *Euthanasia Is Not the Answer* (1992, Totowa NJ: Humana Press), is convinced that the answer to euthanasia lies with proper pain control. Dr. Cundiff, a hospice physician, received some of his training in England and discovered that he had not been taught how to control pain for terminal cancer patients in American medical school, nor did he realize that he did not know. Cundiff feels that this is true of the vast majority of doctors and nurses in this country. Americans, he proposes, are too afraid of creating drug addicts (not a problem especially for a terminally ill patient) and too aggressive in their use of anticancer therapies. Cundiff also credits England's socialized medicine with supporting superior palliative care. Their system encourages less health care, and one of the results of good palliative care is that a patient who can manage his own pain at home does not require the services of a hospital intensive care unit.

Cundiff's experience as a consultant in pain management for cancer and AIDS patients has brought him to the conclusion that patients whose needs are met do not ask for death.

Depression

Doctors Yeates Conwell and Eric Caine, in the *New England Journal of Medicine* (October 10,

1991, "Rational Suicide and the Right to Die," vol. 325, no. 15) warned about the psychiatric component to suicide. As geriatric psychiatrists (psychiatrists for the elderly), they are concerned that the doctors who are most likely to encounter patients who ask for death are not trained to diagnose depressive illness in older patients. Suicide is the eighth leading cause of death in the United States, and the rate of suicide is highest among elderly white men (Table 5.2). Although suicide in medical cases often goes unreported, based on the available data, 90 to 100 percent of suicides have a diagnosable psychiatric illness. Furthermore, the elderly appear to be more prone than younger victims to suffer acute depressive episodes that often respond well to available treatment. Conwell and Caine found that 75 percent of those elderly who had taken their lives had seen a primary physician in the month prior to death, yet their psychiatric problems either were not noted or were inadequately treated.

Pain

Dr. Cundiff (see above) sees pain, rather than depression, as the major factor in asking for death. He defines four types of pain: physical pain from the disease; psychological pain from fear, anxiety, and depression; social pain from the isolation the patient feels from his family and friends when his attention is dominated by fighting physical pain; and spiritual pain when life has lost its meaning and value.

Not everyone would agree, however, that pain is to be avoided at all costs. In a televised discussion, Malcolm Muggeridge, the leader of the British right-to-life movement said, "I think this horror of pain is a rather low instinct and if I think of human beings I've known and of my own life, such as it is, I can't recall any case of pain which didn't on the whole, enrich life." The archbishop of the Russian Orthodox Church concurred, ". . . people who try to escape it from cowardice miss something extremely precious." This attitude is reflected in the traditional Catholic theology that suffering brings a person closer to Christ in his martyrdom. Carlos Gomez, in his research on euthanasia in the Netherlands (see below), found that fear of indefinite dependence, either on a machine or on other people, was a major factor for many people who requested to die.

Cundiff disputes some commonly held assumptions about cancer pain. Patients do not become immune to the effects of the opioids (usually mor-

TABLE 5.2

[Data are based on the National Vital Statistics System]

Sex, race, and age	1950[1]	1960[1]	1970	1980	1985	1986	1987	1988	1989
All races	Deaths per 100,000 resident population								
All ages, age adjusted.................	11.0	10.6	11.8	11.4	11.5	11.9	11.7	11.4	11.3
All ages, crude.......................	11.4	10.6	11.6	11.9	12.3	12.8	12.7	12.4	12.2
Under 1 year........................	...	...	...	...	...	...	...	...	...
1–4 years...........................	...	...	...	...	...	...	...	...	...
5–14 years..........................	0.2	0.3	0.3	0.4	0.8	0.8	0.7	0.7	0.7
15–24 years.........................	4.5	5.2	8.8	12.3	12.9	13.1	12.9	13.2	13.3
25–34 years.........................	9.1	10.0	14.1	16.0	15.2	15.7	15.4	15.4	15.0
35–44 years.........................	14.3	14.2	16.9	15.4	14.6	15.2	15.0	14.8	14.6
45–54 years.........................	20.9	20.7	20.0	15.9	15.6	16.4	15.9	14.6	14.6
55–64 years.........................	27.0	23.7	21.4	15.9	16.7	17.0	16.6	15.6	15.5
65–74 years.........................	29.3	23.0	20.8	16.9	18.5	19.7	19.4	18.4	18.0
75–84 years.........................	31.1	27.9	21.2	19.1	24.1	25.2	25.8	25.9	23.1
85 years and over....................	28.8	26.0	19.0	19.2	19.1	20.8	22.1	20.5	22.8

Source: *Health - United States, 1991 and Prevention Profile*, National Center for Health Statistics, (Hyattsville, MD, 1992)

phine) and can successfully take the medication for years if necessary. Pain medication does not make the patient sleepy or less alert. The first two or three days may have that effect, but the body adjusts quickly and Cundiff asserts that part of the sleepiness is the result of exhaustion from battling the previously unrelieved pain. Pain medication should not be given as needed (in medical terminology that means when the patient reports feeling pain). Health care providers stop the medication each time the patient falls asleep and they wait for the patient to complain of pain before giving another dose. This leads to a cycle of sleepiness followed by agony rather than continuous pain relief. Sufficient pain medication properly administered does not shorten life. Instead it can lengthen a patient's life by avoiding the complications of chronic pain.

Cundiff is particularly disturbed that doctors question whether the patient is truly feeling pain or not. In one medical center 60 percent of the physicians and nurses gave patients placebos to test if a patient had "real" pain or was "faking it." Cundiff asserts that doctors, in an effort to control a difficult patient or a patient who has not responded to treatment the way the physician wanted, will sometimes give patients a placebo. An enlightened physician, however, will realize that pain reduction from a placebo does not mean that the pain was imaginary. The Medical Knowledge Self-Assessment Program published by the American College of Physicians reports, "One third of hospitalized patients treated with opioids are undermedicated, usually because of physician misinformation, underdosage, or exaggerated fears of addiction."

Cundiff concludes:

With widespread availability of good hospice care for the terminally ill, the question of euthanasia would become moot. . . . We have the knowledge and the means to assure that no terminally ill person need beg for death to end his or her suffering. . . . Universally available, excellent quality hospice medicine is the life affirming alternative to the hopelessness of euthansia.

DOCTORS WHO KILL

Jack Kevorkian

In June of 1990 and again in October 1991, Dr. Jack Kevorkian, a Michigan pathologist, helped three women kill themselves. In the first case, Janet Adkins, a 54 year old woman with Alzheimer's disease, did not wish to let the disease destroy her mind. She contacted Kevorkian, who, after meeting her, determined that she was still untouched enough by her illness to make a reasoned decision. He used a home-made machine which allowed her to push a button and receive a lethal injection. The suicide took place in the back of Kevorkian's van. Dr. Howard Brody, head of the ethics committee of the Michigan State Medical Society, felt that the mainly positive public reaction to this unprofessional method underscored the public interest in the right to suicide.

We thought patients would be horrified by the rusty van in the parking lot, the unsterile solutions — it sounded so sleazy. Instead a significant number want to erect a statue to the man. It became clear that many people see doctors as the enemy when it comes to death and dying and you have to see that as a terrible failing.

In 1991, Kevorkian assisted Sherry Miller, a patient with multiple sclerosis, and Margery Wantz, suffering from an unspecified pelvic disease, to commit suicide. Sherry Miller, who had begged Dr. Kevorkian for two years to help her, told a court in the civil hearing for Kevorkian's first suicide, "I can't walk. I can't write. It's hard for me to talk. I can't function as a human being. What can anybody do? Nothing. I want the right to die." The brother of an AIDS patient who was unable to get help from Kevorkian before his painful death, testified that Dr. Kevorkian was a "hero and a trailblazer in a field of processionary caterpillars." Margery Wantz in a letter to her husband to be opened after death, wrote "No doctor can help me anymore. If God won't come to me, I'm going to find God. I can't stand it any longer."

In February 1992, a grand jury indicted Dr. Kevorkian on two counts of murder and one count of delivery of a controlled substance. The case has not yet been tried, although the charge of murder brought against Dr. Kevorkian in Janet Adkins' death was dismissed because the judge ruled there was no law against assisting suicide in Michigan. In May 1992, Kevorkian was at the side of a fourth woman who took her life by placing a mask attached to a tank of carbon monoxide on her face. It is not clear if Kevorkian actually helped her or merely counseled her and was present at her death.

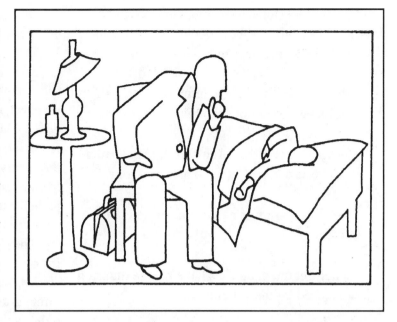

Other Doctors

Dr. Kevorkian is seen as an eccentric, quirky person (opponents to euthanasia would be more likely to describe him as a dangerous murderer) who has always been outside the mainstream of medical care. His business card reportedly reads, "Bioethics and Obitiatry, Special Death Counseling, by Appointment Only." Nonetheless, he is not the only doctor to admit to practicing euthanasia. Dr. Timothy Quill, in "Death and Dignity — a case of individualized decision making" (1991, vol. 324, *New England Journal of Medicine*), revealed his role in the death of a leukemia patient known as Diane. When Diane suffered a relapse, she refused a second course of treatment (chemotherapy, full body radiation, and a bone marrow transplant) which would have given her a one in four chance for recovery. She asked Dr. Quill for a lethal prescription that she could use before she became too ill. He told her how to use the barbiturates for sleep but also advised her on the number she would have to take to commit suicide. Dr. Quill admits to having felt uneasiness when he wrote the prescription, but at his grand jury hearing he said, "I hope a deeper appreciation of the suffering of dying people is achieved as a result of this process." The grand jury ruled that there was no criminal liability on Dr. Quill's part.

AIDS has lead to an increase in the private use of euthanasia. An anonymous doctor who treated over 400 AIDS patients told them that if the treatment or disease ever became too much for them, he would provide medicine for a painless suicide. Only four accepted his offer, but the doctor claimed that all felt they had regained control over their lives and treatments knowing that the possibility for choosing a quick death existed. When the doctor himself developed AIDS, he took his own prescription. His death was not listed as a suicide.

EUTHANASIA IN THE NETHERLANDS

The Netherlands is the only country where active euthanasia openly occurs. The Netherlands' State Commission on Euthanasia (1985) defines euthanasia as, "the deliberate action to terminate life, by someone other than, and on request of, the patient concerned." Euthanasia is a criminal offense under article 293 of the Penal Code of the Netherlands punishable by imprisonment of up to 12 years or a fine. At the same time, however, section 40 of the same penal code states that someone is not punishable if the person who committed the act was driven by an "overwhelming power" — a conflict of interests between providing mercy or continuing a life in a situation in which a choice must be made.

In 1991, the Dutch parliament guaranteed doctors that they will not be prosecuted if they have observed the following guidelines:

- an explicit and repeated request by the patient that leaves no doubt as to his desire to die;

- the mental or physical suffering of the patient must be severe and have no prospect for relief;

- the decision must be well-informed and not coerced;

- other treatment options have been exhausted or refused by the patient; and

- the doctor consults another physician.

What are the Statistics?

There has been a great deal of controversy over the Dutch attitude, and both proponents and critics cite the experiment as an example of either the benefits or detriments of euthanasia. Reports from Holland contradict each other, some lauding the success of euthanasia and others claiming that indiscriminate killing is widespread and condoned.

How many patients are helped to die is unknown because, although doctors are not prosecuted, most do not choose to report the euthanasia to the authorities. Recently, unconfirmed reports from Holland suggest that the change made by parliament guaranteeing safety from prosecution has encouraged doctors to be much more open in their practices. In January 1992, 339 mercy killings were reported for that one month compared to the 591 which were reported for all of 1991.

Estimates have varied widely from about 2,000 per year (2 to 3 percent of all deaths) to as high as 18,000 to 20,000 (a staggering 16 percent). Estimates have been made that approximately 11 percent of Dutch AIDS patients and 15 percent of terminal cancer patients die by active euthanasia.

In a recent study (1991), the *Netherlands Journal of Medicine* sent anonymous questionnaires to 1,042 physicians. Of the 676 who responded, 388 gave detailed information. The typical patient who asks for euthanasia is a terminal cancer patient (85 percent), in his or her early 60's who fears "dependence, loss of dignity, humiliation, and pain." The lethal injection is usually administered at home by the family doctor. The remaining 15 percent suffer from AIDS or multiple sclerosis. Very few cardiac patients asked for death.

The researchers were surprised that the majority of patients who asked for help were in their sixties, while those in their seventies and eighties rarely asked for help. They speculated that perhaps older people were better able to accept the effects of their illness or they were less assertive or informed about asking.

The study claimed that strong indications put the number of patients who receive euthanasia at about 3,000 a year, about half of the normally accepted figures. (If the January 1992 figure is accurate and complete, the rate would be around 4,100 patients a year.) The research also showed that more people asked for euthanasia than actually received it. Home care physicians received about 5,000 requests a year and complied in about 2,000 cases. In nearly two-thirds of the cases the doctors estimated that the patients had less than two weeks to live. In 83 percent of the cases, the patient raised the issue, in 10 percent the physician broached the subject, and in the remaining 7 percent the family brought it up.

"A Case Against Dutch Euthanasia," by Richard Fenigsen in the *Hastings Center Report* on euthanasia ("Mercy, Murder, and Morality"), catalogues abuses and horrors that he claims are carried out in the Dutch system. Fenigsen, a cardiologist in the Netherlands, insists that doctors allow at least 300 babies to die each year by preventing surgery for heart defects and Down's syndrome, that they refuse to implant pacemakers for patients older than 75, and that they neglect to treat pneumonia in the elderly and single people without close family*. (Dr. Fenigsen did include references for the data in his article but because they were in Dutch they were omitted in the American publication.) The doctor cites a letter to the Parliamentary Committees for Health Care and Justice from a group of severely handicapped adults :

> We feel our lives threatened. . . . We realize that we cost the community a lot. . . . Many people think we are useless . . . often we notice that we are being talked into desiring death . . . we will find it extremely dangerous and frightening if the new medical legislation includes euthanasia.

Fenigsen tells of a doctor who allegedly told his nurse, "When I come back from the weekend. I don't want to find this man here anymore." Fenigsen's reports, however, have been repudiated even by other critics of euthanasia. One ethicist who opposes mercy killing accused him of exaggerating.

Henk Rigter, executive director of the Health Council of The Netherlands, in "Euthanasia in The Netherlands: Distinguishing Facts from Fiction," denies the assertions made by Fenigsen (published in the same *Hastings Center Report*). Claims that patients are fearful of entering health care facilities is proven wrong by the continued need for more funds to shorten the waiting lists of potential patients. Rigter estimates that fewer than the frequently cited figure of 5,000 to 8,000 cases of euthanasia occur each year. He estimates that in 1987, there were 200 to 300 cases in Amsterdam, 10 percent of which were reported to the public prosecutor. Rigter did not specifically address Fenigsen's claims of wholesale murder, but in a reference to an article by Fenigsen that appeared in the *Wall Street Journal* (September 29, 1987), Rigter stated that there was no data to support Fenigsen's allegations.

Carlos Gomez, MD, in *Regulating Death: Euthanasia and the Case of the Netherlands* (1991, New York: The Free Press) remarks on the lack of official statistics from the Netherlands. The government cannot include "illicit" practices in its official health statistics, and private universities or research groups have either not done the work or it has been inadequate. Some believe the topic does not lend itself to research — it is a private matter, it is an unhappy subject to raise with grieving families, and it is not a practice doctors like, but use only when they are "pushed to the wall." Gomez finds that the low estimates of euthanasia do not fit with published mortality statistics, while the high estimates from people like Fenigsen, who are strongly opposed to the practice, are unsupported. Middle estimates put the rate of euthanasia at 4 to 8 percent of the deaths in the Netherlands.

Gomez interviewed doctors to determine under what circumstances they would resort to euthanasia. He was concerned that the practice is badly regulated and the integrity of euthanasia rests on the good character of the medical profession. He does not believe that the practice is controlled because doctors in theory only agree to requests for euthanasia when they are pushed to the limit. "Public policy instructs the physician to resist euthanasia (because physicians should not intentionally kill), yet it simultaneously gives physicians license to kill. What is offered, on the one hand, as a safeguard against abuse of the practice, is taken away by giving permission to perform euthanasia." Gomez questions the eagerness to believe the best about the Dutch situation and thinks a healthy skepticism would be wiser. He reports that he had a sense that, rather than euthanasia being a last resort, some proponents felt certain patients were better off dead and that it was humane to kill them. A better solution, he proposes, would be to improve the care and concern offered to the terminally ill.

---

* Several studies of the British National Health Plan reveal similar choices are made in Britain as a method of curtailing expenses in a financially overburdened health plan. See Chapter VIII for more information.

INITIATIVE 119

In 1991, Washington State voters were given the opportunity to permit physician aid-in-dying. An amendment to the 1979 Natural Death Act, initiative 119 would have legalized "a medical service provided in person by a physician that will end the life of a conscious and mentally competent qualified person in a dignified, painless and humane manner, when requested voluntarily by the patient through a written directive executed at the time the service is desired." The initiative tried to be specific enough to avoid claims by critics that uncontrolled murder would result. In addition to the limitations stated above, the initiative required that the written request be witnessed by two people who were not employees of the health care facility or family members or heirs of the patient; two doctors had to certify that the patient was terminal (less than six months to live); physicians could not be forced to provide aid-in-dying; the patient could revoke her request at any time; and the physician could require a psychological evaluation if there were any question of the patient's competency.

At first it appeared that the initiative would have no trouble passing. A poll taken one month before the election showed that 61 percent of likely voters supported it, while 27 percent opposed it, and 12 percent were undecided. On election day, however, 54 percent opposed the measure and 46 percent supported it. Voters reported that, on the one hand, they were moved by personal stories of prolonged death, but on the other hand, they were wary of being the first in the world to legally approve euthanasia and were concerned that people might be pressured into death to spare their families expense and suffering.

Derek Humphry of the Hemlock Society (see above) attributed the loss partly to proponents who used the ambiguous term "aid-in-dying" and shied away from the terms their critics used with relish — "suicide" and "euthanasia." Furthermore, Humphry felt that the law was not worded precisely enough and the safeguards were not clear — a sign that the general public has some distrust of the medical and legal professions. Some analysts thought that Kevorkian's assisted suicide of two women just two weeks prior to the election frightened people, not so much by what Kevorkian did, but because they suddenly thought that Washington would become the "suicide mecca" with terminally ill patients from all over country coming to die in their state.

Supporters of euthanasia have not given up. Initiatives are being prepared for California and Oregon in upcoming elections.

CHAPTER VI

LIVING WILLS AND ADVANCE DIRECTIVES

"Given the new medical technology that can sustain life even when the brain is gone, we must think about the right to die and the need for dignity in departing life. We owe it to ourselves and the ones we love to make provision for that moment." Jacob K. Javits

Today, part of taking responsibility for one's life includes taking responsibility for one's death. Advance directives, or living wills, are quasi-legal documents that make known a person's wishes regarding terminal health care. A "living will" is a signed, dated, and witnessed declaration which permits a person to state in advance his or her wishes for the use of life sustaining treatment. A "durable power of attorney" is a signed and notarized document delegating health decision-making powers to a surrogate (a substitute with power to make decisions) should the document's author become incompetent. "Health care proxies" have become the current official term for a document in which patients designate a surrogate who has legal authority to make medical decisions should the patient become too sick to do so.

LIVING WILLS

Living wills were first introduced in 1930 by Luis Kutner, a lawyer and human rights activist. The first widely circulated will was distributed in 1968 by Choice in Dying, a non-profit council to improve the care of dying patients. Choice in Dying, (formerly Concern for Dying and the Society for the Right to Die) supports patient autonomy and open discussion of issues surrounding terminal care.

The living will is intended to provide a patient with the greatest possible control over medical decisions if, in the future, the patient should be-

come incapable of expressing her needs. Signing the will while of sound mind presumably ensures that the patient has control over the end of his life. It can also help the doctor and the patient's family in the emotional and difficult process of choosing treatment for a dying patient.

Although most people initially think that they know just what they want, deciding what to include in a living will is complicated. Choice in Dying distributes a brochure ("Medical Treatments and Your Living Will") to help choose which medical treatments the author of the will would like or not like to receive if he were dying or unable to communicate. The brochure discusses different medical treatments that need to be considered in writing the document. (See Chapter IV for a further discussion of medical treatments.)

Cardiopulmonary Resuscitation

Cardiopulmonary resuscitation (CPR) includes several procedures to restart the heart when it stops beating and to provide artificial respiration when breathing stops. CPR can include manual pressure, electrical shock, or intravenous drugs to regulate the heartbeat. Mouth-to-mouth resuscitation, or pumping air into the lungs, or a tube inserted into the windpipe for mechanical ventilation may be used to provide respiration (breathing). If CPR is started promptly, the patient will return to the previous state of health; if not, permanent brain damage can result. Intensive care treatment often follows resuscitation, but the patient's prognosis has not been improved. For a terminally ill patient, cardiopulmonary arrest can be a peaceful way to die.

Mechanical Ventilators

When a person's lungs are working inadequately, mechanical ventilators take over breathing by providing oxygen through a tube inserted into the windpipe. The ventilator can cause discomfort, but if a patient is gasping for breath, mechanical help is usually preferable. Ventilation can temporarily ease a patient through a crisis like pneumonia, although, in some cases, breathing is never restored and the patient becomes permanently dependent on the ventilator. If a person with severe breathing problems is disconnected from a ventilator, she will quickly lose consciousness. An oxygen mask, muscle relaxants, and sometimes narcotics can ease discomfort if the patient has chosen to die.

Tube Feeding

Tube feeding is used for patients who are unable (or unwilling) to swallow foods and fluids. Tubes can be placed through the nose (nasogastric tube) or directly into the abdomen (gastrostomy or jejunostomy tube). Tube feeding is usually given to unconscious or severely brain-damaged patients. Unconscious patients cannot feel hunger or thirst and are unaware of whether they are being fed or not. Some survive for years with tube feedings. Patients with severe brain damage (Alzheimer's, stroke, Parkinson's) may be unable to say they do not want food or that the amount of food is more than their bodies can handle. If nutrition is stopped, death occurs in three days to two weeks from dehydration or infection. Most experts agree that unconscious or severely brain-damaged persons do not experience discomfort from this process.

The bodies of persons who are very near death no longer need nutrition, and their digestive systems are unable to handle the input. Reaching this stage is gradual, however, and brain-damaged pa-

tients are often put on tube feeding before they are terminal because the health care staff does not have the time to manually feed a patient who can no longer eat solid food or swallow properly. Some people see artificial feeding as a means of prolonging death, while others consider it the most basic form of care due to all humans.

Antibiotics

Antibiotics fight infection. They are not always successful, but can be very effective, especially in curing pneumonia. If antibiotics are refused, fever and other symptoms caused by the infection can be relieved with other medications. While antibiotics rarely cause side effects (allergic reactions, upset stomach, kidney failure), the infection can cause sleep or coma, easing the body into death. By treating the infection, the hopelessly ill person may be brought back to conscious awareness of his discomfort and death will be delayed. Antibiotics are such a standard part of medical practice and so easily administered that doctors may not pause to consider whether they will actually be of benefit or not.

Dialysis

Dialysis cleanses the blood when the kidneys are unable to perform the task. Dialysis, either through an intravenous line or a tube placed into the abdomen, needs to be done two or three times a week and takes two to three hours. Many people live for years with the help of dialysis, but for a dying person with sudden kidney failure, the discomfort may outweigh the potential benefit, especially since it will not improve the underlying condition. Untreated kidney failure leads to cardiac arrest or coma, and death.

Surgical Procedures

Surgical procedures such as amputation can halt the spread of infection or relieve pain. Some patients, however, would prefer to be treated with pain medication than undergo surgery.

Diagnostic Tests

Some diagnostic tests are simple and routine such as blood or urine analysis. Some tests may be more involved, expensive, and painful. "CAT" scans (images of the soft tissues of the body) or MRI's (magnetic resonance imaging), although they are not painful in and of themselves, require that the patient be moved from bed and then remain perfectly still while the test is being performed. For someone in severe pain, this can be torture that may not serve any useful purpose.

Intravenous Lines

Intravenous lines (IV's) are standard for most hospitalized patients. They generally are painless once they are inserted, however, confused patients may try to pull out the lines, which may lead to placing the patient in restraints.

Chemotherapy and Radiation

Chemotherapy and radiation are treatments for cancer. When cancer is incurable, doctors may still recommend the treatment for pain reduction or to gain a few more months of life. Chemotherapy can have severe side effects of nausea, vomiting, and other complications. Radiation causes fewer problems and can sometimes shrink a tumor that is causing pain. Doctors in America treat cancer more aggressively and longer than in most countries, resulting in some living wills which specifically state that the patient does not want further cancer treatment unless it relieves pain.

Comfort Care

Comfort care includes any help that makes a dying patient more comfortable. It can include oxygen, food and fluids by mouth, cleaning, touching, or simply sitting with a patient who is dying. Medication in high enough doses to relieve pain are often necessary for comfort care. Hospice care provides comfort care, and most persons state in their living wills that they wish to receive all available care that will ease their passing.

When Living Wills Do Not Help

To be effective, living wills need to be as explicit as possible. It is very hard to predict all the potential medical problems that might arise and, if the patient is unable to participate in the medical decisions, how the will will be interpreted. For example, if an AIDS patient has asked not to be given antibiotics and enters the hospital with pneumonia, should the doctor heed the living will and let the patient die or should she administer the antibiotics, knowing that this is a temporary setback in the illness and the patient still has more time before death is imminent? Bedell and Delbanco in "Choices about Cardiopulmonary Resuscitation in the Hospital," (1984, vol. 310, *New England Journal of Medicine*, Boston), found that eight out of 25 resuscitated cancer patients wished, six months later, that they had not been revived.

Stuart J. Eisendrath, MD, and Albert R. Jonsen, PhD, in "The Living Will: Help or Hindrance?" (1983, vol. 249, no. 15, *Journal of the American Medical Association*, Chicago: AMA), found that if a patient discusses his intentions before a medical emergency arises, the physician will have a better understanding of the patient's desires. This is frequently not the case, however, and the doctor must interpret the living will as best as possible. Eisendrath and Jonsen give two examples of how the living will can either help or hinder the medical process.

A Hindrance

In the first case, a 65 year old woman was admitted for preventive heart surgery against a possible stroke. She informed the medical staff that she had a living will and she wished it to be followed if she suffered a disabling stroke as a result of the operation. After surgery the patient did show signs of severe stroke and was readmitted to surgery to remove a large blood clot in an artery. The patient was unresponsive for several days and pneumonia developed. A tracheostomy was necessary to aid her breathing, but the staff questioned whether this would go against her wishes as expressed in her living will. The physician felt that after only one week, it was impossible to judge how much function the patient might regain and therefore, treatment must be continued. Other staff members worried that they were trapping the woman in a useless body — precisely what she most wanted to avoid. The patient's brother wrote a letter stating that legal action might ensue if the hospital continued to treat her against her wishes.

A hospital ethics committee was called in to review the case and decided that the living will should not be acted upon at this time because it was too soon to predict to what extent the conditions stated in the will ("deterioration, dependence, and hopeless pain") would be permanent. Although this decision ran the risk of leaving the woman in the state she wished to avoid, the ethics committee followed the maxim, "when in doubt, favor life." Within three weeks the woman began to improve and regained her ability to speak. When she was discharged to a rehabilitation center, she was asked how she felt about her living will. She thought they were a good thing, but added that her condition had not been what she had meant in her living will. Her intention was that she did not want to become a "vegetable." Her will had stated, "If a situation should arise in which there is no reasonable expectation of my recovery from physical or mental disability, I request that I be allowed to die. . . ." In this woman's case, what did "reasonable" mean?

A Help

The second case involved a 55 year-old woman who was suffering from multiple sclerosis. She was admitted with aspiration pneumonia caused by her diminished gag reflex, a result of her disease. Antibiotics cleared up the pneumonia, but the woman continued to be in danger of aspiration because the nerve damage to her gag reflex was permanent. The most effective method of dealing with the gag reflex was to close the patient's epiglottis (the valve that prevents food from entering the windpipe or larynx). This would require, however, a permanent tracheostomy which would prevent the patient from speaking. For this woman

this was a most serious consideration. She was highly educated and articulate, and her disease had left her confined to bed. Her only interaction with others was through speech. The doctor informed her that she had no pulmonary reserves and the next episode of aspiration would surely kill her. The patient responded that she would rather die than lose the ability to speak.

A psychiatric consultation was requested and the woman was found to have some mild organic brain dysfunction but no real evidence of psychosis. It was, however, difficult to determine if the patient fully understood the implications of her choice.

At this point, her sister came forth with a living will that the woman had signed several years earlier. The will stated that the patient did not want her life maintained if was not a "useful life." According to the sister, a "useful life" meant being able to communicate meaningfully with others. With this information, the physician could agree to not perform the surgery and let the woman take her chances.

These two cases point out the necessity of making one's wishes known to as many responsible people as possible. In the case of the first woman, she had presented the will to the anesthesiology resident the night before her surgery, but he had not taken any time to discuss it with her. In the second case, the woman's sister was able to clarify the issue, but an earlier discussion with the doctor would have saved the woman the uncertainty of getting the care she desired.

Are Living Wills a Mistake?

The ambiguity in interpreting living wills has led some to question their usefulness, however, since the *Nancy Cruzan* Supreme Court decision (see Chapter VII), they have taken on added significance and importance. They give patients a sense of control in case of a loss of competency and reassures them that excessive treatment will not be imposed against their wishes. They further avoid discussions about the quality of life and give per-

FIGURE 6.1

SAMPLE HEALTH CARE PROXY

1. I, _____(name)_____, hereby appoint _____ (name, home address and telephone number)_____ as my health care agent to make any and all health care decisions for me, except to the extent that I state otherwise. This proxy shall have effect when and if I become unable to make my own health decisions.

2. Optional instructions: I direct my agent to make health care decisions in accord with my wishes and limitations as stated below, or as he or she otherwise knows. _____. (Example: I have discussed with my agent my wishes about artificial nutrition and hydration and I want my agent to make all decisions about these measures.)

3. Name of substitute or fill-in agent if the person I appoint above is unable, unwilling or unavailable to act as my health care agent. _____(name, home address and telephone number) _____

4. Unless I revoke it, this proxy shall remain in effect indefinitely, or until the date or conditions stated here

_____

5. Signature, address and date

_____

Statement by two witnesses, other than the proxy; both must by 18 or older.

Source: Proxy, (NY, 1992)

mission to withhold treatment, permitting doctors to act (or not, as the case may be) without fear of legal repercussions.

Despite their intended benefits, most people do not have living wills, and even when they do, doctors are sometimes reluctant to follow them. The most serious problem, for some, however, as noted by John A. Robertson, a law professor at the University of Texas (1991, "Second Thoughts on Living Wills," *Hastings Center Report*, vol. 21, no. 6, Briarcliff, NY), is that the wills are drawn up by competent people who have not yet faced the actual medical emergency that will call the will into use. Society has come to accept that a competent person knows what the best interests of the incompetent person are. For Robertson, however, the will does not take into account that the person's values may change when he is faced with the real situation. "Although still the same person, the patient's interests have changed radically once she becomes incompetent. Yet the premise of the prior directive is that the patient's interests and values remain significantly the same. . . . "

Although people are encouraged to update their wills frequently, they do not necessarily do so, and the wills may not reflect the fact that people's interests change as they go through life. While no statistical research is available, anecdotes of patients thanking their doctors for not having followed their wills are not uncommon. Robertson believes that the central issue is to determine the best interests of the incompetent patient based on a proxy (surrogate) decision. Rather than simply enforce earlier directives, family and physicians should be able to decide whether or not treatment is in the best interests of the patient. "A procedure that avoids an over rigid vitalism will have to be devised to resolve these conflicts." Robertson does not offer any procedure, but concludes that what quality of life is worth protecting is really the issue, but this is too politically divisive to be discussed openly. As a second best solution, substituted judgment, he feels, is preferable to the vitalist approach of always treating.

HEALTH CARE PROXIES

Because of the problems associated with living wills, they are being replaced or amended by health care proxies. A health care proxy designates a surrogate to have legal authority to make medical decisions if a patient is too sick to do so. (See Figure 6.1. and Appendix IV.) As of February 1992, 42 states and the District of Columbia accepted both living wills and the appointment of a health care agent, four states authorized living wills only, and four states authorized a health care agent only. (See Figure 6.2.) The situation in the states is changing rapidly since the Supreme Court permitted the termination of life support in *Cruzan* (see Chapter VII); state laws that had previously prohibited this would no longer be able to withstand a court challenge.

State Laws

New York's law on the termination of life support is both the most strict and the most subject to interpretation. Surrogates can only reject nutrition and hydration if they can claim specific knowledge of the subject's desires through a written statement or prior conversations, a limitation imposed as a result of lobbying by Roman Catholic groups. The frustrated husband of a woman who choked on food and is in an irreversible coma claimed that the hospital told him he needed five witnesses to swear the woman had specifically said she did not want this tube or that in order to have them removed. The law requires "clear and con-

vincing evidence" of the patient's desires but it leaves the interpretation of what "clear and convincing" means up to the hospital.

The New York legislation is based on a 1988 legal decision (*O'Connor v. Westchester Medical Society* — see Chapter VII) by Judge Wachtler who admitted that the strict interpretation of "clear and convincing" was based on his own personal feelings about his mother's experience with a stroke. Judge Wachtler's mother had suffered a stroke, and eventually, when she was able to say a few words, said, "Let me go." The judge chose not to listen and, today Mrs. Wachtler, 90 years old, has recovered and works in another son's jewelry store. In March 1992, the Governor's Task Force on Life and the Law released proposed legislation to permit surrogates to make decisions in the patient's best interests.

Missouri, the only other state with seriously restricted rights for surrogates, will also have a proposal for the voters in November 1992 that would broaden a surrogate's authority. In Kentucky and Tennessee, surrogates are not permitted to decide to terminate life support for persistent coma victims, but can for patients who are in imminent likelihood of death.

The Nutrition and Hydration Act

The Nutrition and Hydration Act was sponsored by right-to-life organizations in Oklahoma in 1987. The principal portion of the law establishes a legal presumption that "every incompetent patient has directed his health care providers to provide him with hydration and nutrition to a degree that is sufficient to sustain life." The act does have an exception for patients who, while competent and suffering a specific illness or injury, made a decision to have nutrition withheld or withdrawn. The provision was included to prevent right to die advocates from winning a legal battle against the act. The act also excepted cases where two physicians have determined that nutrition or hydration will cause pain or is not medically possible or the patient is the final stage of a terminal illness and

FIGURE 6.2

State Law Governing Living Wills/Declarations and Appointment of a Health Care Agent

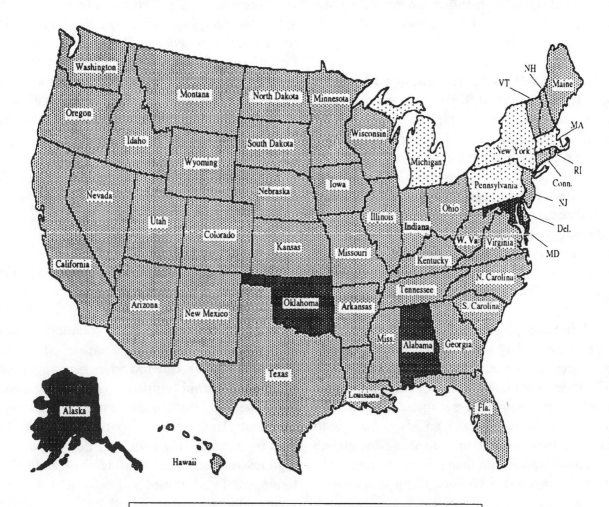

Appropriate documents for each state are available from Choice in Dying.

Jurisdictions with legislation that authorizes both Living Wills/Declarations and the appointment of a health care agent* (**the District of Columbia and 42 states: Arizona, Arkansas, California, Colorado, Connecticut, Delaware, Florida, Georgia, Hawaii, Idaho, Illinois, Indiana, Iowa, Kansas, Kentucky, Louisiana, Maine, Minnesota, Mississippi, Missouri, Montana, Nebraska, Nevada, New Hampshire, New Jersey, New Mexico, North Carolina, North Dakota, Ohio, Oregon, Rhode Island, South Carolina, South Dakota, Tennessee, Texas, Utah, Vermont, Virginia, Washington, West Virginia, Wisconsin and Wyoming**).

States with legislation that authorizes only Living Wills/Declarations (**4 states: Alabama, Alaska, Maryland and Oklahoma.**)

States with legislation that authorizes only the appointment of a health care agent (**4 states: Massachusetts, Michigan, New York and Pennsylvania***).

Note: The specifics of living will and health care agent legislation vary greatly from state to state. In addition, many states also have court-made law that affects residents' rights. For information about specific state laws, please contact Choice in Dying.

* Pennsylvania has no statutory document for this purpose.

Source: Choice in Dying (formerly Concern for Dying/Society for the Right to Die), (NY, 1992)

53

will die of the disease and not starvation. The act prohibits any guardian, court, or third party from withdrawing or withholding nutrition from an incompetent patient, except in the above circumstances. Finally, the act provides that no health care provider shall be required to participate in the care of an incompetent patient who is dying of starvation and dehydration.

Choice in Dying, an organization which had carefully tracked the different laws in each state, feels it is no longer necessary. The Supreme Court has made the termination of life support possible, and the states are rapidly following with the legislation that permits surrogates to make this decision. For vitalists this is a serious blow, although they have now turned their attention to the question of euthanasia (see Chapter V), which is where the next legislative battles will be fought.

The Power of Proxies

Living wills, because of their imprecision, can be circumvented by a determined doctor or hospital ethics committee. Furthermore, most living wills refer to terminal illness, not the situation that develops from many illnesses such as Alzheimer's or stroke. Proxies, however, are given the right to make decisions as needed, something doctors are more comfortable with than a piece of paper written perhaps many years before. Because a patient's right to refuse medical treatment is legally accepted in the United States, this right has also been conferred on the incompetent patient. A designated surrogate is now accepted as the most likely person to serve the patient's best interests.

Making Life Support Decisions

Few states have standards to determine when a patient is no longer able to make rational decisions. This is often left to the physician in consultation with perhaps a psychiatrist or an evaluation by a hospital ethics committee. Occasionally the question will be decided in court. Most legal scholars agree that the ability to make a health care decision requires that the patient have: 1) the ability to understand the treatment choice presented; 2) the capacity to appreciate the implications of the alternatives presented; and 3) the ability to make a choice and to communicate that choice.

Choice in Dying publishes a brochure to help appointed surrogates with the necessary steps to make a medical decision for someone else. The first step is to fully understand the patient's condition and likely outcome. Does this condition apply to any terms stated in the patient's living will? How would the patient wish to be treated in this situation? Has he spoken about this kind of situation? Inform the medical team of the patient's desires and see that they are carried out. (See Figure 6.3.)

THE PATIENT SELF-DETERMINATION ACT

In November 1990, Congress passed the Patient Self-Determination Act (part of the Omnibus Budget Reconciliation Act of 1990 — PL 101-508), partly in response to the situation faced by Nancy Cruzan's family (see Chapter VII), requiring that all health-care providers receiving Medicare and Medicaid (virtually every hospital, nursing home, and health maintenance organization in the country) must inform all patients over age 18 of their rights to plan in advance for their care. It also requires that hospitals educate their staff about living wills and advance directives. Choice in Dying estimates that no more than 20 percent of the population has made an advance directive.

Many hospitals ask a patient on admission if, as ordered by federal law, he has a living will and provide him with the necessary information if he does not but would like to make one. Patients either with wills or those who ask for more information will be visited by someone trained to discuss the issue. Physicians are often reluctant to begin a conversation about the possibility of death, and this law opens the door to all patients to have the opportunity to express their wishes. Some health care workers are worried that patients will react badly to being confronted with the issue, particularly if they have come to the hospital for minor care.

The staff at New York's Beth Israel Hospital have found that the patients are receptive rather than frightened. Since January 1990, hospital representatives have visited every patient within 24 hours to discuss the state law for advance directives and to encourage patients to complete their own document.

The Right to Life Opinion

The National Right to Life Committee objected to the legislation because they believe it encourages people to make living wills and advance directives without fully understanding the implications. Furthermore, it has led states to pass laws permitting these documents without being explicit that these documents often include the right to refuse what vitalists see as non-negotiable care — nutrition and hydration. Thomas Marzen, lawyer for the National Legal Center for the Medically Dependent and Disabled speaks for vitalists when he says,

> What people don't understand is that these rights usually include the ability to refuse the most minimal care — food and fluids, antibiotics, insulin — whatever the condition of the person. Current durable power of attorney laws are a far greater threat than living will laws ever were from this point of view but they are passing state legislatures with little or no resistance.

The National Right to Life Committee has developed a living will to ensure continued medical care for its members which supports a vitalist approach to sustaining life. (See Appendix IV.)

The original bill, as presented by Senator John Danforth (R-MO) and Daniel Moynihan (D-NY),

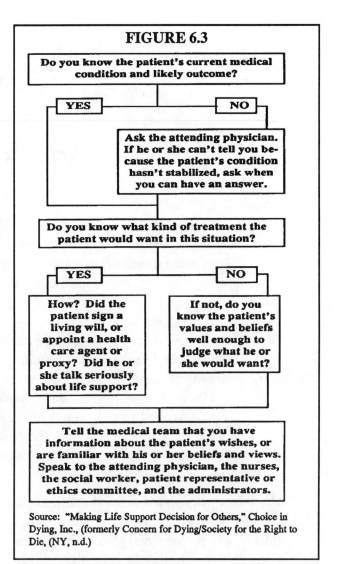

FIGURE 6.3

Do you know the patient's current medical condition and likely outcome?

YES   NO

Ask the attending physician. If he or she can't tell you because the patient's condition hasn't stabilized, ask when you can have an answer.

Do you know what kind of treatment the patient would want in this situation?

YES   NO

How? Did the patient sign a living will, or appoint a health care agent or proxy? Did he or she talk seriously about life support?

If not, do you know the patient's values and beliefs well enough to judge what he or she would want?

Tell the medical team that you have information about the patient's wishes, or are familiar with his or her beliefs and views. Speak to the attending physician, the nurses, the social worker, patient representative or ethics committee, and the administrators.

Source: "Making Life Support Decision for Others," Choice in Dying, Inc., (formerly Concern for Dying/Society for the Right to Die, (NY, n.d.)

included a provision that all states must enact both living will and durable power of attorney legislation in order to receive federal health care funds. Pressure from vitalist groups succeeded in removing that provision, while pro-life representative Brian Donnelly (D-MA) added a clause to preserve the rights of any health care provider who, as a matter of conscience, cannot implement an advance directive.

CHAPTER VII

THE LEGAL RIGHT TO DIE

*When cherished values of human dignity and personal privacy, which
belong to every person living or dying, are sufficiently transgressed by what
is being done to the individual, we should be ready to say: enough.*
Judge J. Handler, dissenting *In the Matter of Conroy*

*. . . I can think of nothing more degrading to the human person than the
balance which the court struck today in favor of death against life. It is but
another triumph for the forces of secular humanism (modern paganism)
which have now succeeded in imposing their anti-life principles at both
ends of life's spectrum.*
Judge J. Nolan, dissenting *Patricia E. Brophy
v. New England Sinai Hospital*

Black's Law Dictionary defined death as "a total stoppage of the circulation of the blood," until, in 1979, an additional entry was added under the heading of "brain death." In 1968, the Ad Hoc Committee of the Harvard Medical School published their report which included irreversible coma as a new criterion for death. The courts, sticking with tradition, continued to use *Black's* definition into the 1970s, mainly in cases involving homicide and organ transplants. But confusion as to the definition of death (see also Chapter II) and a patient's right to die was growing as medical technology became increasingly able to keep the circulation of a comatose person functioning independently.

THE RIGHT OF PRIVACY:
KAREN ANN QUINLAN

The case of Karen Ann Quinlan (*In re Quinlan*, 70 NJ 10, 355 A2d 647, 1976) was the first to confront the complexities of terminating life sup-

port for a patient who was not dead, not terminally ill, and yet not really "alive." In ruling on this landmark case, the New Jersey Supreme Court changed the accepted practice of permitting doctors and families to make private decisions about terminating life support and turned instead to the courts for judicial resolution.

Karen Quinlan was a 22 year old woman who, after the alleged ingestion of tranquilizers and alcohol, stopped breathing for at least two 15-minute periods, which resulted in a permanent coma. Dr. Fred Plum, a neurological expert, described her as a "subject who remains with the capacity to maintain the vegetative parts of neurological function but who . . . no longer has any cognitive function." She made grimaces, chewing motions, sounds, kept a normal blood pressure, but could not respond.

Karen's father asked to be appointed her guardian and have the power to authorize "the discontinuance of all extraordinary procedures for sustaining his daughter's vital processes." Experts believed she could not breathe without the respirator and that she would die soon after its removal. (It is interesting that her father did not include nutrition in his request and when Karen's respirator was finally removed, she lived on for nine years, breathing on her own. Her father never asked to have the tubal feeding stopped.) Her doctor refused to disconnect Karen's respirator because he felt that she was not brain dead, and according to medical ethics, a doctor should not interrupt the life-saving benefits of the respirator if the patient were not dead.

Karen's father lost his case in Superior Court and appealed to the Supreme Court of New Jersey where he was granted the right to disconnect the respirator. The court examined several arguments before deciding on the basis of the decision, a decision which has now been used as legal precedent in almost all right-to-die cases.

The Right to Privacy

The court rejected the right of free exercise of religious freedom and protection from cruel and unusual punishment as irrelevant and settled on the right to privacy. They believed the right to privacy had the greatest bearing on the case and made it the basis of their decision. Although the U.S. Constitution does not explicitly mention a right to privacy, certain areas of privacy have been recognized by the courts. The right to self-determination of one's body has been upheld in *Griswold v. Connecticut* (the right to use contraception — 381 US 479), *Roe v. Wade* (the right to abortion — 410 US 174), and in many cases upholding the right to refuse medical treatment. If Karen had the legal right to refuse treatment, did it then follow that her guardian also had the right to refuse for her?

The court had no doubt that Karen would not wish to be maintained in her present condition.

... in these unhappy circumstances, that if Karen were herself miraculously lucid for

an interval (not altering the existing prognosis of the condition to which she would soon return) and perceptive of her irreversible condition, she could effectively decide upon discontinuance of the life-support apparatus, even if it meant the prospect of natural death.

Balanced against Karen's right to privacy was the state's interest in preserving life. The court, however, found that the state's interest "weakens and the individual's right to privacy grows as the degree of bodily invasion increases and the prognosis dims. Ultimately there comes a point at which the individual's rights overcome the State interest." The New Jersey court found that care for Karen was highly invasive (24-hour nursing care, antibiotics, respirator, catheter, and feeding tube). Some later court rulings have argued that, because the patient is unaware of the treatment, it cannot be interpreted as invasive.

Is It Homicide?

Karen's doctor was concerned that terminating life support would violate normal medical practice and perhaps would also subject him to criminal prosecution. The court found that while respirators could be considered "ordinary" care for a curable patient, they were "extraordinary" for an "irreversibly doomed" patient.

The evidence in this case convinces us that the focal point of decision should be the prognosis as to the reasonable possibility of return to cognitive and sapient life, as distinguished from the forced continuance of that biological vegetative existence to which Karen seems to be doomed.

To help avoid criminal liability, the court suggested that doctors turn to hospital ethics committees. This would diffuse responsibility and screen out cases which were "contaminated by less than worthy motivations of family or physician." The court felt that, in general, the court was not the right place for these decisions because it infringed on the medical profession's field of competence and because it was too cumbersome. Furthermore, the court rejected the notion that terminating life support could be interpreted as homicide. Death would result from existing natural causes and could not be construed as "unlawful" since it was due to the removal of life support as a matter of self-determination.

Guardianship

While the lower court had found Karen's father to be "very sincere, moral, ethical and religious," the judges thought his having to make a choice for Karen would be a "source of anguish to him and would distort his 'decision-making processes.'" The higher court disagreed and found that his strength of character far outweighed any of these other considerations and concluded that there was no reason to overrule the normal preference for appointing next of kin to serve as guardian. In this case the court did not question whether or not a guardian should make a decision for an incompetent patient — this issue would arise in later cases concerning terminating life support.

The New Jersey court established important precedents in their decision, especially the right to privacy, guardianship, and the recommendation of hospital ethics committees. Recognizing their responsibility, the court wrote,

> Put in another way, the law, equity and justice must not themselves quail and be helpless in the face of modern technological marvels presenting question hitherto unthought of. Where a Karen Quinlan, or a parent, or a doctor, or a hospital, or a State seeks the process and response of a court, it must answer with its most informed conception of justice in the previously unexplored circumstances presented to it. That is its obligation and we are here fulfilling it, for the actors and those having an interest in the matter should not go without remedy.

SUBSTITUTED JUDGMENT

Superintendent of Belchertown State School v. Joseph Saikewicz

Joseph Saikewicz was a mentally incompetent resident of the Belchertown Institution suffering from acute myeloblastic monocytic leukemia. The superintendent of the school petitioned the court for a guardian *ad litem* (a temporary guardian for the time of the trial) who would appeal to the court for permission not to treat the resident. Saikewicz was 67 years old, but had a mental age of about two and half years when he was diagnosed with the fatal leukemia. Chemotherapy, the normal treatment of choice, achieved remission in only 30 to 50 percent of the cases. If remission did occur, it typically lasted between two and 13 months. Age is a factor in remission, thus Saikewicz was considered too old to respond well to treatments.

The effects of chemotherapy would make Saikewicz feel much sicker than he presently did from the disease. He would become severely anemic and need blood transfusions to prevent his dying from the treatment. If treatments were not given, Saikewicz would probably live for a matter of weeks, perhaps months, and he would die without pain. Although a competent adult would normally choose to receive the chemotherapy, the judge in the probate court found that because of the patient's profound retardation, he would be unable to cooperate with treatment or to understand why he was having the side effects (nausea, hair loss, bladder irritation, pain, etc.) of chemotherapy.

In fact, Joseph Saikewicz died on September 4, 1976 from pneumonia, a complication of the leukemia. Nevertheless, his case was heard by the Supreme Court of Massachusetts in order to establish a precedent on the question of substituted judgment (*Superintendent of Belchertown State School v. Joseph Saikewicz*, Mass, 370, N.E.2d 417, 1977).

The court agreed that extraordinary measures should not be used if there is no hope for recovery, and furthermore, "Recovery should not be defined simply as the ability to remain alive; it should mean life without intolerable suffering" (Lewis, 1968, "Machine Medicine and Its Relation to the Fatally Ill", Vol 387, *Journal of the American Medical Association*). The court also found that a person has a right to his body integrity and can refuse medical invasion. The Massachusetts court turned to *Quinlan* in support of the right of privacy.

The Rights of an Incompetent Patient

Once the right to refuse treatment had been established, the court then had to decide the rights of the incompetent patient.

> The recognition of that right must extend to the case of an incompetent, as a competent, patient because the value of human dignity extends to both. . . . To presume that the incompetent person must always be subjected to what many rational and intelligent persons may decline is to downgrade the status of the incompetent person by placing a lesser value on his intrinsic human worth and vitality.

Although the *Saikewicz* court referred to *Quinlan*, the recommendation of the Massachusetts court was not to give the treatment that most people would choose. (Unlike some later courts, *Quinlan* accepted the premise that a vegetative patient would not want to remain "alive.") The court had to make a subjective decision, "to determine with as much accuracy as possible the wants and needs of the individual involved." "Substituted judgment" was preferable "because of its straightforward respect for the integrity and autonomy of the individual." The court took pains, however, to point out that the probate judge's use of the term "quality of life" in making the decision not to treat the patient referred only to the pain and disorientation of the treatment and not to Saikewicz's ability to appreciate life.

In evaluating the role of the hospital and the guardian in the decision-making process, the court rejected the *Quinlan* court's recommendation that ethics committees should be the source of decisions. The court instead concluded:

> We do not view the judicial resolution of this most difficult and awesome question - whether potentially life-prolonging treatment should be withheld from a person incapable of making his own decision — as constituting a "gratuitous encroachment" on the domain of medical expertise. Rather, such questions of life and death seem to us to require the process of detached but passionate investigation and decision that forms the ideal on which the judicial branch of government was created. Achieving this ideal is our responsibility and that of the lower court, and is not to be entrusted to any other group purporting to represent the "morality and conscience of our society," no matter how highly motivated or impressively constituted.

In the Matter of John Storar

Like Saikewicz, John Storar was a mentally retarded man (he had a mental age of about 18 months and a chronological age of 52 years) with terminal cancer. His mother petitioned the court to discontinue blood transfusions which were delaying her son's death, which would probably occur within three to six months. At the time of the hearing, Storar required two units of blood every week or two. He found the transfusions disagreeable and had to be given a sedative prior to and be restrained during the procedure. Without the transfusions, however, there would be insufficient oxygen in the patient's blood, causing his heart to beat faster and his breathing to increase. After transfusions, the doctor reported, John had more energy and was able to resume most of his normal activities.

The Probate Court had granted Mrs. Storar the right to terminate the treatments, but the order was stayed and treatment was continued pending the appeal to the New York Appellate Division (*In the Matter of John Storar* N.Y., 420 N.E.2d 64, 1981). John Storar died before the case could be heard, rendering the decision moot, but the issues were considered to be of public importance, and so the court heard the case anyway.

The Appeals Court agreed with the lower court that a guardian can make medical decisions for an incompetent patient, but the parent/guardian "may not deprive a child of life saving treatment." In this case, there were two threats to Storar's life — the cancer that was incurable and the loss of blood which could be remedied with transfusions. Because the transfusions did not, in the eyes of the majority opinion (written by Judge Wachtler — see also *O'Connor*, below), cause much pain, the court overturned the lower court's ruling.

In a dissenting opinion, Judge Jones wrote that the problem of medical treatments is one which the judicial system is ill-equipped to handle. The time lapse, the lack of medical expertise, the adversarial system of the court, and the weighing of theological and human values are all factors that make a court a poor choice for such decisions. Judge Jones did not think that the treatments served Storar's best interests. They did not relieve his pain. In fact, they caused him additional pain and, in this case, they served as extraordinary treatment because they offered no cure. Finally, the judge reasoned that John's mother, after a life-time of care, knew best what her son needed, and her opinions should be respected.

COMPETENT PATIENTS' WISHES

Satz v. Perlmutter

Not all the cases of patients who are seeking to terminate life support are about incompetent persons. Abe Perlmutter (73 years old) was suffering from amyotrophic lateral sclerosis (ALS, sometimes called Lou Gherig's Disease), a disease that is always fatal after a prolonged physical degeneration, but which does not lessen mental acuity. Mr. Perlmutter asked the court for the right to have his respirator removed. The court questioned whether the patient truly understood the consequences of his request. Mr. Perlmutter's response to a judge at a bedside hearing was that if the respirator were removed, "it can't be worse than what I'm going through now."

The Florida court found that Perlmutter's right to refuse treatment overrode the State's interests and found in Perlmutter's favor (*Satz v. Perlmutter*, Fla. App., 362 So.2d, 160, 1978).

The State's Interests

Legally, a state has four interests to protect:

1. Interest in the preservation of life;
2. Need to protect innocent third parties;
3. Duty to prevent suicide;
4. Requirement that it help maintain the ethical integrity of medical practice.

The court found that the preservation of life is an important goal, but not when the affliction is incurable, and the issue is not whether, but when, for how long, and at what cost to the individual a life may be extended. The protection of third parties refers to cases in which a parent refuses to treat a minor, thus abandoning that child. That was clearly not the case for Mr. Perlmutter. Mr. Perlmutter was also not committing suicide; he was exercising his right to refuse medical treatment. In regard to the fourth point, ethical medical practice, the court turned to *Quinlan* and *Saikewicz* in finding that there are times when medical care dictates that a patient needs comfort more than treatment. The court concluded:

> Abe Perlmutter should be allowed to make his choice to die with dignity, notwithstanding over a dozen legislative failures in this state to adopt suitable legislation in this field. It is all very convenient to insist on continuing Mr. Perlmutter's life so that

there can be no question of foul play, no resulting civil liability and no possible trespass on medical ethics. However, it is quite another matter to do so at the patient's sole expense and against his competent will, thus inflicting never ending physical torture on his body until the inevitable, but artificially suspended, moment of death. Such a course of conduct invades the patient's constitutional right of privacy, removes his freedom of choice and invades his right to self-determine.

John F. Kennedy Hospital v. Bludworth

In a case similar to *Perlmutter*, *John F. Kennedy Hospital v. Bludworth* (Fla., 452 So.2d 921, 1984), the hospital questioned whether a terminal patient with a living will needed the court to appoint a guardian in order to obtain court approval to terminate life support in accordance with the will. Without court approval, would family members, attending physicians, and the hospital and its administrators be civilly or criminally liable? The court found that, not only was a court decision not necessary, but neither was a court appointed guardian, nor was a hospital ethics committee review as recommended by *Quinlan*. While the court is available if there are disagreements, substituted judgment with the persuasive evidence of a living will is sufficient basis for a decision.

THE SUBJECTIVE, LIMITED-OBJECTIVE, AND PURE-OBJECTIVE TEST

In the Matter of Claire C. Conroy

Claire Conroy was an 84-year-old nursing home patient with serious and irreversible mental and physical impairments and with a limited life expectancy. Her nephew and guardian (her only living relative) petitioned the court to remove her nasogastric tube. Conroy's guardian *ad litem* opposed the petition. A trial court approved the nephew's request and the guardian *ad litem* appealed. Mrs. Conroy died with the nasogastric tube

in place while the appeal was pending. Nonetheless, the Appellate Court chose to hear the case, reversing the trial court's ruling (*In the Matter of Claire C. Conroy*, N.J., 486 A.2d 1209, 1985).

Claire Conroy had multiple problems: heart disease, hypertension, and diabetes; her left leg was gangrenous to the knee, she had several bed sores, she had an eye problem that required irrigation, she could not control her bowels, she could not speak, and her ability to swallow was very limited. She was not, however, comatose or in a vegetative state, and she had some very limited interaction with her environment. One expert witness characterized her as awake, but severely demented; she was "unable to respond to verbal stimuli, and as far as he could tell, had no higher functioning or consciousness." A second expert witness testified that "although she was confused and unaware, 'she responds somehow.'"

The experts did not agree as to what Mrs. Conroy could feel. The first expert was unsure whether the nasogastric tube caused her discomfort and thought it was "an open question whether she [felt] pain," although, it was possible that she was in a great deal of pain. The second doctor proposed that her contracted legs were a symptom of her pain, but that she did not necessarily feel pain from the sores on her legs. On the other hand, the doctors seemed to feel that she would suffer pain from her death from dehydration if they removed her tube.

Mrs. Conroy's nephew testified that she would never have wanted to be maintained in this manner. She had avoided doctors all her life, even refusing to have her gangrenous leg amputated in 1982. Because Mrs. Conroy was Roman Catholic, a priest was brought in to testify. In his judgment, the removal of the tube would be ethical and moral even though the death might be painful.

The Appeals Court held that the right to terminate life support "was limited to incurable and terminally ill patients who are brain dead, irreversibly comatose, or vegetative, and who would gain no medical benefit from continued treatment."

Furthermore, a guardian's decision "may never be used to withhold nourishment" from an incompetent patient who does not fit the terms above. Withholding food and water, according to the court, hastens death rather than simply allowing an illness to take its course, and removing Ms. Conroy's tube would be "tantamount to killing her." "Such active euthanasia [see Chapter V] would be ethically impermissible."

The Three Tests

The court proposed three tests to determine if the feeding tube should be removed from Claire Conroy's nose. The subjective test was to determine "not what a reasonable or average person would have chosen to do under the circumstances but what the particular patient would have done if able to choose for himself." The court listed acceptable expressions of intent which should be considered by surrogates or the court: spoken expressions, living wills, oral directives, prior behavior, and religion.

> . . . the probative value of such evidence may vary depending on the remoteness, consistency, and thoughtfulness of the prior statements or actions and the maturity of the person at the time of the statements or acts. Thus, for example, an offhand remark about not wanting to live under certain circumstances made by a person when young and in the peak of health would not in itself constitute clear proof twenty years later that he would want life-sustaining treatment withheld under those circumstances. In contrast, a carefully considered position, especially if written, that a person had maintained over a number of years or that he had acted upon in comparable circumstances might be clear evidence of his intent.

If the court determines that the patient, like Claire Conroy, has not made her wishes explicit, two other "best interests" tests can be applied. The limited-objective test permits suspending life sustaining treatment if the pain that the patient would experience would outweigh any "physical pleasure, emotional enjoyment, or intellectual satisfaction that the patient may still be able to derive from life." The limited-objective test also requires some trustworthy evidence that the patient would have wanted the treatment stopped.

The pure-objective test applies when there is no trustworthy evidence, or perhaps any evidence at all, to help guide a decision. The treatment again must outweigh the benefits — "the recurring, unavoidable and severe pain of the patient's life with the treatment should be such that the effect of administering life-sustaining treatment would be inhumane."

Quality of Life and Nutrition are Not Factors

The court did not, however, want to give the impression that they were establishing a "quality of life" basis for judgment.

> Although we are condoning a restricted evaluation of the nature of a patient's life in terms of pain, suffering, and possible enjoyment . . . we expressly decline to authorize decision-making based on assessments of the personal worth or social utility of another's life, or the value of that life to others. We do not believe that it would be appropriate for a court to designate a person with the authority to determine that someone else's life is not worth living simply because, to that person, the patient's "quality of life" or value to society seems negligible.

In addition, the court emphasized that the question of food was not the crucial factor. Although food has a symbolic meaning, like "ordinary" and "extraordinary" treatment, its relevance is to the wishes and needs of the patient only. Food may actually increase the distress of a dying patient and the proposed pain of dying from dehydration may well be either no more painful than any other form of death or not painful at all to some dying patients.

Claire Conroy, the court concluded, failed the tests. Her intentions, while perhaps clear enough to help support a limited-objective test, were not strong enough for the subjective test, and the information on possible pain versus benefits was not sufficient for either the limited-objective or pure-objective test. Had Ms. Conroy survived the Appellate Court's decision, more information to support the subjective test and the limited-objective test would have been necessary to terminate her life support.

A Dissenting Opinion

Judge Handler, dissenting in part with the majority's opinion, wrote,

I harbor the most serious doubts as to the justice, efficacy or humaneness of a standard that would require a person to die in this fashion. The Court should, therefore, formulate a standard that would, in these circumstances, permit a natural death with dignity and compassion. Such a standard should not give determinative weight to the element of personal pain, which necessarily obviates other extremely important considerations. Rather it should accommodate as comprehensively, fairly, and realistically as possible all concerns and values that have a legitimate bearing on the decision whether to provide particular treatment at the very end of an individual's life.

The judge felt that the standards set by the majority's tests focused on pain as the critical factor. First, pain is not always the operative factor; it can be controlled through drugs in many cases. Second, pain levels cannot always be determined as was shown by Ms. Conroy's case. Finally, the pain requirement negates other highly relevant considerations. Not all patients make a decision based on fear of pain. Other individuals fear being dependent, or value personal privacy or dignity. Bodily integrity may be more important than simply prolonging life. Judge Handler supported

reliance on knowledgeable, responsible surrogates, not standards set in a series of tests.

CAN DOCTORS BE HELD LIABLE?

Barber v. Superior Court of the State of California

Other than Dr. Kevorkian (see Chapter V), physicians have been mostly free from prosecution for terminating life support. A precedent was set in 1983 when two doctors were charged with murder and conspiracy to commit murder, based on agreeing to requests from a patient's family to discontinue life support (*Barber v. Superior Court of the State of California*, 147 Cal. App. 3d.1006, 195 Cal. Rptr. 484, 1983).

The deceased, Clarence Herbert, suffered cardio-respiratory arrest following surgery. He was placed on a respirator, and after three days his condition was diagnosed as deeply comatose. The prognosis was that he would likely never recover. The family drafted a written request that the patient's respirator be removed. The doctors complied, but Mr. Herbert continued to breathe on his own. The family stayed by his bedside, requesting that the nursing staff not disturb him. After two days, the family asked the doctors to remove the intravenous tubes that provided nourishment and hydration. "From that point until his death, Mr. Herbert received nursing care which preserved his dignity and provided a clean and hygienic environment."

The court began by stating that "It appears to us that a murder prosecution is a poor way to design an ethical and moral code for doctors who are faced with decisions concerning the use of costly and extraordinary 'life support' equipment." "Murder," they declared, "is the *unlawful* killing of a human being, . . . with malice aforethought." The doctors' behavior was not the cause of death, the patient's physical condition was responsible; there was no malice, and they had acted in good faith and sound ethical judgment.

A lower court had ruled that because the doctors' behavior had intentionally shortened the patient's life, they had committed murder. The higher court, however, found that a patient's right to refuse treatment and a surrogate's right to refuse for an incompetent superseded any liability that could be attributed to the doctors. In addition, although food has a symbolic meaning, in this case it was a medical treatment, and doctors have the right to discontinue treatments that are of no benefit to the patient. For these reasons the court found in favor of the doctors.

Estate of Leach v. Shapiro

Edna Marie Leach suffered from respiratory distress. In July 1980 she had a respiratory-cardiac arrest which left her in a vegetative state. In October, Mr. Leach, as guardian, petitioned to have life support terminated. In December it was granted, and Mrs. Leach died three weeks later. On July 9, 1982 Mrs. Leach's family sued for damages for the time Mrs. Leach was on life support systems. The trial court dismissed the motion, but the Appeals Court reversed the lower court, permitting the Leaches to sue (*Leach v. Shapiro*, Ohio App. 469 N.E.2d 1047, 1984).

Mrs. Leach's family alleged that the hospital had hidden her true condition from them for two months and during that period had administered experimental drugs without the family's consent to see what effects these drugs would have on a person in Mrs. Leach's condition.

The Ohio Appeals Court did not rule on the Leachs' specific situation, but on whether or not they had the right to sue for damages. The court found that

> A physician who treats a patient without consent commits a battery, even though the procedure is harmless or beneficial. . . .the patient's right to refuse treatment is absolute until the quality of the competing [state] interests is weighed in a court proceeding. We perceive this

right as the logical extension of the consent requirement and conclude that a patient may recover for battery if his refusal is ignored.

The court ruled that the relationship of trust between patient and doctor flowed to the person acting in the patient's behalf and the family did, therefore, have the right to sue for damages incurred by the invasion of Mrs. Leach's right to privacy.

WHAT ARE THE HOSPITAL'S RIGHTS?

Patricia E. Brophy v. New England Sinai Hospital, Inc.

Paul Brophy suffered an aneurysm in 1983 that left him in a persistent vegetative state. He was not brain dead, nor was he terminal. He had been a fireman and emergency medical technician and often expressed the opinion that he never wanted to be kept alive artificially. When the aneurysm ruptured he had said to his daughter, "If I can't sit up to kiss one of my beautiful daughters, I may as well be six feet under."

Patricia Brophy brought suit when physicians refused to remove or clamp a gastrostomy tube (G-tube) that was maintaining her husband's vegetative state. The Appeals Court ruled against Mrs. Brophy, but the State Supreme Court reviewed the case and found that substituted judgment was sufficient to permit removal of the tube. However, if the hospital felt that they were ethically unable to remove the tube, they were to have the patient moved to another facility which would terminate life support (*Brophy v. New England Sinai Hosp., Inc.* Mass. 497 N.E.2d 626, 1986).

The court accepted substituted judgement for a comatose patient who had made his intentions clear, although they had not been written out. The majority decision also accepted the hospital's right to refuse to remove the G-tube although it noted, "A significant portion of the medical community disagrees with New England Sinai Hospital and considers it appropriate to withhold hydration and nutrition from individuals like Brophy when that is the wish of the patient and his family." This point referred to the state's fourth interest of maintaining the ethical standards of the medical community (above). "A patient's right to refuse medical treatment does not warrant such an unnecessary intrusion upon the hospital's ethical integrity in this case."

Vitalist Dissensions

Two judges strongly disagreed with the majority opinion to permit removing the G-tube. Justice Nolan wrote, "The court today has rendered an opinion which affronts logic, ethics, and the dignity of the human person." For Nolan, the decision fell apart because it was built on the "outrageously erroneous premise" that food and liquid are medical treatments that can be refused. In his view, food and water are basic human needs, and by permitting removal of the G-tube the court had given approval to "euthanasia and suicide."

Justice Lynch felt that the court had not paid enough attention to the state's interests in preserving life. The state has an interest in preserving this particular life and in the sanctity of all human life. Did an individual have "a legal right to choose to die, and to enlist the assistance of others to effectuate that choice on the ground that, irrespective of the nature of available life prolonging treatment, life in any event is not worth living and its continuation is intolerable." Lynch saw the court's approval of Brophy's request as condoning the right to suicide, because Brophy would be terminating his life through his action, and the right to euthanasia because the person who removed the tube was aiding in ending that life. "Such rights should never be recognized." Lynch concluded,

> Whether the court is establishing an absolute legal right to commit suicide or a right that depends on judicial measurement of the quality of the life involved, neither principle is consistent with this nation's traditional and fitting reverence for human life.

Even in cases involving severe and enduring illness, disability and "helplessness," society's focus must be on life, not death, with dignity. By its very nature, every human life, without reference to its condition, has a value that no one rightfully can deny or measure. Recognition of that truth is the cornerstone on which American law is built. Society's acceptance of that fundamental principle explains why, from time immemorial, society through law has extended its protection to all, including, especially, its weakest and most vulnerable members. The court's implicit, if not explicit, declaration that not every human life has sufficient value to be worthy of the State's protection denies the dignity of all human life, and undermines the very principles on which American law is constructed.

In the Matter of Beverly Requena

Beverly Requena was a competent 55 year old woman with ALS (amyotrophic lateral sclerosis). She would soon lose the ability to swallow and had informed the hospital that she would refuse a feeding tube at that time. The Roman Catholic hospital filed a suit to remove her from the hospital, citing that the hospital has a strong institutional policy against participating in withholding food or fluids.

Time was running very short for Beverly Requena. She was paralyzed from the neck down, unable to make sounds, although she could form words with her lips, and could suck some nutrients through a straw. During the two weeks prior to her hearing, she lost 18 pounds. Judge Stanton described her in his decision:

> Her body is now almost totally useless. She is trapped within it. Most understandably, she feels enormous frustration and experiences a pervasive sense of helplessness and hopelessness. Her situation is desperately sad.

The court did not question her right to refuse nutrition. That was a right that had been upheld in many prior cases. Nor did the hospital question that right, but the hospital board of trustees stated,

> . . . food and water are basic human needs and that such fundamental care cannot be withheld from patients in the Medical Center and that neither the Medical Center nor personnel will participate in the withholding or withdrawal of artificial feeding and/or fluids.

The hospital offered to transfer Ms. Requena to another facility which would be willing to assist her.

Ms. Requena, however, had spent the last 17 months in the hospital, she had developed a relationship of trust and affection for the staff, and was familiar with her surroundings. To move her would be psychologically stressful and "would also have significant elements of rejection and casting out which would be burdensome for Mrs. Requena." The staff at the hospital was feeling stress as well because of their fondness for Ms. Requena and did not want to see her die a presumably painful death from dehydration.

She Does Not Have to Leave

Unlike the decision in *Brophy*, the judge found that Beverly Requena could not be removed from the hospital without her consent and that the hospital would have to accede to her wishes (N.J.Super.A.D. 517 A.2d 869, 1986). The judges' conclusion included the primacy of the patient's right to make informed, autonomous decisions. The hospital's role is to counsel her and give her the information she needs, but the decision must be her free choice. The court found the hospital to be "coercive" because they saw the issue as "pro-life" versus "anti-life." Beverly Requena was not "anti-life," she had consciously accepted her death and surrendered to the dying process. The court decision concluded,

In unconscious ways, some of the management and treating personnel are being inappropriately judgmental. They are, in effect, telling this poor woman that it is wrong for her not to accept more suffering. Beverly Requena is sorely tried by her ordeal. Putting her out of the Hospital would be a hard psychological and emotional blow to her. . . . I realize that by keeping Mrs. Requena in the Hospital I will be imposing a real burden on its nurses and technicians. I do not like to do that. But they are well and whole people. . . . In the final analysis, it is fairer to ask them to give than it is to ask Beverly Requena to give. Also, I suggest, with deference, that by rethinking more carefully their own attitudes, the health care workers at the Hospital might find it possible to be more fully accepting and supportive of Mrs. Requena's decision. If they were able to do that, I think that some of the special stress of this situation might disappear.

In closing, the judge quoted the words of Jesus, "Come to me, all you who are weary and find life burdensome, and I will refresh you" (Matthew 11:28).

In the Matter of Nancy Ellen Jobes

Since 1980 Nancy Jobes had been in a nursing home in a persistent vegetative state. At age 24 and four and half months pregnant, she had an automobile accident that killed her fetus. During the operation to remove the fetus she sustained severe loss of oxygen and blood flow to the brain. She never regained consciousness. In 1985 her husband brought a suit to have the feeding tube removed. The trial court appointed a guardian *ad litem* who, after reviewing the case, filed in favor of the Jobeses. The nursing home moved to appoint a "life advocate" which was turned down by the trial court. The nursing home then appealed the decision (*In the Matter of Nancy Ellen Jobes*, N.J. 529 A2d 434, 1987).

Differing Medical Interpretations

Whether or not Nancy Jobes was in a persistent vegetative state (PVS) was hotly debated in this trial and revealed how different medical interpretations of the same patient can lead to different conclusions. After Mr. Jobes initiated the suit, Nancy was transferred to Cornell Medical Center for four days of observation by order of the guardian *ad litem*. Dr. Plum, a world renowned expert in the field and the man who first identified PVS, and his associate, Dr. Levy, found that, after hours of observation, a positron-emission tomograph scan, and a nuclear magnetic resonance scan, Nancy Jobes was in a persistent vegetative state and would never improve.

The nursing home also asked for expert opinions. Dr. Victor, a neurosurgeon from Case Western Reserve, observed Nancy for about one and one-half hours. He found that, although she had suffered severe and irreversible brain damage, he would not characterize her condition as PVS. He had no written record of his impressions, but testified that on four or five occasions she had responded to his request to pick up her head, or wiggle her toes, or stick out her tongue. Dr. Ropper, of the Harvard Medical School, also observed Mrs. Jobes for the same amount of time and found that her range of motions excluded her from his definition of PVS. (His definition differed from Dr. Plum's in that it excludes patients who make reflexive responses from being in PVS, a definition that would have also excluded Karen Quinlan.) Testimony from the nurses who had cared for Nancy over the last several years was also contradictory, with some asserting that she smiled or responded to their care, while others said they saw no movement that could be interpreted as anything more than reflexive.

The court chose to base their decision on the testimony of Dr. Levy because he had spent the most time observing Nancy and he had been hired by the two most disinterested parties, the Public Advocate and the guardian *ad litem*.

Nancy's friends and family testified that in general conversation, Nancy had always said that she never wanted to be kept alive in these kinds of circumstances. The court found the evidence to be "trustworthy" but not clear and convincing enough to satisfy the subjective test (see above). The court did, however, find that family members are the best qualified to represent an incompetent patient's best interests. It is they who "treat the patient as a person, rather than as a symbol of a cause." In fact, the court did not really see why a case such as this even needed to come to the court. Legal precedent supported Nancy Jobes' right, as expressed through her husband, to terminate treatment and it was unfortunate that through the cumbersome court process too many patients died while waiting for a decision (*Conroy, Bludworth, Perlmutter, Saikewicz, Storar*, etc.).

The Nursing Home's Responsibility

The trial court had found that the nursing home could refuse to participate in the withdrawal of the feeding tube. The Appeals Court reversed that decision. "Mrs Jobes' family had no reason to believe that they were surrendering the right to choose among medical alternatives when they placed her in the nursing home." The nursing home had not informed the family of their policy until 1985 when the family made the request to remove the tube. At this point it would have been very difficult to find another facility to take Nancy, leading the court to rule that the nursing home was frustrating Nancy's right of self-determination.

Justice O'Hern dissented on both issues decided in this case. He questioned the precedent set by giving the responsibility to the family. Not all families are as loving and caring as the Jobes family. "It is not possible for us to construct a substantive principle of law based upon the intact family status. We must construct a substantive principle of law that will endure in all circumstances." He also disagreed that the nursing home had a responsibility to furnish treatment contrary to its ethical standards. This decision impinges on the privacy rights of the nursing professionals. "I find it difficult to understand how we can order nursing professionals with an abiding respect for their patients to cease to furnish the most basic of human needs to a patient in their care."

CLEAR AND CONVINCING

Throughout the history of right-to-die cases, there has been considerable debate as to how to determine a patient's wishes. How clearly must a patient have expressed his or her opinions before becoming incompetent? Does a parent or other family member best represent the patient? Is casual conversation sufficient to reveal intentions, or must they be written down?

In the Matter of Philip Eichner, On Behalf of Joseph C. Fox

The case of Joseph Fox was the first in which the reported attitudes of an incompetent patient were accepted as "clear and convincing." Fox was an 83-year-old member of the religious order, the Society of Mary. He was in a persistent vegetative state as the result of a hernia operation. The local director of the society, Philip Eichner, filed suit asking for permission to have the respirator removed.

The court reasoned that "the highest burden of proof beyond a reasonable doubt should be required when granting the relief that may result in the patient's death." The need for high standards "forbids relief whenever the evidence is loose, equivocal or contradictory." Brother Fox, however, had discussed his feelings in the context of formal religious discussions and only two months before his final hospitalization had stated he would not want his life prolonged if his condition were hopeless. "These were obviously solemn pronouncements and not casual remarks made at some social gathering, nor can it be said that he was too young to realize or feel the consequences of his statements" (*In the Matter of Eichner*, N.Y., 420 N.E.2d 64, 1981).

In the Matter of Westchester County Medical Center on Behalf of Mary O'Connor

Most patients do not have the foresight to express their views in solemn religious discussions, nevertheless, courts have supported evidence of "best interest" or "substituted judgments." The cases of *O'Connor* and *Cruzan* challenged those notions and the right to die.

Mary O'Connor was a 77-year-old widow, who, as a result of several strokes, was incompetent and unable to eat without assistance. The hospital petitioned the court for permission to insert a nasogastric tube. Mrs. O'Connor's two daughters objected because they claimed she would never have wanted to be kept alive if she were unable to care for herself. The lower court found in favor of Mary O'Connor's daughters but, the Court of Appeals of New York reversed the decision (*In the Matter of Westchester County Medical Center on Behalf of Mary O'Connor* N.Y. 531 N.E.2d 607, 1988).

At the time of Mary O'Connor's second stroke her daughters had submitted a statement signed by them to be entered in their mother's medical record stating that their mother had expressed the wish in many conversations that "no artificial life support be started or maintained in order to continue to sustain her life."

After a few months in a long-term geriatric center and suffering from dehydration, infection, and probably pneumonia, she was transferred to the hospital. She had lost her gag reflex making it difficult, if not impossible, for her to swallow foods. After antibiotic treatment she became more alert and was able to answer simple questions. At this point her doctor wanted to insert a nasogastric tube, but her daughters objected.

What was Mary's Condition and What Would She Have Wanted?

Mrs. O'Connor was not in a coma, but she was unable to express her wishes, a condition which would not change. Intravenous feedings would not be enough to sustain her much longer, and if all nutrition were stopped, her doctor testified, she would experience a painful death. An expert called in by the daughters testified that she might not feel pain due to her brain damage and that, if she did, it could be relieved. This witness also noted that Mrs. O'Connor appeared to have made some improvement in her condition and could now say her name and that she had a gag reflex. Whether she would ever be able to swallow was not clear.

Friends and family testified that Mrs. O'Connor had often expressed the opinion that it was "monstrous" to keep someone alive with "machinery." The court agreed that a patient had a right to refuse treatment, but that there had to be "clear and convincing" evidence of the patient's wishes as there had been in *Eichner*. Mrs. O'Connor's wishes, according to the court, were not as clear. She had only spoken in casual conversations, and she had never specifically expressed an opinion on food and water. Judge Wachtler*, writing for the majority, stated,

> Every person has a right to life, and no one should be denied essential medical care unless the evidence clearly and convincingly shows that the patient intended to decline the treatment under some particular circumstances. This is a demanding standard, the most rigorous burden of proof in civil cases. It is appropriate here because if an error occurs it should be made on the side of life.

Judge Hancock, in a concurring decision, wrote that the court should be required to consider several factors before deciding about life support:

1. [t]he intention of the patient under the existing circumstances, *to whatever extent it can be ascertained* from past expressions [Hancock feels it is impossible to truly determine present intentions from past expressions];

2. any moral, ethical, religious or other deeply held belief, insofar as it might bear on the patient's probable inclinations in the matter;

3. the medical condition of the patient, including the level of mental and physical functioning and the degree of pain and discomfort;

4. the nature of the prescribed medical assistance, including its benefits, risks, invasiveness, painfulness, and side effects;

5. the prognoses with and without the medical assistance, including life expectancy, suffering and possibility of recovery;

6. the sentiments of the family or intimate friends; and

7. the professional judgment of the involved physicians.

The majority concluded that both the evidence of Mary O'Connor's physical condition and her expression of her wishes were not "clear and convincing" enough to permit her to die.

This is Too Restrictive

The dissenting judges found that the majority opinion was too restrictive and that citizens of New York would be subjected to unnecessary suffering because their courts did not accept the validity of a substituted judgement.

---

* Judge Wachtler later indicated that he had been influenced by his own mother's recovery from a stroke. See Chapter VI.

Judge Simons saw O'Connor's condition very differently from the majority. Her "limited conversations" were actually only sounds she could phonate with an occasional "yes," and the doctors could not even be sure that this limited ability reflected any understanding of the question. Her inability to feed herself was not comparable to an infant who needs to be spoon fed; "Mrs O'Connor's ability to swallow, necessary to continued existence, is gone and cannot be restored. . . . This breakdown is a substantial loss of a bodily function, analogous to a patient's loss of kidney function." While Karen Quinlan and Brother Fox needed respirators to stay alive, Mrs. O'Connor needed nutrition. Furthermore, her "improvement" stemmed from the antibiotics which cured her infections, not any change in her basic physical condition. She may not have been terminally ill, but she was dying and medical intervention would not cure her, it would only prolong her death.

Judge Simons disagreed with the majority's determination of Mrs. O'Connor's intentions as they had been presented by the lower court. While the trial court had found her statements to be credible proof of intent, the Appellate Court took exactly the same evidence and "makes its own finding and draws its own inferences to support its contrary decision." Simons cited the majority's statement that Mrs. O'Connor's reactions to life support were only in reaction "to the unsettling experience of seeing or hearing of another's unnecessarily prolonged death." (Mrs. O'Connor had worked in the health care field and had recently lost several family members to prolonged illnesses.) In Simon's opinion, the majority had chosen not only to devalue Mrs. O'Connor's experience in the field, but also to ignore the statement she had made that was in specific reference to her own condition. When she had left the hospital at an earlier stage of her illness, she had told her daughter she hoped never to return and she "would never want any sort of intervention, any sort of life support systems to maintain or prolong her life." For Simon, the majority trivialized Mrs. O'Connor's statements to support their own point of view.

Instead, the majority, disguising its action as an application of the rule on self-determination, has made its own substituted judgment by improperly finding facts and drawing inferences contrary to the facts found by the courts below. Judges, the persons least qualified by training, experience or affinity to reject the patient's instructions have overridden Mrs. O'Connor's wishes, negated her long held values on life and death, and imposed on her and her family their ideas of what her best interests require.

Cruzan, by Cruzan v. Harmon

While *O'Connor* set a rigorous standard of proof for the state of New York, *Cruzan* was the first right-to-die case heard by the U.S. Supreme Court confirming the legality of such standards for the entire country.

In January 1983, Nancy Cruzan lost control of her car and was thrown face down into a ditch. The trooper who found her could not detect a pulse or cardiac function. When the paramedics arrived, they revived her, but the final diagnosis estimated that she had suffered anoxia (lack of oxygen) for 12 to 14 minutes. After six minutes of oxygen deprivation, the brain is permanently damaged. At the time of the trial, Nancy was able to breathe on her own, but was being nourished with a gastrostomy tube. She was oblivious to her environment, except for reflexive responses to sound and perhaps painful stimuli. Her response was limited to grimaces. She had no hope of improvement. Her medical insurance had expired in January 1986, and she was a ward of the state.

Nancy Cruzan's case was first heard by a circuit court of Missouri which gave Nancy's guardian the right to terminate life support. The state and the guardian *ad litem** appealed to the state Supreme Court where the decision was reversed on the basis that the subject's wishes were not sufficiently or reliably expressed to support the substi-

---

*The guardian *ad litem* personally felt Cruzan had the right to die, but was legally obliged to appeal the decision.

tuted judgment of the guardian (*Cruzan v. Harmon*, Mo. 760 S.W.2d 408, 1988).

The majority opinion described the case:

This is a case in which we are asked to allow the medical profession to make Nancy die by starvation and dehydration. The debate here is thus not between life and death; it is between quality of life and death. We are asked to hold that the cost of maintaining Nancy's present life is too great when weighed against the benefit that life conveys both to Nancy and her loved ones and that she must die.

Nancy was not terminal, but her condition would never improve. She was capable of existing in her condition for another 30 years. Because there was no hope of improvement, the court found that arguments to terminate her life were "but a thinly veiled statement that her life in its present form is not worth living. Yet a diminished quality of life does not support a decision to cause death."

The Wrong Precedents

The Missouri court observed that other states' decisions had been based primarily on *Quinlan*, *Saikewicz*, and *Eichner/Storar* (see above). These three cases (*Eichner/Storar* had been decided as a joint ruling by the same court and, although they were different cases, they are sometimes presented as different aspects of the same issue) "limit themselves to circumstances in which the patient is terminally ill. Cases which follow, however, recognize no such restraint, *but extend the principles upon which the Quinlan-Saikewicz-Eichner/Storar*

trilogy rely, to persons who are not terminally ill."* The court determined that, although other states may have been content with the reasoning proposed in those seminal cases, this court was not. In a footnote the majority stated, "It is our duty . . . not only to consider precedents from other states, but also to determine their strength. We have found them wanting and refuse to eat 'on the insane root which takes the reason prisoner' (Shakespeare, *Macbeth*, I, iii)."

The majority considered the three tests of validity as presented in *Conroy*, the right to privacy, and the state's interests. Like Claire Conroy, in the judges' assessment, Nancy's expression of intent was not clear and convincing and her burden of suffering and pain did not outweigh the benefits of continued care. As to the right of privacy, the court did not find that it was expressly provided by either the federal Constitution or the constitution of the state of Missouri.

. . . this Court was asked to recognize an unfettered right of privacy. We decline to do so. This is consistent with our view that Missouri's constitution must be interpreted according to its plain language and in a manner consistent with the understanding of the people who adopted it. We thus find no unfettered right of privacy under our constitution that would support the right of a person to refuse medical treatment in every circumstance.

Quinlan based the right to privacy on *Griswold* (the right to use contraception) and *Roe* (the right to have an abortion) and,

---

* Karen Ann Quinlan was actually no more terminal than Nancy Cruzan — both were in a persistent vegetative state and dependent on tube feeding - however, in *Quinlan*, the court described Karen as "moribund" (in a dying state; near death). The majority in *Cruzan* may have chosen to use this description of Quinlan because it supported their argument that later court decisions have been improperly based on the wrong precedent. On the other hand, it can be argued that it is irrelevant whether Quinlan was terminal or not. The point of the majority argument is that Nancy Cruzan was not terminal and her situation was what was being decided by this court.

"without further analysis states, 'presumably this right is broad enough to encompass a patient's decision to decline medical treatment under certain circumstances.'"

This court disagreed.

The State's Interest in Life

The majority ruled that the state's interest was confined to its interest in the preservation of life. "The state's concern with the sanctity of life rests on the principle that life is precious and worthy of preservation without regard to its quality." The state of Missouri, in its constitution, strongly favors life for the unborn and the dying. The Uniform Rights of the Terminally Ill Act, which provided the basis for many of the state's statutes, does *not* support death prolonging treatment, however, "*Death-prolonging procedure shall not include. . . the performance of any procedure to provide nutrition or hydration.*" (Emphasis added by the court.) The court was mindful that their decision would not apply only to Nancy Cruzan and feared treading the slippery slope. "Were the quality of life at issue, persons with all manner of handicaps might find the state seeking to terminate their lives.* Instead, the state's interest is in life; that interest is unqualified."

A Guardian's Rights

After the court found that Nancy Cruzan had no constitutional right to die, they further found that her guardian had no right to express this right for her. Autonomy means self-law. "It is logically inconsistent to claim that rights which are found lurking in the shadow of the Bill of Rights and which spring from concerns from personal autonomy can be exercised by another absent the most rigid of formalities." Cases which have accepted a guardian's right to choose have based

that power on the incompetent's right to choose, if competent. In the opinion of the majority, third party consent "allows the truly involuntary to be declared voluntary." In conclusion:

We find no principled legal basis which permits the coguardians in this case to choose the death of their ward. In the absence of such a legal basis for that decision and in the face of this State's strongly stated policy in favor of life, we choose to err on the side of life, respecting the rights of incompetent persons who may wish to live despite a severely diminished quality of life.

The State Does Not Have an Overriding Interest

In his dissent, Judge Blackmar indicated that the state need not be involved in these cases. These are decisions that are most often made in private by the patient or relatives with their doctor. The judge also questioned the state's strong interest in life. If the state values life above all else, why does it permit capital punishment? If it values life above all else, why does it not finance the preservation of life without regard to cost? Citing a case known personally to him, Judge Blackmar asked why, if the state has an overwhelming interest in life, had it been unwilling to pay for the extraordinary and expensive medical treatment needed by a judge to preserve his life?

Judge Blackmar was equally skeptical regarding the majority decision's opinion that the quality of life cannot be evaluated, finding it "appropriate to consider the quality of life in making decisions about the extraordinary medical treatment." He was not "impressed with the crypto-philosophers cited in the principal opinion, who declaim about the sanctity of any life without regard to its quality.

---

* According to the federal government's Office of Technology Assessment, there are approximately 5,000 to 10,000 PVS patients in the United States. In addition, there are an estimated 1.5 million people who suffer dementia, a population which is expected to increase as much as 60 percent by the year 2000, as the elderly population grows. (See Chapter IX.)

They dwell in ivory towers." Finally, he was not swayed by arguments of the slippery slope. One decision does not mean the court has opened the door to "wholesale euthanasia." A decision is precedent only for the facts of the particular case.

"Erroneous Declaration of Law"

In Judge Higgins' dissenting opinion, the judge supported Nancy's "right to liberty," which permits an individual to refuse medical treatment. "To decide otherwise that medical treatment once undertaken must be continued irrespective of its lack of success or benefit to the patient in effect gives one's body to medical science without their consent." His main disagreement, however, was with the majority's basic premise that all the precedent setting cases from 16 other states were based on an "erroneous declaration of law."

> A reader of the ensuing opinion searches and waits in vain for citation of a single authority to support the majority's bold assertion and its drastic action. . . . Should not a reader ask the majority why it projects the irony of recognizing yet rejecting this abundance of evidence of dispositive case law in favor of its non-supported assertion of "erroneous declaration of law?". . . is it simply because the majority elects to ignore the facts and law of this case and "chooses to err" on the side of life of incompetent persons who may wish to live, a case not before the Court at this time?

Cruzan v. Missouri Department of Public Health

Nancy's father appealed, and in December of 1989, the U.S. Supreme Court heard arguments in the Cruzan case. They did not pass judgement on Nancy Cruzan's particular situation, but simply on whether or not the federal Constitution prohibits the state of Missouri from insisting on and defining clear and convincing evidence. Chief Justice Rehnquist wrote the opinion with White, O'Connor, Scalia, and Kennedy joining. Justices Brennan, Marshall, Blackmun, and Stevens dissented (58 LW 4916, 1990).

The Court considered whether Missouri can require that the evidence of an incompetent's wishes be clear and convincing. "The question, then, is whether the United States Constitution forbids the establishment of this procedural requirement by the State. We hold that it does not." When a decision to terminate life support might result in the erroneous death of a patient, and the decision not to do so leads to a maintenance of the status quo, it is permissible to uphold rigorous standards. There will be cases where this requirement of proof will frustrate the not-fully expressed wishes of some patients (including Nancy Cruzan), "But the Constitution does not require general rules to work faultlessly; no general rule can." The majority opinion concluded,

> No doubt is engendered by anything in this record but that Nancy Cruzan's mother and father are loving and caring parents. If the State were required by the United States Constitution to repose a right of "substituted judgement" with anyone, the Cruzans would surely qualify. But we do not think the Due Process Clause* requires the State to repose judgment on these matters with anyone but the patient herself. Close family members may have a strong feeling — a feeling not at all ignoble or unworthy, but not entirely disinterested either — that they do not wish to witness the continuation of the life of a loved one which they regard as hopeless, meaningless, and even degrading. But there is no automatic assurance that the view of close family members will necessarily be the same as the patient's would have been had she been confronted with the prospect of her situa-

---

* The Fourteenth Amendment provides that no State shall "deprive any person of life, liberty, or property, without due process of law."

tion while competent. All of the reasons previously discussed for allowing Missouri to require clear and convincing evidence of the patient's wishes lead us to conclude that the State may choose to defer only to those wishes, rather than confide the decision to close family members.

It is a "Fundamental Right"

Justice Brennan, dissenting, pointed out that the state's interests cannot override a "fundamental right" unless those state interests are sufficiently important and "closely tailored to effectuate only those interests." While the majority conceded that the patient had a "general liberty interest in medical treatment" (liberty interests are not as inviolate as fundamental interests), and, therefore the right to reject it, the decision avoided discussing the strength of that interest. In Brennan's opinion it has been upheld in other cases as fundamental, surpassing state interests. Brennan, quoting from Justice Stevens' opinion in the abortion case of *Hodgson v. Minnesota* (58 LW 4957, 1990), insisted that

> The only state interest asserted here is a general interest in the preservation of life. But the State has no legitimate general interest in someone's life, completely abstracted from the person's choice to avoid medical treatment. [T]he regulation of constitutionally protected decisions . . . must be predicated on legitimate state concerns *other than* disagreement with the choice the individual has made. . . . Otherwise, the interest in liberty protected by the Due Process Clause would be a nullity.

Furthermore, artificially delivered food and water cannot be excluded as somehow more basic than a medical treatment. They are, according to the medical profession and the federal government, "medical." (See the President's Commission for the Study of Ethical Problems in Medicine and Biomedical and Behavioral Research in Chapter III.) Medicare reimburses artificial feedings under medical expenses, and the food itself is a medicine

regulated by the Food and Drug Administration.) The Justice pointed out that Missouri appears to be the only state to suggest otherwise.

State's Interests

Brennan did not understand the logic of the state's insistence on their interest in the preservation of life. In his view, Missouri does not, and cannot, claim that society will benefit from Nancy's continued medical treatment. Moreover, the state runs the risk of impairing rather than serving any interest in preserving life. Current medical practice recommends the use of any treatment that offers the smallest hope of the patient's recovery, a practice that should be encouraged. However, when the President's Commission approved the withdrawal of life support from PVS patients, they explained that an "even more troubling wrong occurs when a treatment that might save life or improve health is not started because the health care personnel are afraid that they will find it very difficult to stop the treatment if . . . it proves to be of little benefit and greatly burdens the patient." The state interest should have been in seeing that Nancy's wishes were accurately determined, not in blocking them.

Finally, for Brennan, Missouri imposed an uneven burden of proof. While the proof to terminate life support must be clear and convincing, no proof is required to support the decision that a patient would want treatment continued. In addition, the justification that to err on the side of life maintains the status quo, while on the other hand an error leads to death, might appear logical, but Brennan disagrees. For a PVS patient, an erroneous decision "robs a patient of the very qualities protected by the right to avoid unwanted medical treatment. His own degraded existence is perpetuated; his family's suffering is protracted; the memory he leaves behind becomes more and more distorted."

Nancy as a Symbol

Justice Stevens, in a separate dissenting opinion, echoed Brennan's objections. The Court, in the guise of protecting state interests has denied

Nancy her personhood and made her a symbol. In Stevens' opinion the Missouri court subordinated Nancy's body to their

> effort to define life, rather than to protect it. . . . the Court errs insofar as it characterizes this case as involving "judgments about the 'quality' of life that a particular individual may enjoy." . . . The State's unflagging determination to perpetuate Nancy Cruzan's physical existence is comprehensible only as an effort to define life's meaning, not as an attempt to preserve its sanctity.

The state's claim that maintaining the status quo does no harm ignores Nancy's interests in favor of their own.

> Insofar as Nancy Cruzan has an interest in being remembered for how she lived rather than how she died, the damage done to those memories by the prolongation of her death is irreversible. Insofar as Nancy Cruzan has an interest in the cessation of any pain, the continuation of her pain is irreversible. Insofar as Nancy Cruzan has an interest in a closure to her life consistent with her own beliefs rather than those of the Missouri legislature, the States' imposition of its contrary view is irreversible. To deny the importance of these consequences is in effect to deny that Nancy Cruzan has interests at all, and thereby to deny her personhood in the name of preserving the sanctity of her life.

What Was Established By the Supreme Court Decision?

The Supreme Court made three points in *Cruzan v. Director, Missouri Department of Public Health*. The first is that under the U.S. Constitution, a person has a right to refuse medical treatment. As the Supreme Court has curtailed some of the rights to privacy (see *Webster v. Reproductive Health Services* decision on abortion in *Abortion: An Eternal Social and Moral Issue*, 1992, Wylie, Texas: Information Plus), states have turned to their own constitutions to determine whether or not a patient has the right to refuse treatment. In *Cruzan* the Court re-established this right as a liberty interest.

The second is that incompetent patients also retain a right to refuse treatment with that right to be exercised by a surrogate decisionmaker. Some experts have argued that without an advance directive, it is impossible to correctly judge an incompetent's wishes, but the Court made no such requirement.

The third is that, although the Court upheld Missouri's right to require "clear and convincing evidence," it did not say that the guidelines adopted by other states which permit a guardian's "best interests" decision were not permissible. While Missouri can maintain its rigorous requirements, other states can legally establish more flexible guidelines.

A number of points were also inferred by the Supreme Court decision:

> 1. The right to refuse medical treatment is not limited to terminally ill patients .
>
> 2. The right to refuse medical treatment includes the right to refuse artificially supplied nutrition and hydration.
>
> 3. The right to refuse medical treatment may be exercised through a living will, durable powers of attorney, or other advance directives.

Many state statutes had limited advance directives to terminal patients, or excluded the removal of feeding tubes, or did not specifically allow surrogate decisions through proxies (see Chapter VI). With this decision any clear and convincing evidence is permissible for any patient to refuse unwanted treatment.

Postscript

On December 14, 1990, nearly eight years after the car accident, a county probate judge ruled that new evidence from some of Nancy's friends constituted "clear and convincing" evidence and gave permission to remove her feeding tube. The attorney who had represented the State of Missouri asked that the state be dismissed as a party to the action; the state had no interest now that the legal standard had been established. At the hearing, the guardian *ad litem* questioned Nancy's doctor, taking him through pages of medical records reporting her incontinence, ailments of the stomach, eyes, and gums, her alternating diarrhea and constipation, her rashes and obesity, her vomiting, seizures, and contorted limbs. The guardian asked if the doctor still thought that it was in Nancy's best interest to continue her existence. The doctor replied, "No, sir, I think it would be personally a living hell."

Within two hours of the ruling, Nancy's family asked the doctor to remove the feeding tube. The nursing staff at the Missouri Rehabilitation Center was very bitter and angry at the ruling. Some refused to speak to Nancy's family or to have anything more to do with the patient. Nancy's family kept a 24-hour vigil with her until she died on December 26, 1990, 12 days after her feeding tube was removed.

CHAPTER VIII

THE EXPENSE OF HEALTH CARE

WHAT DOES HEALTH CARE COST?

Health care is in crisis in the United States. Costs continue to rise, and, despite efforts to contain expenses, nothing so far has been successful. In 1970 the U. S. spent a little more than 7 percent of its gross national product (the value of all the goods and services produced by the nation) on health care. This was equal to its expenditures on education. In 1991, however, health care had risen to 13 percent ($738 billion) of the GNP, twice as much as education and five times the amount dedicated to research and development.

Many factors contribute to this increase including: high salaries for doctors, malpractice insurance, hospitals that are trying to pay off expensive, redundant technology, cumbersome medical insurance programs, a lack of a national health plan, and the increasing number of elderly.

The Problem

In 1990, $666 billion was spent on national health — 12.2 percent of the gross national product and $2,566 for every man, woman, and child in America (Table 8.1). Compared to other industri-

---

TABLE 8.1

Gross national product, national health expenditures, and Federal government expenditures: United States, selected years 1929–90

[Data are compiled by the Health Care Financing Administration]

Year	Gross national product in billions	National health expenditures			Federal government expenditures		
		Amount in billions	Percent of gross national product	Amount per capita	Total in billions	Health in billions	Health as a percent of total
1929.	$ 103.1	$ 3.6	3.5	$ 29	$ 2.7	- - -	- - -
1935.	72.2	2.9	4.0	23	6.6	- - -	- - -
1940.	99.7	4.0	4.0	29	10.0	- - -	- - -
1950.	284.8	12.7	4.5	80	41.2	$ 1.6	3.9
1955.	398.0	17.7	4.4	101	68.6	2.0	2.9
1960.	515.3	27.1	5.3	143	93.9	2.9	3.1
1965.	705.1	41.6	5.9	204	125.3	4.8	3.8
1966.	772.0	45.9	5.9	222	145.3	7.5	5.2
1967.	816.4	51.7	6.3	248	165.8	12.2	7.4
1968.	892.6	58.5	6.6	278	182.9	14.1	7.7
1969.	963.9	65.7	6.8	309	191.3	16.1	8.4
1970.	1,015.5	74.4	7.3	346	207.8	17.7	8.5
1971.	1,102.7	82.3	7.5	379	224.8	20.4	9.1
1972.	1,212.8	92.3	7.6	421	249.0	22.9	9.2
1973.	1,359.3	102.5	7.5	464	269.3	25.2	9.4
1974.	1,472.8	116.1	7.9	521	305.5	30.5	10.0
1975.	1,598.4	132.9	8.3	592	364.2	36.4	10.0
1976.	1,782.8	152.2	8.5	672	393.7	42.9	10.9
1977.	1,990.5	172.0	8.6	753	430.1	47.6	11.1
1978.	2,249.7	193.7	8.6	839	470.7	54.3	11.5
1979.	2,508.2	217.2	8.7	932	521.1	61.4	11.8
1980.	2,731.9	250.1	9.2	1,063	615.1	72.0	11.7
1981.	3,052.6	290.2	9.5	1,221	703.3	84.0	11.9
1982.	3,166.0	326.1	10.3	1,358	781.2	93.3	11.9
1983.	3,405.7	358.6	10.5	1,479	835.9	103.2	12.3
1984.	3,772.2	389.6	10.3	1,592	895.6	112.6	12.6
1985.	4,014.9	422.6	10.5	1,710	985.6	123.6	12.5
1986.	4,231.6	454.8	10.7	1,822	1,034.8	133.1	12.9
1987.	4,515.6	494.1	10.9	1,961	1,071.9	144.0	13.4
1988.	4,873.7	546.0	11.2	2,146	1,114.2	156.7	14.1
1989.	5,200.8	602.8	11.6	2,346	1,187.2	175.0	14.7
1990.	5,465.1	666.2	12.2	2,566	1,275.7	195.4	15.3

NOTES: These data include revisions back to 1978 and differ from previous editions of Health, United States. These data reflect Bureau of Economic Analysis, Department of Commerce revisions to the gross national product and Federal government expenditures as of May 1991 and Social Security Administration population revisions as of May 1991.

SOURCE: Office of National Health Statistics, Office of the Actuary: National health expenditures, 1990. Health Care Financing Review. Vol. 13, No. 1. HCFA Pub. No. 03321. Health Care Financing Administration. Washington. U.S. Government Printing Office, October 1991.

TABLE 8.2

Total health expenditures as a percentage of gross domestic product and per capita expenditures in dollars: Selected countries and years 1960–90

Country	1960	1965	1970	1975	1980	1985	1988	1989	1990
	Health expenditures as a percent of gross domestic product								
Australia	4.9	5.1	5.7	7.5	7.4	7.8	7.7	7.6	7.5
Austria	4.4	4.7	5.4	7.3	7.9	8.1	8.4	8.4	8.4
Belgium	3.4	3.9	4.1	5.9	6.7	7.4	7.5	7.4	7.4
Canada	5.5	6.0	7.1	7.2	7.4	8.5	8.7	8.7	9.0
Denmark	3.6	2.7	6.1	6.5	6.8	6.3	6.5	6.4	6.2
Finland	4.2	4.9	5.7	6.3	6.5	7.2	7.2	7.2	7.4
France	4.2	5.2	5.8	7.0	7.6	8.5	8.6	8.8	8.9
Germany	4.8	5.1	5.9	8.1	8.4	8.7	8.9	8.2	8.1
Greece	2.9	3.1	4.0	4.1	4.3	4.9	5.0	5.3	5.3
Iceland	3.5	4.2	5.2	6.2	6.5	7.4	8.5	8.6	8.5
Ireland	4.0	4.4	5.6	7.6	9.0	8.3	7.9	7.3	7.1
Italy	3.3	4.0	5.2	6.1	6.9	7.0	7.6	7.6	7.7
Japan	2.9	4.3	4.4	5.5	6.4	6.4	6.6	6.6	6.5
Luxembourg	---	---	4.1	5.6	6.8	6.8	7.3	7.4	7.2
Netherlands	3.9	4.4	6.0	7.6	8.0	8.0	8.2	8.1	8.0
New Zealand	4.3	---	5.2	6.7	7.2	6.6	7.4	7.3	7.2
Norway	3.3	3.9	5.0	6.7	6.6	6.4	7.5	7.6	7.2
Portugal	---	---	3.1	6.4	5.9	7.0	7.1	7.2	6.7
Spain	---	2.6	3.7	4.8	5.6	5.7	6.0	6.3	6.6
Sweden	4.7	5.6	7.2	7.9	9.2	8.8	8.5	8.7	8.7
Switzerland	3.3	3.8	5.2	7.0	7.3	7.6	7.8	7.6	7.4
Turkey	---	---	---	3.5	4.0	2.8	3.7	3.9	4.0
United Kingdom	3.9	4.1	4.5	5.5	5.8	6.0	6.0	6.0	6.2
United States	5.2	6.0	7.4	8.4	9.3	10.7	11.4	11.7	12.4
	Per capita health expenditures [1]								
Australia	$95	$121	$205	$433	$595	$952	$1,102	$1,123	$1,151
Austria	60	81	149	336	618	871	1,046	1,112	1,192
Belgium	50	76	123	286	541	802	949	1,007	1,087
Canada	117	165	274	478	806	1,315	1,585	1,683	1,795
Denmark	64	64	209	335	571	770	892	922	963
Finland	58	91	163	305	513	826	998	1,090	1,156
France	66	109	192	365	656	991	1,174	1,277	1,379
Germany	86	119	199	420	739	1,046	1,243	1,224	1,287
Greece	17	29	62	110	196	292	343	382	406
Iceland	60	96	152	321	638	964	1,350	1,353	1,372
Ireland	37	52	99	225	448	577	639	658	693
Italy	46	75	147	270	548	766	990	1,061	1,138
Japan	26	63	126	252	515	785	978	1,060	1,145
Luxembourg	---	---	150	319	616	879	1,140	1,190	1,300
Netherlands	71	102	207	411	693	908	1,048	1,109	1,182
New Zealand	89	---	174	354	523	667	811	341	853
Norway	55	86	154	350	624	900	1,223	1,219	1,281
Portugal	---	---	46	158	252	385	479	528	529
Spain	---	37	82	186	322	437	571	648	730
Sweden	92	145	274	475	842	1,125	1,258	1,344	1,421
Switzerland	87	127	250	482	742	1,115	1,308	1,363	1,406
Turkey	---	---	---	57	100	100	165	175	197
United Kingdom	76	98	146	272	454	662	817	864	932
United States	142	206	346	592	1,063	1,711	2,145	2,346	2,566

[1]Per capita health expenditures for each country have been adjusted to U.S. dollars using the annual average daily exchange rate for each year.

NOTES: Gross domestic product differs slightly from gross national product shown in the previous table. For definitions, see Appendix II. Some numbers in this table have been revised and differ from previous editions of Health, United States.

SOURCE: Organization for Economic Cooperation and Development: Measuring Health Care 1960–1983, OECD Pub. No. 43239. Paris, France, 1985; OECD Health Data 1991, and OECD Health Systems: Facts and Trends. Forthcoming.

TABLE 8.3

National health expenditures, percent distribution, and average annual percent change, according to type of expenditure: United States, selected years 1960–90

[Data are compiled by the Health Care Financing Administration]

Type of expenditure	1960	1965	1970	1975	1980	1985	1987	1988	1989	1990
	Amount in billions									
Total	$27.1	$41.6	$74.4	$132.9	$250.1	$422.6	$494.1	$546.0	$602.8	$666.2
	Percent distribution									
All expenditures	100	100	100	100	100	100	100	100	100	100
Health services and supplies	94	92	93	94	95	96	97	96	97	97
Personal health care	88	86	87	88	88	87	89	88	88	88
Hospital care	34	34	38	39	41	40	39	39	39	38
Physician services	19	20	18	18	17	17	19	19	19	19
Dentist services	7	7	6	6	6	6	5	5	5	5
Nursing home care	4	4	7	7	8	8	8	8	8	8
Other professional services	2	2	2	3	3	4	4	4	4	5
Home health care	0	0	0	0	1	1	1	1	1	1
Drugs and other medical nondurables	16	14	12	10	9	9	9	8	8	8
Vision products and other medical durables	3	3	3	2	2	2	2	2	2	2
Other personal health care	3	2	2	2	2	2	2	2	2	2
Program administration and net cost of health insurance	4	5	4	4	5	6	5	5	6	6
Government public health activities	1	2	2	2	3	3	3	3	3	3
Research and construction	6	8	7	6	5	4	3	4	3	3
Noncommercial research	3	4	3	3	2	2	2	2	2	2
Construction	4	5	5	4	2	2	2	2	2	2

Type of expenditure	1960–65	1965–70	1970–75	1975–80	1980–85	1985–87	1987–88	1988–89	1989–90
	Average annual percent change								
All expenditures	8.9	12.3	12.3	13.5	11.1	8.1	10.5	10.4	10.5
Health services and supplies	8.5	12.6	12.5	13.9	11.3	8.2	10.3	10.6	10.5
Personal health care	8.3	12.8	12.4	13.5	11.0	9.0	9.9	9.8	10.5
Hospital care	8.6	14.7	13.4	14.3	10.4	7.4	9.2	9.7	10.1
Physician services	9.2	10.6	11.4	12.5	12.1	12.1	13.1	8.0	10.7
Dentist services	7.3	10.8	12.1	11.7	10.1	8.0	8.5	7.3	7.6
Nursing home care	11.6	23.4	15.4	15.0	11.3	7.8	7.8	11.5	11.4
Other professional services	7.4	11.8	18.3	19.9	13.8	12.8	12.4	14.0	16.6
Home health care	9.6	19.7	23.2	27.2	23.3	3.6	9.6	24.9	22.5
Drugs and other medical nondurables	6.8	8.4	8.1	10.7	10.8	9.3	7.2	9.3	7.9
Vision products and other medical durables	9.0	10.1	8.8	8.2	9.4	12.7	11.8	12.9	6.1
Other personal health care	3.5	10.7	14.6	11.0	6.9	10.6	12.1	11.2	16.4
Program administration and net cost of health insurance	10.5	7.5	12.8	19.3	15.5	–4.6	16.9	26.6	14.1
Government public health activities	10.8	17.1	17.0	18.9	11.3	8.9	13.5	10.4	5.6
Research and construction	15.2	9.0	9.2	6.4	6.4	5.9	14.9	4.3	10.2
Noncommercial research	17.1	5.1	11.2	10.4	7.4	7.6	14.5	6.8	11.9
Construction	13.9	11.8	8.0	3.3	5.4	4.2	15.3	1.5	8.3

NOTE: These data include revisions back to 1978 and differ from previous editions of Health, United States.

SOURCE: Office of National Health Statistics, Office of the Actuary: National health expenditures, 1990. Health Care Financing Review. Vol. 13, No. 1. HCFA Pub. No. 03321. Health Care Financing Administration. Washington. U.S. Government Printing Office, October 1991.

alized countries, the United States spent more on health care than any other country. (See Table 8.2.) Almost all of the expense went to personal health care (88 percent) with most of that going to hospital expenses (38 percent) and 19 percent for physician services. Between 1989 and 1990 hospital expenses increased 10.1 percent, while the cost of doctor's services grew 10.7 percent (Table 8.3).

From 1985 to 1990, the consumer price index (a measure of the average change in prices paid by consumers) has increased at a greater rate for medical care than any other commodity. Inflation has been low for most goods, but in 1989-1990, medical care increased 9 percent (Table 8.4). In 1990, 28.9 percent of the medical bill was paid for by private business through insurance and contributions through Social Security which are used to fund Medicare; 34.9 percent was paid by private households through private insurance, tax contributions to Medicare, and out-of-pocket expenses; 33.1 percent was paid out by the federal or state governments (Figure 8.1).

Why are Prices Increasing?

Henry Aaron, director of the Economic Studies program of the Brookings Institution (an economic think tank in Washington, DC), in *Serious and Unstable Condition: Financing America's Health Care* (1991, WDC: Brookings Institution), looked at why health care costs keep rising. He found five factors that have contributed to the increase:

1. The growth of third-party payments which encourages the demand for health care because the recipient is either not paying or is paying a greatly reduced rate. The increased coverage by private insurance for hospital and physician expenses in the 1950s and 1960s reduced patients' out-of-pocket price of health care and increased demand

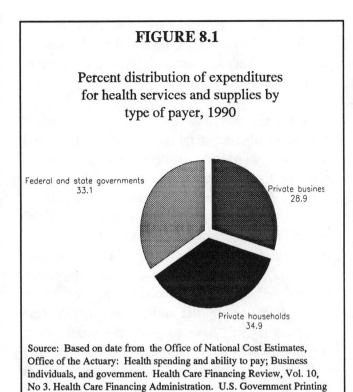

FIGURE 8.1

Percent distribution of expenditures
for health services and supplies by
type of payer, 1990

Federal and state governments
33.1

Private busines
28.9

Private households
34.9

Source: Based on date from the Office of National Cost Estimates,
Office of the Actuary: Health spending and ability to pay; Business
individuals, and government. Health Care Financing Review, Vol. 10,
No 3. Health Care Financing Administration. U.S. Government Printing
Office, Spring 1989; Unpublished data.

for care. Between 1950 and 1970 the percentage of bills paid by the individual fell from 30 percent to 9 percent.

2. An increase in the price of medical services. How much the relative price of health care has changed is difficult to measure. According to the Bureau of Labor Statistics, the wages earned by health care workers has risen sharply in comparison to other workers. Between 1963 and 1989 the pay of head nurses rose 75.9 percent, nurse supervisors, 62.5 percent; nursing instructors, 50 percent; licensed practical nurses, 44 percent; physical therapists, 35.2 percent; and radiographers, 33.5 percent. Average earnings rose 7 percent in manufacturing and fell 25.7 percent in the retail trade. Physician's median earnings increased from $132,200 in 1980 to $214,500 in 1988. The highest paid doctors, cardiovascular surgeons, earned an average of $485,900 in 1988. The increase in the price of medical care is difficult to measure, however, because the care changes constantly. A hospital stay in 1960 did not include the same services that are offered in a hospital stay in 1990. Part of the increased price is increased quality of care.

3. The aging of the American population. Older people use health care at much greater rates than do young people. Per capita annual health care spending in 1987 was $745 for people under 19 years old, $1,535 for those 19 through 64, $5,360 for people over 65, and $9,178 for those aged 85 or older. A major reason for the link between rising health care spending and age is the high cost of care in the last year or two before death (see below). Another group that is now surviving longer than ever before is the disabled. Their medical expenses are about five times higher than those without disabilities.

4. Malpractice insurance and law suits which not only increase the cost of medical care, but allegedly cause physicians to treat unnecessarily to avoid the risk of litigation. According to Aaron, malpractice litigation has been overrated as a factor in the increase of medical costs. Insurance premiums add to the costs for doctors and hospitals, but economists find that premiums for physicians totalled only about 3.4 percent of the doctor's income and 0.8 percent of personal medical spending in 1989. A potentially more expensive charge may be that doctors practice "defensive medicine" — unnecessary tests and care that would not be ordered if there were no threat of a law suit.

5. A technological revolution which has remade medicine in only a generation. Aaron concludes that medical technology has had the greatest influence on the cost of medical care. Bypass surgery, organ transplants, artificial hips, dialysis, bone marrow transplants, and neonatology (the care of seriously ill newborns) are only some of the procedures that are available today that were unknown not so long ago. Antibiotics, which appear to reduce health care costs by curing diseases at much lower cost than was previously possible, have actually added greatly to medical care costs. Patients who once died peacefully and inexpensively from pneumonia (the "widow's friend") now have an increased chance of dying of more expensive and protracted diseases such as Alzheimer's or cancer. In addition, antibiotics have permitted great advances in the success of costly cancer

therapies and transplants that would be lethal without antibiotic drugs. Technologies like CT scanners have reduced the amount of expensive exploratory surgeries, but, the saving is more than absorbed by the vastly increased number of relatively expensive tests which are performed.

RATIONING

Many people believe that rationing health care is the only way to help solve the financial crisis. In fact, some claim the United States already rations health care by not covering the uninsured; it just does not call it that. Others insist that if the waste were eliminated from the system, there would be adequate funding to give everyone health coverage.

Rationing is Not Necessary

Opponents of rationing claim that if the U.S. improved the efficiency of the health care system, there would be enough money saved to make health care available to all. Robert Brook and Kathleen Lohr of the Rand Corporation (a research and policy think tank), in "Will We Need to Ration Effective Health Care?" (1991, Santa Monica, CA: Rand), propose that one-third of the nation's health care expenses offer little or no benefit. If these services were eliminated, there would be resources for beneficial care for all who need it. They claim that if the country rations effective services, no matter how well it is done, it will have a greater impact on the elderly, the poor, and the chronically ill.

Brook and Lohr point out that rates of use of certain medical services vary widely across the country for similar population groups. Per-person medical expenditures for the elderly of Miami are more than twice as high as in Rochester, the use of coronary angiography varies by as much as threefold across the United States, the rates of hysterectomies varies by a factor of three, while gall bladder removal in women varies by a factor of five. If the figures at the low end represent appropriate care, 30 to 50 percent of the nation's health bill is spent on care which may have no demonstrable benefit. If, however, the high end represents adequate care, then our expenditures on health care are not out of line.

Unfortunately, data on unnecessary care is not readily available. Rights of privacy, technical problems, and ethical considerations make an evaluation of the efficacy of health care difficult to obtain. Another hard-to-measure factor that results in unnecessary care is the "do something" mentality of doctors and patients. Nonetheless, Brook and Lohr estimate from studies of treatment rates and hospital stays that approximately one-third of medical care is ineffective or unproductive. To eliminate waste, the authors feel that doctors and patients will have to give up some of their privacy in order to assess the benefits of care, and doctors and hospitals will have to agree to peer review of their performance.

Anthony Tartaglia, in "Is Talk of Rationing Premature?," published in *Rationing America's Medical Care: the Oregon Plan and Beyond* (1992, WDC: Brookings Institution) insists that it is not hard to see what problems in the system need tackling in order to avoid rationing. (He does not, however, offer the solutions to these problems.)

· It is generally agreed that the United States does not have enough primary care physicians.

· A huge amount of money can be saved if more emphasis is placed on preventive care. If strategies were developed to prevent destructive behavior like smoking or alcohol abuse, billions of dollars could be saved. (Smoking alone has been estimated to cost the health care system $65 billion a year.)

· Overuse and inappropriate use of medical care (see Rand, above).

· The use of medical treatments that were assumed to be beneficial but have never actually been found to be effective. Examples of treatments that are no longer considered worthwhile include the widespread performance of tonsillectomies and the dictum, "Once a cesarean, always a cesarean" which banned women from ever trying to vaginally deliver subsequent children.

· The amount of money spent on the care of the terminally ill. Although preserving life at all costs is a wonderful ideal, it must be looked at realistically. Is it worth the millions of dollars for a few extra months of life?

· The high cost of administration of the American health system. A single payer of health care as in the Canadian system (Tartaglia does not, however, say the United States should adopt the entire Canadian system) would streamline the administration of whatever health care system was adopted.

· Overregulation of the American system. An outcome-monitoring (a measure of benefit to the patient) quality assurance program would ensure quality medicine and cost less.

· The malpractice system which costs doctors $9.2 billion a year and yet does not show a correlation between those who receive malpractice settlements and those who were injured by malpractice.

Doctors, lawyers, and insurance companies stand to lose if reforms are implemented in the health care system, but Tartaglia feels Americans need to stand up and insist before the United States moves to a rationing system in which, he feels, the poor will be the losers.

There Is No Choice But to Ration

Supporters of rationing argue that rationing is inevitable because health care costs are not rising from inefficiency, but because the population is aging, technological innovation continues to raise the price of care, and the price of labor and supplies will inevitably increase. There are different proposed ways to ration health care which will be examined below.

Daniel Callahan, director of the bioethical institute, The Hastings Center, thinks the issue of rationing is much more than simply a financial question. In "Modernizing Mortality: Medical Progress and the Good Society" (1990, vol. 20, no. 1, *The Hastings Center Report*), Callahan examined the relationship between good health and the good society. Current social values reject anything but the promise of health for all, but this cannot be a realistic approach to health care. Callahan points out that the basic values of our society rejects failure. He quotes Michael Ignatieff (December 1988, "Modern Dying," *The New Republic*), "Cultures that live by the values of self-realization and self-mastery are not especially good at dying, at submitting to those experiences where freedom ends and biological fate begins. Why should they be? Their strong side is Promethean ambition . . . Their weak side is submitting to the inevitable."

The American obsession with health has become an end in itself as seen in the endlessly growing investment in health care as opposed to other needs like education. Callahan argues that this is a quest that will impoverish us, and that a re-evaluation of health is required. Two requirements must be fulfilled: a sufficient level of general good health to assure the viability of society's cultural, political, and social institutions, and a willingness to guarantee all citizens a baseline of public health and then beyond that only as much individualized cure of disease as is compatible with overall societal needs. Callahan's priorities are, first, caring for those we cannot cure — no one should be abandoned; second, preventive care, primary care, and emergency care; and finally, depending on the available funding, technologically advanced care that benefits comparatively few individuals.

A change of perspective from an individual point of view to a search for the collective good will be necessary. According to Callahan, the nation's system of health care costs too much for what it delivers and fails altogether to deliver to millions of uninsured. The U.S. has spent too much on health in comparison to other needs, too much on

TABLE 8.5

INFANT MORTALITY RATE, SELECTED COUNTRIES, 1989

Rank	Nation	Rate*
1	Japan	4
2	Finland	6
2	Sweden	6
4	Canada	7
4	Hong Kong	7
4	Netherlands	7
4	Switzerland	7
8	Australia	8
8	Austria	8
8	Denmark	8
8	East Germany	8
8	France	8
8	Norway	8
8	Singapore	8
8	United Kingdom	8
8	West Germany	8
17	Ireland	9
17	Spain	9
	U.S., White	9
19	Belgium	10
19	Israel	10
19	Italy	10
19	New Zealand	10
19	**United States**	**10**
24	Cuba	11
24	Czechoslovakia	11
24	Greece	11
27	Portugal	13
28	Bulgaria	14
29	Trinidad and Tobago	15
30	Hungary	16
30	Jamaica	16
30	Poland	16
33	Kuwait	17
34	Costa Rica	18
	U.S., Black	**18**

* Infant deaths per 1,000 live births.

SOURCE: UNICEF, except race specific data for the United States. Race specific data for the U.S. are from the National Center for Health Statistics for 1988.

the old in comparison to the young, too much on curing and not enough on caring, too much on extending the length of life and not enough on enhancing the quality of life.

A health care system which understood that it was meant to be part of, and to serve the needs of, a broader social and political system, would be one less prone to think only of its own needs, or to forget that health is only a means to the living of a life, not its goal. A system that guaranteed a minimally decent level of health care for all, in turn asking each of us to rein in our private demands, would be a decent and manageable one. That is not an impossible ideal.

THE UNITED STATES' SYSTEM IN COMPARISON WITH OTHER COUNTRIES

The American system of health care is often compared unfavorably to other countries. The proof of American failure, many claim, is our high infant mortality rates. In 1988, the United States lagged behind nearly every industrialized nation in infant mortality (Table 8.5). The rate for black infants, in particular, is shocking — higher than in underdeveloped countries like Jamaica or Bulgaria. Experts warn, however, that while this is a serious problem that needs to be addressed and may be mitigated by a changed health care system, it is not exclusively the fault of our health system. Infant mortality is linked to the high rate of poverty in certain groups and may reveal that certain behavior patterns have a larger bearing on health outcomes than the type of health system. There is virtually no difference in black and white infant mortality from nonpreventable causes such as congenital anomalies, but large differences in preventable causes. In 1988, black infants were 3.88 times more likely to die from disorders relating to low birth weight and short gestation, 3.2 times more likely to die from homicide, and twice as likely to die from accidents and adverse effects (Table 8.6).

The British National Health Plan

The United Kingdom's British National Health Service offers universal (everyone is covered) health care. Originally the intention was to "universalize the best." The theory was that the cost of developing the service would be offset by the fall in demand which would result once the backlog of need had been taken care of as the population became healthier from improved medical care. The result has been just the opposite. Not only did demand for medical care continue to increase because it was "free," when improved care and life saving technologies became available, costs escalated because patients were living longer and needed continued care.

TABLE 8.6

INFANT MORTALITY RATES* FOR THE LEADING CAUSES OF INFANT DEATH, BY RACE, U.S., 1988

	All Races	White	Black	Nonwhite	Ratio of Black to White
All Causes	995.3	851.1	1,762.0	1,504.0	2.07
1 Congenital anomalies	208.2	211.5	209.8	196.8	0.99
2 Sudden infant death syndrome	140.1	123.8	226.2	197.5	1.83
3 Disorders relating to short gestation and low birthweight	83.6	56.7	219.9	178.6	3.88
4 Respiratory distress syndrome	81.4	70.5	142.4	119.7	2.02
5 Maternal complications of pregnancy	36.1	28.7	75.7	62.1	2.64
6 Accidents and adverse effects	23.9	20.9	41.8	34.5	2.00
7 Complications of placenta, cord, or membranes	23.2	20.2	39.9	33.8	1.98
8 Perinatal infections	22.5	18.8	41.5	35.2	2.21
9 Hypoxia and birth asphyxia	19.9	17.3	34.5	29.0	1.99
10 Pneumonia and influenza	16.4	12.7	33.3	29.4	2.62
11. Neonatal hemorrhage	8.3	6.5	17.3	14.6	2.66
12 Homicide	8.1	5.9	18.9	15.6	3.20
13 Septicemia	6.3	5.1	12.2	10.4	2.39
14 Birth trauma	5.5	4.9	8.8	7.9	1.80
15 Meningitis	5.2	4.4	9.2	8.1	2.09

* Deaths per 100,000 live births.

SOURCE: National Center for Health Statistics. Calculations by the Children's Defense Fund.

Waiting lists for care became common (the longest in the industrialized world) and those with the funds sought out private medical care that they paid for out of their own pockets. Critics of Britain's system point out that rationing was achieved by concealing from the public how much health care they were not receiving. Doctors redefined standards of care to fit what was available. For example, physicians tell patients with end-stage renal disease (kidney failure) that dialysis is painful and burdensome and they would be better off without it. The need for kidney dialysis increases with age. However, in England, men over 50 years old receive dialysis at half the rate of older men in other European countries. Women are discriminated against even more. English women over 65 years old are dialysized at a rate that is one-third to one-fifth the rate of the rest of Europe.

The End Stage Renal Disease Program in the U.S.

In the United States, dialysis, the treatment for kidney failure, is provided free to nearly all (7 percent of those with end stage renal disease [ESRD] do not meet Medicare requirements for benefits) regardless of age under the Social Service Act (PL 92-603). The decision to cover ESRD expenses was made at a time when resources seemed unlimited, and it was easier to offer treatment to all than to resolve the difficult ethical dilemma of who should receive and who should not. It was predicted that program enrollment would level out at about 900,000 patients by 1995; instead, it reached that level a decade earlier and has shown no signs of tapering off.

When the program began in 1974, it cost Medicare $229 million. By 1989, the most current data showed expenses had risen to $3.689 billion. Predictions for 1990 expenses are $4.134 billion, which will more than double to $8.425 billion by 1996. Both the number of patients and the cost per patient are expected to increase at similar rates. The cost per patient is expected to rise 34.3 percent from $26,811 per person, per year in 1989 to $40,861 in 1996 and the number of patients will increase from 137,585 to 206,198 in the same amount of time. (See Table 8.7.)

The Canadian System

Canada's health insurance plan is frequently proposed as the cure for what ails the American system. In contrast to the fragmented and complex system of third party payment in the United States, the Canadian system is based on provincially controlled, single-payer health plans, eliminating much of the administrative costs. Primary and emergency care is universally insured. Critics of the system claim that, as in Britain, there are waiting lists for treatment, and Canadians with enough money come across the border to the United States for high-tech medical care (a charge denied by proponents of the plan). For Americans to embrace the Canadian system, the insurance industry would likely have to be restructured and rationing of high-cost, experimental health care would be imposed.

TABLE 8.7

ESRD MEDICARE BENEFICIARIES AND PROGRAM EXPENDITURES

[Expenditures in millions]

Fiscal year	Expenditures (HI & SMI)	HI beneficiaries	Per person
1974	$229	15,993	$14,300
1975	361	22,674	15,900
1976	512	28,941	17,700
1977	641	35,889	17,900
1978	800	43,482	18,400
1979	1,010	52,636	19,200
1980	1,250	60,814	20,600
1981	1,472	68,288	21,500
1982	1,651	70,303	23,484
1983	1,908	78,019	24,458
1984	2,083	87,857	23,710
1985	2,377	97,119	24,476
1986	2,665	106,740	24,970
1987	2,884	116,658	24,723
1988	3,158	127,192	24,831
1989	3,689	137,585	26,811
1990	4,134	148,351	27,869
1991	4,721	159,088	29,674
1992	5,338	169,655	31,465
1993	5,985	179,797	33,288
1994	6,729	189,334	35,540
1995	7,542	198,176	38,057
1996	8,425	206,198	40,861

Note: Estimates for 1983–96 are subject to revision by the Office of the Actuary, Office of Medicare Cost Estimates; projections for 1992–96 are under the fiscal year 1993 budget assumptions.

Source: Office of the Actuary, Health Care Financing Administration, Department of Health and Human Services, for fiscal years 1989–96.

THE OREGON PLAN

Since 1987, the state of Oregon had been working on a new, universal health care plan that would contain costs by limiting services. Unlike other states which have trimmed budgets by eliminating people from Medicaid eligibility, Oregon wanted to eliminate low priority services. To this end, Oregon worked out a table of health care services and ranked them according to need and benefit obtained. (See Table 8.8.)

In setting the priorities, prevention and quality of life were the factors that most influenced the ranking of the choice of treatments. Quality of life (QWB in the Oregon plan, or quality of well-being) drew fire from those who felt such judgments could not be subjectively decided. The Children's Defense Fund criticized the fact that treatment for extremely premature infants (under 500 grams and less than 23 weeks gestation) was rated second to last on the list, just above treatment for babies born without a brain (see Chapter IV). The low placement of this care was not based on the high cost of treatment, but on the likelihood that babies who survived would have a very high chance of low QWB. Similarly, active medical or surgical treatment of terminally ill patients also ranked low because of QWB, while comfort and hospice care was ranked high. The Oregon Health Services Commission emphasized that their QWB judgments were not based on a person's quality of life at a given point in time — such judgments are ethically inappropriate. The non-discriminatory way to deal with quality-of-life is to focus on the change in a person's life. How much better or worse off will a patient be following treatment?

Opponents of the plan objected that the funding would come from reducing services which are currently offered to Medicaid recipients (often poor women and children). Others objected to the rankings and the ethical questions raised by choosing to support some treatments over others. Supporters of the Oregon Plan insisted that the only solution to health care is to offer a basic level of service to all persons on Medicaid and finance it by eliminating high-cost, low benefit services. Americans must come to realize that health care cannot be everything for some and nothing for others. "Life, liberty, and the pursuit of happiness" did not guarantee life to the longest possible age; sacrifices in the pursuit of happiness must be made to allocate more money to housing, education, employment, and the other needs of American society.

In August 1992, the (George) Bush Administration disallowed the Oregon Plan on the basis of discrimination. By limiting health care to those who are terminally ill with AIDS or to alcoholics needing liver transplants, Oregon was discriminating under the newly-passed Americans with Dis-

TABLE 8.8

HSC Categories and Rankings

Rank	Category ID No.

"Essential" Services

1. Acute fatal, prevents death, full recovery — **15**
   Examples: Repair of deep, open wound of neck. Appendectomy for appendicitis. Medical therapy for myocarditis.
2. Maternity care (including care for newborn in first 28 days of life) — **12**
   Examples: Obstetrical care for pregnancy. Medical therapy for drug reactions and intoxications specific to newborn. Medical therapy for low birthweight babies.
3. Acute fatal, prevents death, w/o full recovery — **16**
   Examples: Surgical treatment for head injury with prolonged loss of consciousness. Medical therapy for acute bacterial meningitis. Reduction of an open fracture of a joint.
4. Preventive care for children — **01**
   Examples: Immunizations. Medical therapy for streptococcal sore throat and scarlet fever (reduces disability, prevents spread). Screening for specific problems such as vision or hearing problems, or anemia.
5. Chronic fatal, improves life span and QWB (Quality of Well-Being) — **20**
   Examples: Medical therapy for Type I Diabetes Mellitus. Medical and surgical treatment for treatable cancer of the uterus. Medical therapy for asthma.
6. Reproductive services (excluding maternity and infertility) — **13**
   Examples: Contraceptive management, vasectomy, tubal ligation.
7. Comfort care — **26**
   Example: Palliative therapy for conditions in which death is imminent.
8. Preventive dental (children and adults) — **03/07**
   Example: Cleaning and flouride.
9. Preventive care for adults (A-B-C) — **04**
   Examples: Mammograms, blood pressure screening, medical therapy and chemoprophylaxis for primary tuberculosis.

"Very Important" Services

10. Acute nonfatal, return to previous health — **17**
    Examples: Medical therapy for acute thyroiditis. Medical therapy for vaginitis. Restorative dental service for dental caries.
11. Chronic nonfatal, one time treatment improves QWB — **23**
    Examples: Hip replacement. Laser surgery for diabetic retinopathy. Medical therapy for rheumatic fever.
12. Acute nonfatal, w/o return to previous health — **18**
    Examples: Relocation of dislocation of elbow. Arthroscopic repair of internal derangement of knee. Repair of corneal laceration.
13. Chronic nonfatal, repetitive treatment improves QWB — **24**
    Examples: Medical therapy for chronic sinusitis. Medical therapy for migraine. Medical therapy for psoriasis.

Services "Valuable to Certain Individuals"

14. Acute nonfatal, expedites recovery — **19**
    Examples: Medical therapy for diaper rash. Medical therapy for acute conjunctivitis. Medical therapy for acute pharyngitis.
15. Infertility services — **14**
    Examples: Medical therapy for anovulation. Microsurgery for tubal disease. In-vitro fertilization.
16. Preventive care for adults (D-E) — **05**
    Examples: Dipstick urinalysis for hematuria in adults less than 60 years of age. Sigmoidoscopy for persons less than 40 years of age. Screening of nonpregnant adults for Type I Diabetes Mellitus.
17. Fatal or nonfatal, minimal or no improvement in QWB (non-self-limited) — **25**
    Examples: Repair fingertip avulsion that does not include fingernail. Medical therapy for gallstones without cholecystitis. Medical therapy for viral warts.

Oregon Basic Health Services Program
22 February 1991

abilities Act (PL 101-336), a law to give disabled persons the same rights as able persons.

HEALTH CARE FOR SPECIAL GROUPS

Health Insurance for the Elderly

Americans paid $666.2 billion for health care in 1990. The elderly made up 12 percent of the U. S. population, but accounted for one-third of total personal health care expenditures. Almost all Americans 65 years and older receive help with at least some medical expenses from government programs such as Medicare and Medicaid (see below) and/or are covered by private medical insurance. Many elderly people mistakenly believe that Medicare will pay for all their health costs. No single government or private program covers all health costs. It is possible, however, to obtain total financial coverage for almost all medical costs with a combination of government programs and private health insurance. The cost of such a package, though, is prohibitive for many elderly people, and qualifications for enrollment in some programs may be difficult or impossible for older people to meet.

The United States is one of the few industrialized nations that does not have a national health care program. In most other developed countries, government programs cover almost all health-related costs, from maternity care to long-term care.

In the United States, the major government health care programs are Medicare and Medicaid. They provide financial assistance for the elderly, the poor, and the disabled. Before the existence of these programs, a large number of older Americans could not afford adequate medical care. Public funds are the major source of health care payments

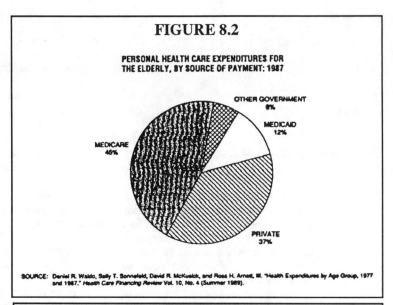

FIGURE 8.2

PERSONAL HEALTH CARE EXPENDITURES FOR THE ELDERLY, BY SOURCE OF PAYMENT: 1987

OTHER GOVERNMENT 6%

MEDICAID 12%

MEDICARE 45%

PRIVATE 37%

SOURCE: Daniel R. Waldo, Sally T. Sonnefeld, David R. McKusick, and Ross H. Arnett, III. "Health Expenditures by Age Group, 1977 and 1987." Health Care Financing Review Vol. 10, No. 4 (Summer 1989).

TABLE 8.9

PERCENT DISTRIBUTION OF PERSONAL HEALTH CARE EXPENDITURES, BY SOURCE OF FUNDS FOR PEOPLE 65+, BY TYPE OF SERVICE: 1987

| Source of funds | Total care | Type of service | | | |
		Hospital	Physician	Nursing home	Other care
Total spending	100.0	100.0	100.0	100.0	100.0
Private	37.4	14.8	35.5	58.4	70.0
Public	62.6	85.2	64.5	41.6	30.0
Medicare	44.6	69.7	60.6	1.7	14.7
Medicaid	12.0	4.9	1.5	36.4	13.3
Other	6.0	10.6	2.4	3.5	2.0

SOURCE: Daniel R. Waldo, Sally T. Sonnefeld, David R. McKusick, and Ross H. Arnett, III. "Health Expenditures by Age Group, 1977 and 1987." Health Care Financing Review Vol. 10, No. 4 (Summer 1989).

for people over 65 years old (Figure 8.2 and Table 8.9), providing 62.6 percent of the cost. Medicare mainly reimburses for hospital and physician care, while Medicaid provided 36 percent of the cost of nursing home care.

Medicare

The Medicare program, enacted under Title XVIII ("Health Insurance for the Aged") of the Social Security Act (PL 89-97), went into effect on July 1, 1966. The program is composed of two parts:

Part A provides hospital insurance. Coverage includes doctors' fees, nursing services, meals, a semiprivate room, special care units, operating room costs, laboratory tests, and some drugs and supplies. Part A also covers rehabilitation services, limited post-hospital skilled nursing facility care, home health care, and hospice care for the terminally ill.

Part B (Supplemental Medical Insurance or SMI) is elective medical insurance, that is, enrollees must pay premiums to get coverage. It covers private physicians' services, diagnostic tests, outpatient hospital services, outpatient physical therapy, speech pathology services, home health services, and medical equipment and supplies.

In 1991, 30.4 million older persons (and more than 3 million disabled persons) were enrolled in Part A of the program, and 6.8 million of those received reimbursed services (Table 8.10). Average annual Medicare costs in 1987 were $2,017 for individuals 65 to 74 years and $3,215 for those 85 years and older. Experts point out that by 2040, the average age of a baby boomer will be 85 years old and the level of Medicare spending could range from $147 to $212 billion (in 1987 dollars).

Doctors are reimbursed on a fee-for-service basis. This system presents a number of problems: because of paperwork, lack of proper compensation, and delays in reimbursements, some doctors will not provide service under the Medicare program; the system includes incentives that may encourage doctors to treat patients in a hospital rather than in a less-expensive outpatient setting; and patients may receive treatment that provides only marginal health benefits.

Medicaid

Medicaid ("Grants to States for Medical Assistance Programs," Title XIX of the Social Security Act) is a federal/state program established in 1966 to provide medical assistance to certain categories of low-income Americans: the aged, blind, disabled, or members of families with dependent children. Medicaid covers hospitalization, doctors' fees, laboratory fees, x-rays, and long-term nursing home care.

The elderly made up only 10.7 percent of all Medicaid recipients in 1990 (out of over 24 mil-

TABLE 8.10

NUMBER OF AGED AND DISABLED ELIGIBLE ENROLLEES AND BENEFICIARIES, AND AVERAGE AND TOTAL MEDICARE BENEFIT PAYMENTS

[Persons in thousands]

	1975 (actual)	1980 (actual)	1985 (actual)	1987 (actual)	1988 (actual)	1989 (actual)	1990 (actual)	1991 (actual)	1993 [1] (estimate)	1995 [1] (estimate)	1975–95 [1]	1985–90	1990–95 [1]
Part A:													
Persons with hospital insurance protection (monthly average):													
Aged......	21,795	24,571	27,123	28,239	28,779	29,366	29,801	30,456	31,534	32,437	2.2	1.9	1.7
Disabled..	2,047	2,968	2,944	3,042	3,115	3,200	3,270	3,380	3,581	3,772	3.7	2.1	2.9
Total.......	23,842	27,539	30,067	31,281	31,894	32,566	33,071	33,036	35,115	36,209	2.3	1.9	1.8
Beneficiaries receiving reimbursed services:													
Aged......	4,906	5,943	6,168	6,041	6,074	6,137	6,070	6,100	6,350	6,640	2.3	−.3	1.8
Disabled..	456	721	672	666	653	657	680	700	740	785	4.0	.2	2.9
Total.......	5,362	6,664	6,840	6,707	6,727	6,794	6,750	6,800	7,090	7,425	2.5	−.3	1.9
Average annual benefit per person enrolled: [2] [3]													
Aged......	$326	$853	$1,563	$1,572	$1,617	$1,749	$1,971	$2,007	$2,341	$2,771	17.0	4.7	7.1
Disabled..	$345	$948	$1,806	$1,777	$1,749	$1,908	$2,139	$2,177	$2,521	$2,976	18.0	3.4	6.8
Total.......	$327	$863	$1,587	$1,592	$1,630	$1,765	$1,987	$2,024	$2,359	$2,792	17.1	4.6	7.0

Source: Health Care Financing Division, Division of Budget

lion), but they received one-third of Medicaid payments. Medicaid is the principal source of public financing for nursing home care. It is the primary source of prescription drug coverage for a large number of the poor elderly. Although home health services presently account for a small share of Medicaid expenditures for the aged, it is the fastest growing expense (Figure 8.3).

Medicaid is designed to take care of those people who, through poverty or disability, cannot afford medical treatment. However, in 1989, only one-third of elderly poor were protected by Medicaid. In addition, Medicaid recipients are often required to travel long distances and endure prolonged waits before they receive attention, and the care they do receive may not be adequate.

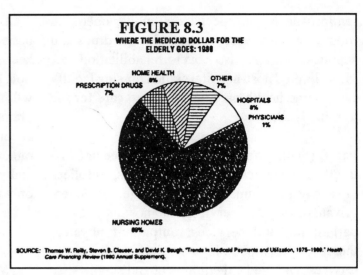

FIGURE 8.3

WHERE THE MEDICAID DOLLAR FOR THE ELDERLY GOES: 1988

HOME HEALTH 6%
PRESCRIPTION DRUGS 7%
OTHER 7%
HOSPITALS 6%
PHYSICIANS 1%
NURSING HOMES 69%

SOURCE: Thomas W. Reilly, Steven B. Clauser, and David K. Baugh. "Trends in Medicaid Payments and Utilization, 1975–1989." Health Care Financing Review (1990 Annual Supplement).

LONG-TERM HEALTH CARE

Perhaps the most pressing and most difficult health care problem facing America today is long-term care. Long-term care refers to services needed by individuals with chronic illnesses or mental or physical conditions so severe that they cannot care for themselves on a daily basis. Longer life spans and improved life-sustaining technologies are increasing the possibility that an individual may eventually require long-term care.

Options are Limited and Expensive

The options for good, affordable long-term care in the United States are few. One year's stay in a nursing home currently costs an average of $30,000, with actual costs ranging from $20,000 to $50,000 depending on the amount of care required. Even hiring an unskilled caregiver who makes home visits can cost over $25,000 a year; skilled care costs much more. Most elderly people, and young families, cannot afford this expense. Life-time savings can be consumed before the need for care ends.

Forty-five percent of elderly nursing home residents are 85 years or older. According to census projections, by 2040 there may be two to three times as many nursing home residents who are 85+ compared to those who are 65 and older. The cost of nursing home care in 1985 dollars could rise to between $84 and $139 billion by the year 2040. If Medicaid covers approximately 40 percent of the expense, the cost to the government in 1985 dollars could be as high as $56 billion.

These increasing costs for health care frighten advocates for the elderly because they worry that the new proposals for rationing will cut off support to the elderly. Daniel Callahan of the Hastings Center and former Governor Lamm of Colorado have both recommended that after a natural life span (somewhere in the seventies or eighties), health care should be limited to relieving suffering. Opponents fear that rationing for the elderly will happen by age, not by possible benefit to the patient (see Britain, above). This would be a form of age discrimination that most find unacceptable. Health care decisions must be made individually, not by an arbitrarily chosen age.

The Dying

Terminal patients often receive sophisticated medical treatments that cannot save their lives but can extend it. Countries with national health care plans have made decisions to ration terminal care, but in the United States, the malpractice system, the medical educational system, and the government reimbursement system all encourage continued medical care. About 27 percent of Medicare costs are spent on the last year of life.

In addition to the terminally ill, there are from 5,000 to 10,000 persons* in a persistent vegetative state costing from $2,000 to $10,000 a month to maintain. That adds up to between $120 million and $1.2 billion annually.

There are several factors that influence a patient's death. Most people (80 percent) die in institutions. Most people die after an extended period of gradually deteriorating disease — cancer, heart disease, chronic obstructive pulmonary disease, and stroke. Health care providers can almost always find more therapies to try which will sustain a patient's life. Most deaths (an estimated 70 to 75 percent) follow a medical decision that life will no longer be prolonged. Generally there is a time when patients, their families, and the health care staff need to decide whether or not to withhold treatment.

Overtreatment

Dr. S., a surgeon, had back pain. Several internists examined him and found nothing wrong. Two CAT scans later, pancreatic cancer was diagnosed. For Dr. S., it was a death sentence. He told his son, also a doctor, "I have seen physicians torture dying patients in vain attempts to prolong life. I have taken care of you most of your life. Now I must ask for your help. Don't let them abuse me. No surgery, no chemotherapy." The son thought he had made his father's wishes clear to the doctors and returned to his home out of town. But almost immediately a series of surgical and radiological procedures were started.

The son realized that specialists with procedure-based practices were running up thousands of dollars in inflated consulting fees. He insisted that his father be seen only by internists who had no financial stake in futile treatments. The doctors agreed and promised to keep in close contact. They never called again. When the other son, a lawyer, came to visit, Dr. S. pleaded, "They are treating me like an animal. Please get me out of here." Despite threats of legal action, the patient spent two weeks receiving unnecessary "billable" high-technology therapy that could not possibly cure him or relieve his pain. Many treatments were done to correct the problems caused by earlier treatments.

When Dr. S. became incoherent, the attorney told the hospital administrators that he was invoking his power of attorney and explicitly forbade the hospital to do anything other than relieve his father's pain. Dr. S. spent that night in surgery again. The sons could not find another hospital to take their father, and the continuous tests left him too unstable to be moved to a hospice. When they finally did get him to a hospice, he died the following morning.

All the medical bills (more than $150,000 for a patient who needed a bed and morphine) were covered by Medicare. The physician-son called the Medicare inspector general's office. He was told that if the hospital had billed for unauthorized procedures it was a possible violation; however, in that particular state, there are so many fraud cases exceeding a million dollars that they could not become involved in one for only $150,000.

AIDS

The rise of AIDS has also increased medical costs. In 1988, the average lifetime cost (the treatment cost over the life of the patient) of treating an AIDS patient was $57,000, in 1991 it was $85,333, and because of new, expensive drug therapies, it has shot up to $102,000 in 1992. The yearly cost of treating an HIV infected patient who has not yet developed AIDS doubled from $5,100 to $10,000 from 1991 to 1992, while AIDS patients now cost about $38,300 a year, up from $32,000. In comparison, the yearly expense of treatment of AIDS in Europe costs approximately $22,300, $2,000 in Latin America, and $393 in Africa,

---

*Some estimates are as high as 25,000 persons in PVS.

although treatment in Latin America and Africa is usually minimal.

Some of the recently marketed drugs which have inflated the cost of care in the United States include:

• Didanosine (DID), a treatment for those who cannot take AZT, at $40 a week.
• Erythropoietin to treat anemia at $200 a week,
• a drug to increase white blood cells usually used for cancer patients but prescribed to some AIDS patients at $1,000 a week.
• Foscarnet to treat retinitis (a blinding condition) at $20,000 a year.

Foscarnet is produced by only one manufacturer, a Swedish drug company, which has been attacked by AIDS activists protesting the company's pricing.

These new therapies offer a better quality of life, but none so far have been shown to increase life span.

Cancer

The final year of a terminal cancer patient's treatment costs twice as much as the last year of a terminal patient with heart disease ($8,021 versus $4,012). There are more options for treatment, more adverse side effects that require treatment, and a greater potential for unrelieved pain with cancer than with heart disease. Hospitalization accounts for 76 percent of the bill, and physician and other medical fees account for 18 percent. The average Medicare costs for a cancer patient over 85 years old ($5,670) are less than for a 75 year old patient ($7,838) which are again less than those for patients 65 to 74 years old ($8,835). The cost is usually higher the younger the patient, because he or she is frequently better able to fight the disease than is the older patient. This financial trend would suggest that the bill for cancer patients who are younger than the age for Medicare eligibility is even higher. Most of these expenses occur at the end of life — 34 percent the last year and 59 percent the last three years. Hospitalization for the initial phase of treatment costs only 38 percent as much as terminal care. In addition, doctors receive nearly three times as much for terminal care as they do for the initial treatment. If more patients were offered hospice care and if they had made out advance directives limiting futile treatment, much of this expense could be spared. (See Chapters V and VI.)

Society and the Individual

In the United States, there is a widespread belief that no one should be denied access to the most advanced medical care. As a result, the dying are often overtreated, sometimes against their will, leaving few resources for preventive and primary care. The needs of society are often at odds with individual desires to do everything possible. When patient M., a terminal patient in intensive care, died after intensive and expensive care, his niece remarked, "I can't see why the doctors shouldn't [have done] as much as possible for him. Cost as a factor should never enter in." At least 80 percent of his bill was covered by Medicare, and he may have had private insurance to cover the rest.

CHAPTER IX

THE ELDERLY

WHO IS OLD?

According to Webster's Dictionary, the word "old" means "having lived or been in existence for a long time." This definition works well for a car or a piece of pottery, but when applied to people, it shows only a small part of a much larger picture — it refers only to the number of years a person has been alive. Even that standard has changed through history. A citizen of ancient Greece had a life expectancy of 20 years. An American Indian warrior in the pre-Columbian Southwest could expect to live 33 years. The low life expectancy was mainly caused by a high infant mortality rate. Once a child survived through childhood, he or she had a reasonable chance of making it into the fifties or sixties. In 1900, the life expectancy of the average American was 47 years; an American male born in 1990 can expect to live 72.1 years and a female, 79.0 years. (See Table 9.1.)

The U. S. government has determined that a person's 65th birthday is the age when U.S. citizens become eligible for government benefits such as full Social Security, Medicare, and reduced taxes. Age 65 was not selected by any scientific process; it follows a precedent set by German Chancellor Otto von Bismark in 1899. In that year, Germany became the first western government to assume financial support of its older citizens by passing the Old Age and Survivors Pension Act. Chancellor von Bismark arbitrarily decided that eligibility for benefits would begin at age 65 (although he himself was an active and vigorous 74 years old at the time).

AMERICA GROWS OLDER

In 1900, one American out of every 25 (4 percent of the total population) was over 65 years old. The 65+ age group made up 12.5 percent of the total population in 1990. By 2050, 22.9 percent of the U.S. population (more than one person out of every five) will be 65 or older (Table 9.2 and Figure 9.1). The national median age (half of all Americans are below and half are above this age) exceeded 32 years for the first time in 1987. The median age was 16.7 in 1820, then reached 30 years in 1950.

TABLE 9.1
PROJECTED LIFE EXPECTANCY AT BIRTH AND AGE 65, BY SEX: 1990-2050
(in years)

Year	At birth			At age 65		
	Men	Women	Difference	Men	Women	Difference
1990	72.1	79.0	6.9	15.0	19.4	4.4
2000	73.5	80.4	6.9	15.7	20.3	4.6
2010	74.4	81.3	6.9	16.2	21.0	4.8
2020	74.9	81.8	6.9	16.6	21.4	4.8
2030	75.4	82.3	6.9	17.0	21.8	4.8
2040	75.9	82.8	6.9	17.3	22.3	5.0
2050	76.4	83.3	6.9	17.7	22.7	5.0

SOURCE: U.S. Bureau of the Census. "Projections of the Population of the United States, by Age, Sex, and Race: 1988 to 2080," by Gregory Spencer. Current Population Reports Series P-25, No. 1018 (January 1989).

TABLE 9.2

ACTUAL AND PROJECTED GROWTH OF THE OLDER POPULATION: 1900-2050

(numbers in thousands)

Year	Total population all ages	55 to 64		65 to 74		75 to 84 years		85+		65+	
		Number	Percent	Number	Percent	Number	Percent	Number	Percent	Number	Percent
1900	76,303	4,009	5.3	2,189	2.9	772	1.0	123	0.2	3,084	4.0
1910	91,972	5,054	5.5	2,793	3.0	989	1.1	167	0.2	3,950	4.3
1920	105,711	6,532	6.2	3,464	3.3	1,259	1.2	210	0.2	4,933	4.7
1930	122,775	8,397	6.8	4,721	3.8	1,641	1.3	272	0.2	6,634	5.4
1940	131,669	10,572	8.0	6,375	4.8	2,278	1.7	365	0.3	9,019	6.8
1950	150,967	13,295	8.8	8,415	5.6	3,278	2.2	577	0.4	12,270	8.1
1960	179,323	15,572	8.7	10,997	6.1	4,633	2.6	929	0.5	16,560	9.2
1970	203,302	18,608	9.2	12,447	6.1	6,124	3.0	1,409	0.7	19,980	9.8
1980	226,546	21,703	9.6	15,580	6.9	7,729	3.4	2,240	1.0	25,549	11.3
1990	250,410	21,364	8.5	18,373	7.3	9,933	4.0	3,254	1.3	31,559	12.6
2000	268,266	24,158	9.0	18,243	6.8	12,017	4.5	4,622	1.7	34,882	13.0
2010	282,575	35,430	12.5	21,039	7.4	12,208	4.3	6,115	2.2	39,362	13.9
2020	294,364	41,087	14.0	30,973	10.5	14,443	4.9	6,651	2.3	52,067	17.7
2030	300,629	34,947	11.6	35,988	12.0	21,487	7.1	8,129	2.7	65,604	21.8
2040	301,807	35,537	11.8	30,808	10.2	25,050	8.3	12,251	4.1	68,109	22.6
2050	299,849	37,004	12.3	31,590	10.5	21,655	7.2	15,287	5.1	68,532	22.9

SOURCES: 1900 to 1980 data are tabulated from the Decennial Censuses of the Population and exclude Armed Forces overseas. Projections, which are middle series projections and include Armed Forces overseas, are from U.S. Bureau of the Census, "Projections of the Population of the United States, by Age, Sex, and Race: 1988 to 2080," by Gregory Spencer. *Current Population Reports* Series P-25, No. 1018 (January 1989).

The Oldest Old

Even more dramatic than the growth of the 65+ population will be the increase in the number of Americans over the age of 85. While the 65 to 84 age group will decline slightly after 2030, the number of people over 85 will continue to grow through 2050. By 2050, the 85+ age group will

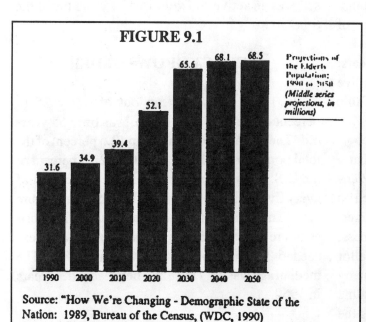

FIGURE 9.1

Projections of the Elderly Population: 1990 to 2050 (Middle series projections, in millions)

Source: "How We're Changing - Demographic State of the Nation: 1989, Bureau of the Census, (WDC, 1990)

make up 5 percent of the total U.S. population and 23 percent will be in the 65+ age group (Table 9.2). Women made up 12 percent of the oldest old in 1989. Because women will continue to have longer life expectancies into the middle of the next century, it is likely that they will make up an even larger proportion in the future (Table 9.3).

Living to be 100

America will likely experience a "centenarian boom" within the next 60 years. The chances of living to age 100 have increased 40 times since 1900. The U. S. had 61,000 centenarians in 1989 (Table 9.3). Dr. Gregory Spencer, a demographer with the U.S. Census Bureau, predicts that America will have 108,000 centenarians by 2000, 441,000 by 2025, and 1.3 million by 2050 - a phenomenal growth when compared to the 4,000 centenarians living in the United States in 1960. Most centenarians live past the age of 100 by only a few years; the majority (90 percent) are less than 105 years.

Reasons For The Aging of America

In addition to the large number of births after World War II, there are other reasons for the aging of the American population. Foremost are medical advances that have greatly reduced infant mortality and death from childhood diseases; people have a much greater chance of surviving the first year of life. Medical advances, life-sustaining technologies, and a greater awareness of and desire for a healthy lifestyle have helped lengthen the lives of Americans.

TABLE 9.3

Total Population, by Sex, Race, and Age: 1989

[In thousands, except as indicated. As of July 1. Includes Armed Forces abroad]

AGE	Total ¹	Male	Female	White	Black	AGE	Total ¹	Male	Female	White	Black
Total	248,762	121,445	127,317	209,326	30,788	50-54 yrs. old . .	11,377	5,511	5,866	9,790	1,223
						50 yrs. old . .	2,411	1,165	1,247	2,063	267
Under 5 yrs. old.	18,752	9,596	9,155	15,050	2,890	51 yrs. old . .	2,312	1,123	1,189	1,991	245
Under 1 yr. old	3,945	2,020	1,925	3,163	619	52 yrs. old . .	2,209	1,070	1,139	1,896	240
1 yr. old . . .	3,717	1,904	1,813	2,983	577	53 yrs. old . .	2,210	1,073	1,137	1,908	234
2 yrs. old . . .	3,660	1,872	1,788	2,931	567	54 yrs. old . .	2,235	1,079	1,155	1,931	237
3 yrs. old . . .	3,710	1,898	1,812	2,983	561	55-59 yrs. old. .	10,726	5,121	5,605	9,310	1,116
4 yrs. old . . .	3,721	1,904	1,816	2,989	565	55 yrs. old . .	2,102	1,010	1,092	1,809	228
5-9 yrs. old . . .	18,212	9,321	8,891	14,626	2,802	56 yrs. old . .	2,076	995	1,081	1,796	219
5 yrs. old . . .	3,605	1,844	1,761	2,895	550	57 yrs. old . .	2,176	1,039	1,137	1,886	230
6 yrs. old . . .	3,678	1,883	1,795	2,950	558	58 yrs. old . .	2,163	1,027	1,135	1,886	219
7 yrs. old . . .	3,733	1,910	1,822	3,000	573	59 yrs. old . .	2,209	1,049	1,160	1,933	219
8 yrs. old . . .	3,573	1,831	1,742	2,874	549	60-64 yrs. old. .	10,867	5,079	5,788	9,569	1,035
9 yrs. old . . .	3,624	1,853	1,770	2,900	573	60 yrs. old . .	2,229	1,053	1,176	1,937	234
						61 yrs. old . .	2,235	1,053	1,182	1,970	212
10-14 yrs. old. .	16,950	8,689	8,260	13,574	2,679	62 yrs. old . .	2,114	984	1,129	1,858	203
10 yrs. old . .	3,563	1,826	1,737	2,846	571	63 yrs. old . .	2,103	978	1,125	1,859	194
11 yrs. old . .	3,418	1,751	1,667	2,740	540	64 yrs. old . .	2,187	1,010	1,176	1,945	192
12 yrs. old . .	3,384	1,735	1,649	2,712	534	65-69 yrs. old. .	10,170	4,631	5,538	9,029	916
13 yrs. old . .	3,257	1,668	1,589	2,608	513	65 yrs. old . .	2,175	1,001	1,174	1,921	204
14 yrs. old . .	3,327	1,708	1,619	2,668	522	66 yrs. old . .	2,045	935	1,111	1,812	187
15-19 yrs. old. .	17,847	9,123	8,725	14,367	2,767	67 yrs. old . .	2,089	954	1,135	1,857	186
15 yrs. old . .	3,278	1,681	1,598	2,619	520	68 yrs. old . .	1,987	905	1,082	1,781	164
16 yrs. old . .	3,355	1,718	1,637	2,672	542	69 yrs. old . .	1,874	837	1,037	1,657	176
17 yrs. old . .	3,536	1,815	1,720	2,832	561						
18 yrs. old . .	3,794	1,936	1,858	3,068	583	70-74 yrs. old. .	8,012	3,464	4,549	7,193	661
19 yrs. old . .	3,884	1,973	1,911	3,177	561	70 yrs. old . .	1,741	772	969	1,552	154
						71 yrs. old . .	1,708	751	956	1,541	134
20-24 yrs. old. .	18,886	9,529	9,356	15,490	2,895	72 yrs. old . .	1,619	700	918	1,457	131
20 yrs. old . .	3,772	1,913	1,859	3,078	549	73 yrs. old . .	1,487	632	855	1,338	120
21 yrs. old . .	3,625	1,835	1,790	2,964	523	74 yrs. old . .	1,458	608	850	1,306	123
22 yrs. old . .	3,671	1,851	1,820	3,014	521	75-79 yrs. old. .	6,033	2,385	3,648	5,430	486
23 yrs. old . .	3,777	1,899	1,879	3,101	538	75 yrs. old . .	1,376	566	811	1,237	113
24 yrs. old . .	4,040	2,031	2,008	3,332	563	76 yrs. old . .	1,297	521	776	1,165	106
25-29 yrs. old. .	21,830	10,979	10,851	18,192	2,861	77 yrs. old . .	1,212	476	735	1,089	98
25 yrs. old . .	4,242	2,136	2,106	3,519	571	78 yrs. old . .	1,120	432	688	1,009	89
26 yrs. old . .	4,282	2,153	2,128	3,564	566	79 yrs. old . .	1,028	391	637	930	79
27 yrs. old . .	4,400	2,210	2,191	3,666	578						
28 yrs. old . .	4,326	2,173	2,153	3,618	555	80-84 yrs. old. .	3,728	1,306	2,422	3,409	256
29 yrs. old . .	4,580	2,307	2,273	3,825	591	80 yrs. old . .	921	338	583	832	72
						81 yrs. old . .	815	290	526	750	51
30-34 yrs. old. .	22,218	11,151	11,068	18,622	2,767	82 yrs. old . .	720	253	467	661	47
30 yrs. old . .	4,575	2,299	2,276	3,812	590	83 yrs. old . .	669	228	441	614	44
31 yrs. old . .	4,483	2,251	2,233	3,764	552	84 yrs. old . .	603	198	405	552	42
32 yrs. old . .	4,507	2,263	2,244	3,778	561	85-89 yrs. old. .	1,962	588	1,374	1,791	142
33 yrs. old . .	4,297	2,149	2,147	3,602	527	85 yrs. old . .	515	164	351	470	37
34 yrs. old . .	4,357	2,189	2,168	3,666	536	86 yrs. old . .	448	137	311	408	32
35-39 yrs. old. .	19,676	9,782	9,894	16,664	2,273	87 yrs. old . .	387	114	272	353	28
35 yrs. old . .	4,204	2,101	2,103	3,545	504	88 yrs. old . .	332	96	237	303	24
36 yrs. old . .	4,033	2,008	2,025	3,417	482	89 yrs. old . .	281	78	203	257	20
37 yrs. old . .	3,934	1,954	1,980	3,332	456						
38 yrs. old . .	3,744	1,853	1,891	3,183	419	90-94 yrs. old. .	790	195	594	719	61
39 yrs. old . .	3,762	1,866	1,896	3,187	431	90 yrs. old . .	234	62	171	213	17
						91 yrs. old . .	190	48	142	174	14
40-44 yrs. old. .	16,908	8,319	8,589	14,571	1,731	92 yrs. old . .	151	36	115	138	12
40 yrs. old . .	3,761	1,856	1,905	3,200	419	93 yrs. old . .	117	26	91	107	9
41 yrs. old . .	3,583	1,768	1,815	3,091	364	94 yrs. old . .	97	23	74	87	9
42 yrs. old . .	3,855	1,903	1,952	3,376	357	95-99 yrs. old. .	229	53	176	200	25
43 yrs. old . .	2,825	1,381	1,444	2,430	287	95 yrs. old . .	77	19	59	69	8
44 yrs. old . .	2,885	1,411	1,473	2,474	303	96 yrs. old . .	58	14	44	51	6
45-49 yrs. old. .	13,528	6,608	6,921	11,678	1,396	97 yrs. old . .	42	10	32	37	5
45 yrs. old . .	2,846	1,391	1,455	2,447	299	98 yrs. old . .	30	7	23	25	4
46 yrs. old . .	3,068	1,499	1,569	2,676	296	99 yrs. old . .	22	5	17	19	3
47 yrs. old . .	2,748	1,339	1,409	2,359	296	100 yrs. old and					
48 yrs. old . .	2,440	1,193	1,247	2,112	246	over	61	13	48	50	9
49 yrs. old . .	2,427	1,185	1,241	2,063	260	Median age (yr.)	32.6	31.5	33.8	33.6	27.7

¹ Includes other races, not shown separately.

Source : U.S. Bureau of the Census, *Current Population Reports*, series P-25, Nos. 1045 and 1057.

One of the reasons people sometimes fear growing older is having to face the loss of mental and physical abilities. Although the human body progressively declines with age, the rate and amount of decline is an individual process. One person may be afflicted with arthritis and senility at age 65 while another is vigorous and active at 80. It is true, however, that older people have more health problems and require more health care than younger ones.

GENERAL HEALTH OF OLDER AMERICANS

The U.S. Department of Health and Human Services, in *Aging America — Trends and Projec-*

tions 1991 Edition, reported that 71 percent of noninstitutionalized elderly people described their health as good or excellent compared to others their age; only 29 percent thought their health was fair or poor (Table 9.4).

The same source indicates that one quarter of all elderly persons and one-half of the oldest old (over 85 years) have at least a mild degree of functional disability. More than four out of five persons 65 and over have at least one chronic (long-lasting or often recurring) illness, and many have multiple chronic conditions.

Chronic conditions are the burden of old age. At the turn of the century, acute conditions (severe illnesses of limited duration, such as infections) were predominant. With the development of antibiotics and cures for many acute infectious diseases, chronic conditions are now the prevalent health problem for the elderly. Because people are now living to an older age, they have more years in which to suffer a chronic condition.

The leading chronic conditions of the elderly are arthritis, hypertension, hearing impairments, and heart disease (Figure 9.2 and Table 9.5). In most cases, the likelihood for disease increases with age. Older men are more likely than women to have acute illnesses that are life threatening, while older women are more likely to have chronic conditions that cause physical limitation.

TABLE 9.4

NUMBER OF ELDERLY PEOPLE AND PERCENT DISTRIBUTION BY RESPONDENT-ASSESSED HEALTH STATUS, BY SEX AND FAMILY INCOME, 1989

Characteristic	All persons[1] (000s)	Respondent-assessed health status[2]					
		All health status[3]	Excellent	Very good	Good	Fair	Poor
All persons 65+[4]	29,219	100.0	16.4	23.1	31.9	19.3	9.2
Sex:							
Men	12,143	100.0	16.9	23.2	30.8	18.4	10.7
Women	17,076	100.0	16.1	23.0	32.8	20.0	8.1
Family income:							
Under $10,000	5,812	100.0	10.3	19.4	29.7	25.0	15.6
$10,000 to $19,999	8,002	100.0	14.8	21.7	33.9	21.1	8.5
$20,000 to $34,999	5,242	100.0	20.2	25.7	32.5	15.7	5.9
$35,000 and over	3,484	100.0	26.0	26.8	30.3	11.7	5.1

SOURCE: National Center for Health Statistics. "Current Estimates from the National Health Interview Survey, 1989." *Vital and Health Statistics Series 10, No. 176* (October 1990). Data are based on household interviews of the civilian, noninstitutionalized population.

NOTE: Percentages may not add to 100 percent due to rounding.

[1] Includes unknown health status.
[2] Excludes unknown health status.
[3] The categories related to this concept result from asking the respondent, "Would you say—health is excellent, very good, good, fair, or poor?" As such, it is based on the respondent's opinion and not directly on any clinical evidence.
[4] Includes unknown family income.

FIGURE 9.2
THE TOP TEN CHRONIC CONDITIONS FOR PEOPLE 65+: 1989

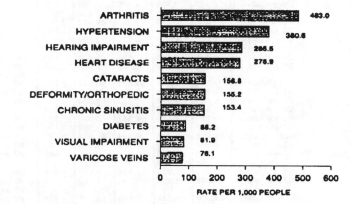

Condition	Rate per 1,000 people
ARTHRITIS	483.0
HYPERTENSION	380.6
HEARING IMPAIRMENT	286.5
HEART DISEASE	278.9
CATARACTS	156.8
DEFORMITY/ORTHOPEDIC	155.2
CHRONIC SINUSITIS	153.4
DIABETES	88.2
VISUAL IMPAIRMENT	81.9
VARICOSE VEINS	78.1

RATE PER 1,000 PEOPLE

SOURCE: National Center for Health Statistics. "Current Estimates from the National Health Interview Survey, 1989." *Vital and Health Statistics Series 10, No. 176* (October 1990).

TABLE 9.5
TOP TEN CHRONIC CONDITIONS FOR PEOPLE 65+, BY AGE AND RACE: 1989
(number per 1,000 people)

Condition	Age				Race (65+)		
	65+	45 to 64	65 to 74	75+	White	Black	Black as % of white
Arthritis	483.0	253.8	437.3	554.5	483.2	522.6	108
Hypertension	380.6	229.1	383.8	375.6	367.4	517.7	141
Hearing impairment	286.5	127.7	239.4	360.3	297.4	174.5	59
Heart disease	278.9	118.9	231.6	353.0	286.5	220.5	77
Cataracts	156.8	16.1	107.4	234.3	160.7	139.8	87
Deformity or orthopedic impairment	155.2	155.5	141.4	177.0	156.2	150.8	97
Chronic sinusitis	153.4	173.5	151.8	155.8	157.1	125.2	80
Diabetes	88.2	58.2	89.7	85.7	80.2	165.9	207
Visual impairment	81.9	45.1	69.3	101.7	81.1	77.0	95
Varicose veins	78.1	57.8	72.6	86.6	80.3	64.0	80

SOURCE: National Center for Health Statistics. "Current Estimates from the National Health Interview Survey, 1989." *Vital and Health Statistics Series 10, No. 176* (October 1990).

The elderly use professional medical equipment and supplies, dental care, prescription drugs, and vision aids more than people under age 65. Table 9.6 indicates a higher hospitalization rate and longer average stay among the elderly than any other age group. The average length of hospitalization for an elderly person has declined over the years (Figure 9.3) from 14.2 days per stay in 1968 to 8.5 days in 1986 and up slightly in 1988 to 8.9 days.

The aging of the American population increases demand for physician care. In 1989, 259 million physician contacts were made by those over 65. Experts predict that in the year 2000, 296 million contacts will be made, an increase of 22 percent (Table 9.7). The year 2030 will reflect a 115 percent increase to 556 million medical visits.

SOCIOECONOMIC DIFFERENCES

Income or socioeconomic status (SES) is directly related to the onset of chronic illness and disability in later years. The more educated and affluent elderly are more likely to be healthy longer. Americans of the lowest SES experience more chronic illness such as cancer, heart attacks, strokes, and lung disease. These illnesses are not as common in upper-SES elderly until after the age of 75.

The number of chronic conditions suffered by an older citizen also varies by SES. Those in the highest SES group reported fewer simultaneous chronic conditions than in the lowest SES. Possible explanations for the health differences among elderly of different SES include:

1. a higher incidence of risk behaviors (smoking, high-fat diet, more sedentary lifestyle) among the lower SES;

2. greater occupational stresses and hazards in the work environments of the lowest SES;

3. acute and chronic stress among the lower SES;

4. decreased access to medical care among the lower SES.

Figure 9.4 shows how elderly persons in all SES segments rated their health. Their self-reports generally mirror the actual condition of their health.

LIFE EXPECTANCY

Life expectancy for all Americans has increased dramatically since the turn of the century. The "average" person born in the United States in 1900 could expect to celebrate no more than 40 birthdays. By current estimates, someone born in the year 2000 will live almost twice that long (73.5 years for a man, 80.4 for a woman). Table 9.8 gives projected life expectancy for those born between 1990 and 2050.

Women Live Longer Than Men

In this century women have lived longer than men and probably will continue to do so. White females have the highest life expectancy of any race/sex group. White males were the second longest-lived group until about 1970, when they were passed by black females. Black males have consistently had shorter life spans than any other group.

Reasons for Increased Life Expectancy

During the first half of the century, increased longevity was a result of reducing or eliminating many diseases that killed infants and children and improved methods of delivering babies (benefitting both the infants and mothers), so that more people survived to middle age. In recent years, increased life expectancy is attributed to decreasing mortality from chronic diseases among the middle-aged and elderly because of new medical knowledge, practices, and life-sustaining technology. In other words, old people are living to be older.

TABLE 9.6

Discharges, days of care, and average length of stay in short-stay hospitals, according to selected characteristics: United States, 1964, 1984, and 1989

[Data are based on household interviews of a sample of the civilian noninstitutionalized population]

Characteristic	Discharges			Days of care			Average length of stay		
	1964	1984	1989	1964	1984	1989	1964	1984	1989
	Number per 1,000 population						Number of days		
Total[1,2]	109.1	114.7	92.6	970.9	871.9	646.6	8.9	7.6	7.0
Age									
Under 15 years	67.6	60.9	44.1	405.7	334.4	256.4	6.0	5.5	5.8
Under 5 years	94.3	96.7	76.6	731.1	595.8	506.2	7.8	6.2	6.6
5–14 years	53.1	41.6	26.7	229.1	193.4	122.8	4.3	4.6	4.6
15–44 years	100.6	81.7	67.0	760.7	530.8	371.8	7.6	6.5	5.5
45–64 years	146.2	160.6	130.5	1,559.3	1,344.5	937.5	10.7	8.4	7.2
65 years and over	190.0	318.0	265.6	2,292.7	2,917.6	2,360.8	12.1	9.2	8.9
65–74 years	181.2	277.7	236.7	2,150.4	2,528.3	2,004.3	11.9	9.1	8.5
75 years and over	206.7	382.6	311.0	2,560.4	3,542.9	2,918.6	12.4	9.3	9.4
Sex[1]									
Male	103.8	114.2	95.0	1,010.2	926.6	690.0	9.7	8.1	7.3
Female	113.7	115.8	91.2	933.4	829.2	615.7	8.2	7.2	6.8
Race[1]									
White	112.4	114.3	92.0	961.4	833.2	635.9	8.6	7.3	6.9
Black[3]	84.0	127.2	105.2	1,062.9	1,247.8	798.9	12.7	9.8	7.6
Family income[1,4]									
Less than $14,000	102.4	150.2	131.3	1,051.2	1,420.3	1,013.0	10.3	9.5	7.7
$14,000–$24,999	116.4	126.6	91.2	1,213.9	991.2	600.5	10.4	7.8	6.6
$25,000–$34,999	110.7	109.4	93.0	939.8	733.1	630.5	8.5	6.7	6.8
$35,000–$49,999	109.2	99.9	75.0	882.6	678.3	476.9	8.1	6.8	6.4
$50,000 or more	110.7	95.9	72.1	918.9	614.8	497.4	8.3	6.4	6.9
Geographic region[1]									
Northeast	98.5	104.5	80.2	993.8	877.5	589.5	10.1	8.4	7.4
Midwest	109.2	125.2	98.4	944.9	965.6	690.2	8.7	7.7	7.0
South	117.8	126.4	106.5	968.0	953.7	721.6	8.2	7.5	6.8
West	110.5	92.9	75.7	985.9	596.7	528.8	8.9	6.4	7.0
Location of residence[1]									
Within MSA	107.5	108.1	89.0	1,015.4	864.6	649.7	9.4	8.0	7.3
Outside MSA	113.3	128.4	105.1	871.9	888.9	639.1	7.7	6.9	6.1

[1]Age adjusted.
[2]Includes all other races not shown separately and unknown family income.
[3]1964 data include all other races.
[4]Family income categories for 1989. Income categories in 1964 are: less than $2,000; $2,000–$3,999; $4,000–$6,999; $7,000–$9,999; and $10,000 or more; and, in 1984 are: less than $10,000; $10,000–$18,999; $19,000–$29,999; $30,000–$39,999; and $40,000 or more.

NOTE: Excludes deliveries.

SOURCE: Division of Health Interview Statistics, National Center for Health Statistics: Data from the National Health Interview Survey.

FIGURE 9.3

TRENDS IN HOSPITAL USAGE BY PEOPLE 65+: 1965–1988

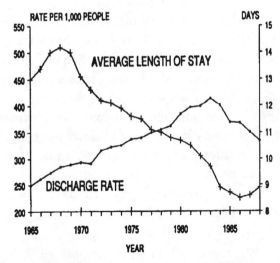

SOURCES: National Center for Health Statistics. "Trends In Hospital Utilization: United States, 1965-1986." Vital and Health Statistics Series 13, No. 101 (September 1988).

TABLE 9.7

PROJECTED PHYSICIAN VISITS AND PERCENT CHANGE IN VISITS FOR YEARS 2000 AND 2030

(number of people and visits in thousands)

Year	Age		
	65+	65 to 74	75+
2000			
Noninstitutionalized population	34,882	18,243	16,639
Total physician contacts	295,613	147,480	148,133
% change in contacts, 1989-2000	14.2	1.0	31.1
2030			
Noninstitutionalized population	65,604	35,988	29,616
Total physician contacts	555,717	290,932	264,785
% change in contacts, 1989-2030	114.6	99.3	134.4

SOURCE: U.S. Administration on Aging. Unpublished projections based on physician visit rates from the 1989 National Health Interview Survey and population projections from the U.S. Bureau of the Census.

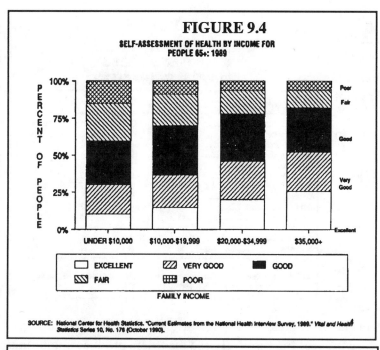

FIGURE 9.4

SELF-ASSESSMENT OF HEALTH BY INCOME FOR
PEOPLE 65+: 1989

SOURCE: National Center for Health Statistics. "Current Estimates from the National Health Interview Survey, 1989." *Vital and Health Statistics* Series 10, No. 176 (October 1990).

TABLE 9.8

PROJECTED LIFE EXPECTANCY AT BIRTH AND AGE 65, BY SEX: 1990-2050
(in years)

Year	At birth			At age 65		
	Men	Women	Difference	Men	Women	Difference
1990	72.1	79.0	6.9	15.0	19.4	4.4
2000	73.5	80.4	6.9	15.7	20.3	4.6
2010	74.4	81.3	6.9	16.2	21.0	4.8
2020	74.9	81.8	6.9	16.6	21.4	4.8
2030	75.4	82.3	6.9	17.0	21.8	4.8
2040	75.9	82.8	6.9	17.3	22.3	5.0
2050	76.4	83.3	6.9	17.7	22.7	5.0

SOURCE: U.S. Bureau of the Census. "Projections of the Population of the United States, by Age, Sex, and Race: 1988 to 2080," by Gregory Spencer, *Current Population Reports* Series P-25, No. 1018 (January 1989).

FIGURE 9.5

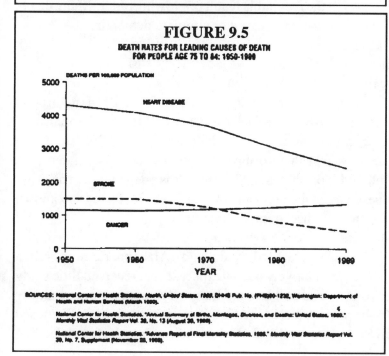

DEATH RATES FOR LEADING CAUSES OF DEATH
FOR PEOPLE AGE 75 TO 84: 1950-1989

SOURCES: National Center for Health Statistics. *Health, United States, 1989.* DHHS Pub. No. (PHS)90-1232. Washington: Department of Health and Human Services (March 1990).

National Center for Health Statistics. "Annual Summary of Births, Marriages, Divorces, and Deaths: United States, 1988." *Monthly Vital Statistics Report* Vol. 30, No. 13 (August 30, 1988).

National Center for Health Statistics. "Advance Report of Final Mortality Statistics, 1988." *Monthly Vital Statistics Report* Vol. 30, No. 7, Supplement (November 28, 1988).

CAUSES OF DEATH

Seven out of every 10 elderly people die from heart disease, cancer, or stroke (Figure 9.5). The leading causes of death and the death rate from each cause in 1988 for age 65 and older are shown in Table 9.9. (Malignant neoplasms refer to cancer, and cerebrovascular diseases include strokes.)

"Still Number One"

The American Heart Association reported that in 1988, 55 percent of all heart attacks occurred in people over 65. Statistically, women have far less coronary heart disease than men until they reach age 65, at which point their numbers approach those of men. Heart disease is the primary cause of death for all Americans, but especially for the elderly. The risk of dying from heart disease increases greatly after age 65, and the death rate more than doubles for each age group between 65 and 85.

The past three decades have shown a marked decline in death rates for heart disease. Several factors account for the decline. Primary factors are better control of hypertension and changes in exercise and nutrition. Also important is the expanding use of trained mobil emergency personnel (paramedics) in most urban areas. The generalized use of CPR (cardiopulmonary resuscitation) and new emergency medication also increase the likelihood of one's surviving an initial heart attack.

Research on heart disease has historically been done on male subjects. However, recent reports indicate that postmenopausal women not only suffer from the disease as do their male counterparts, but those with the disease are more than twice as likely to die from an initial heart attack than men. While the reasons are unknown at this time, it has been suggested that because of the misconception that women do not experience the disease as frequently, their complaints are not taken as seriously as those of men. Also, physiologic factors as yet unknown may play a role in women's succumbing to heart disease. There is a need for research on female subjects which is only just beginning.

Cancer

Cancer is the second leading cause of death among the elderly. Success in the cure of certain tumors (Hodgkin's disease, certain forms of leukemia) is equalled by the rise in rates of other cancers, for example, breast and lung cancer. Progress in treating cancer has largely been related to screenings, early diagnosis, and new drug therapies.

Stroke

Strokes are the third leading cause of death and the primary cause of disability among the elderly. The incidence of stroke is strongly related to age; 72 percent of stroke victims are 65 or older.

MENTAL DISORDERS OF THE ELDERLY: DEMENTIA

Equally devastating as the decline of a once healthy body is the deterioration of the mind. As with other disorders, mental impairments can occur in persons of any age, but certain types of illness are much more prevalent in the elderly. In this area more than any other, the differences between individuals can vary dramatically. Some people may show no decline in mental ability until far into old age. Others experience occasional forgetfulness as they enter their "retirement years." A few are completely robbed of all their mental faculties before they reach 60.

Older people with mental problems were once labeled as "senile." Only in recent years have researchers found that physical disorders can cause

TABLE 9.9

DEATH RATES FOR TEN LEADING CAUSES OF DEATH AMONG OLDER PEOPLE, BY AGE: 1988

(rates per 100,000 population in age group)

Cause of death	65+	65 to 74	75 to 84	85+
ALL CAUSES	5,105	2,730	6,321	15,594
Diseases of the heart	2,066	984	2,543	7,098
Malignant neoplasms	1,068	843	1,313	1,639
Cerebrovascular diseases	431	155	554	1,707
Chronic obstructive pulmonary disease	226	152	313	394
Pneumonia and influenza	225	60	257	1,125
Diabetes	97	62	125	222
Accidents	89	50	107	267
Atherosclerosis	69	15	70	396
Nephritis, nephrotic syndrome, nephrosis	61	26	78	217
Septicemia	56	24	71	199

SOURCE: National Center for Health Statistics. "Advanced Report of Final Mortality Statistics, 1988." Monthly Vital Statistics Report Vol. 39, No. 7, Supplement (November 28, 1990).

progressive deterioration of mental and neurological functions. These disorders produce symptoms that are collectively known as "dementia." Symptoms of dementia include "loss of language functions, inability to think abstractly, inability to care for oneself, personality change, emotional instability, and loss of a sense of time or place" (1987, *Losing a Million Minds*, Washington, DC: Office of Technology Assessment).

It is important to note that occasional forgetfulness and disorientation are normal signs of the aging process. True dementia is a disease and is not the inevitable result of growing older. Many disorders may cause or simulate dementia.

Alzheimer's Disease

The most prevalent form of dementia is Alzheimer's disease, named after the German neurologist Alois Alzheimer who, in 1906, discovered the "neurofibrillary tangles" now associated with the disease. Alzheimer's is a degenerative disorder of the brain and nervous system; there is no known cause, cure, or treatment.

Just 10 years ago, Alzheimer's was still a relatively obscure disease that received little study and still less publicity. Symptoms were generally attributed to aging, and the victims were diagnosed as senile. Today, Alzheimer's is the fourth leading killer of adults behind heart disease, cancer, and strokes, claiming more than 100,000 lives each year. Currently, Alzheimer's is the subject of intense research and is very much in the public consciousness.

Prevalence

As the population ages, Alzheimer's is becoming more of a concern. As many as 10.3 percent of people over the age of 65 with memory problems or other mental impairment probably suffer from Alzheimer's. Up to 3 percent of people between 65 and 74, 19 percent of those between 15 and 84, and 47 percent of those over 85 are likely to have the disease. The National Institute on Aging now estimates that there may be as many as 4 million Alzheimer's victims in the United States today, and by 2050 the number may reach 14 million. These figures far exceed previous estimates and give an added urgency to finding a cause and a cure.

Accurate assessment of the number of patients is difficult because of the stigma attached to the disease. Scientists report that when they try to trace the inheritance of Alzheimer's in families, they often meet denial and resistance among family members in admitting the presence of the disease in their families.

Symptoms

The diagnosis of Alzheimer's disease can be confirmed only after death. An autopsy of the brain of an Alzheimer's victim reveals abnormal tangles of nerve fibers (neurofibrillary tangles), tips of nerve fibers embedded in plaque, and a significant shortage of the enzymes that produce the neurotransmitter acetylcholine. Research is now taking place to develop a diagnostic test for Alzheimer's in living subjects.

The symptoms of living victims usually begin with mild episodes of forgetfulness and disorienta-

TABLE 9.10

Age at symptom onset of 439 patients with a diagnosis of Alzheimer disease only, by sex – California, June 10, 1985–December 31, 1987

Age (yrs) at symptom onset	Men		Women	
	No.	(%)	No.	(%)
Unknown	5	(3.5)	10	(3.4)
45–49	2	(1.4)	3	(1.0)
50–54	6	(4.3)	3	(1.0)
55–59	19	(13.5)	17	(5.7)
60–64	21	(14.9)	35	(11.7)
65–69	22	(15.6)	56	(18.8)
70–74	24	(17.0)	70	(23.5)
75–79	28	(19.9)	58	(19.5)
80–84	12	(8.5)	33	(11.1)
85–92	2	(1.4)	13	(4.4)
Total	141	(100.0)	298	(100.0)

Source: "Alzheimer Disease - California, 1985-1987," *MMWR,* Centers for Disease Control, (Atlanta, GA, February 23, 1990)

tion. Table 9.10 shows the age at onset in one study, reflecting the tendency to develop the disease between the ages of 55 and 80. As the disease progresses, memory loss increases, and mood changes are frequent, accompanied by confusion, irritability, restlessness, and speech impairment. Eventually, the victim may lose all control over his or her mental and bodily functions. Alzheimer's victims survive an average of 10 years after the first onset of symptoms; some live another 25 years.

Suspected Causes

Despite intensified research in recent years, little is known about the cause (or causes) of Alzheimer's. One thing is certain: it is *not* a normal consequence of aging. It is, rather, a disease that is either most likely to strike older people, or, more likely, its symptoms appear and become more pronounced as a person grows older.

There are a several theories on the cause(s) or reasons for the onset of Alzheimer's. Some theories currently being pursued by researchers are:

1. a breakdown in the system that produces acetylcholine;

2. a slow-acting virus that has already left the body before symptoms appear;

AGE	TOTAL [1]			MALE						FEMALE					
				White			Black			White			Black		
	1970	1980	1988	1970	1980	1988	1970	1980	1988	1970	1980	1988	1970	1980	1988
All ages [2]	11.6	11.9	12.4	18.0	19.9	21.7	8.0	10.3	11.5	7.1	5.9	5.5	2.6	2.2	2.4
10-14 years old	0.6	0.8	1.4	1.1	1.4	2.1	0.3	0.5	1.3	0.3	0.3	0.8	0.4	0.1	0.9
15-19 years old	5.9	8.5	11.3	9.4	15.0	19.6	4.7	5.6	9.7	2.9	3.3	4.8	2.9	1.6	2.2
20-24 years old	12.2	16.1	15.0	19.3	27.8	27.0	18.7	20.0	19.8	5.7	5.9	4.4	4.9	3.1	2.9
25-34 years old	14.1	16.0	15.4	19.9	25.6	25.7	19.2	21.8	22.1	9.0	7.5	6.1	5.7	4.1	3.8
35-44 years old	16.9	15.4	14.8	23.3	23.5	24.1	12.6	15.6	16.4	13.0	9.1	7.4	3.7	4.6	3.5
45-54 years old	20.0	15.9	14.6	29.5	24.2	23.2	13.8	12.0	11.7	13.5	10.2	8.6	3.7	2.8	3.8
55-64 years old	21.4	15.9	15.6	35.0	25.8	27.0	10.6	11.7	10.6	12.3	9.1	7.9	2.0	2.3	2.5
65 years and over	20.8	17.8	21.0	41.1	37.5	45.0	8.7	11.4	14.0	8.5	6.5	7.1	2.6	1.4	1.6
65-74 years over	20.8	16.9	18.4	38.7	32.5	35.4	8.7	11.1	12.9	9.6	7.0	7.3	2.9	1.7	2.0
75-84 years over	21.2	19.1	25.9	45.5	45.5	61.5	8.9	10.5	17.6	7.2	5.7	7.4	1.7	1.1	1.3
85 years and over	19.0	19.2	20.5	45.8	52.8	65.8	8.7	18.9	10.0	5.8	5.8	5.3	2.8	-	-

- Represents or rounds to zero. [1] Includes other races, not shown separately. [2] Includes other age groups, not shown separately.

Source: *Vital Statistics of the United States*, National Center for Health Statistics

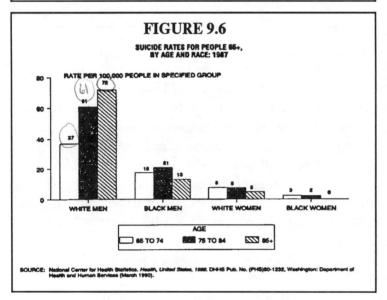

FIGURE 9.6

SUICIDE RATES FOR PEOPLE 65+,
BY AGE AND RACE: 1987

RATE PER 100,000 PEOPLE IN SPECIFIED GROUP

AGE
65 TO 74   75 TO 84   85+

SOURCE: National Center for Health Statistics. *Health, United States, 1989.* DHHS Pub. No. (PHS)90-1232. Washington: Department of Health and Human Services (March 1990).

Table 9.11 shows that, in 1988, the rate of death by suicide for those over 65 was 21 per 100,000 persons, compared to a rate of 12.4 per 100,000 for the general population. White men have, by far, the highest suicide rates, with the oldest old (85+) most likely to kill themselves (Figure 9.6). The incidence among women steadily decreases with age after 55. The increase in suicide among the elderly since 1981 is not an international trend, but peculiar to the U.S.

Suicide figures for the elderly are not always reliable since many suicides are "passive." Persons who are sick, lonely, abandoned, or financially troubled, have been known to starve themselves, not take medication, or mix medications dangerously. Also, the deaths counted as suicides are only those where suicide is named on the official death certificate. Other suicides may be attributed to secondary causes on death certificates. One in six elderly depressives succeeds in committing suicide in contrast to one in 100 in the general population.

The upward trend in suicide among the elderly perplexes health care experts who note that the elderly today are generally more financially secure and healthier than in past generations. It has been suggested that the technological advances being made to extend life (or postpone death) may have resulted in longer, but less satisfying lives. Experts suggest that older males, who have the highest suicide rates, may become depressed at the loss of job, income, and power status when they retire. Some mental health professionals have noted that the concept of "rational suicide" is gaining popularity. The elderly who are faced with the possibility of extending their lives by medical technologies are weighing the costs, and more of them are rejecting that option as society's attitude toward suicide changes.

3. an environmental toxin such as aluminum;

4. a genetic (hereditary) origin.

TROUBLE WITH COPING — SUICIDE

Loss of a loved one is a major cause of depression and suicide for older people. During the first year after the death of a spouse, the risk of suicide for the remaining partner is 2.5 times greater than the general population; in the second year after a loss, the risk is 1.5 times as great.

The suicide rate among the elderly began to increase in 1981, a reversal of a half-century trend.

102

CHAPTER X

THE PUBLIC'S OPINION OF DEATH

FEAR OF DEATH

It is generally accepted that humans are the only species that can understand the inevitability of death. Some philosophers and psychiatrists would suggest that mankind is obsessed with death and that it has a profound influence on thought and daily life.

Public opinion polls of Americans show otherwise. The Gallup Polls' survey, "Mirror of America," published in January 1991, revealed that most Americans are not overly worried about death or even think about it very often. Only 7 percent reported that they thought about their own death very often, while nearly half (47 percent) said they thought about it occasionally, and 36 percent claimed they almost never thought about their death. (See Table 10.1.)

One would expect that older Americans would be more conscious of death than younger ones, but Gallup researchers found no difference in the responses from younger or older people, nor did they find any significant differences in religious and non-religious respondents.

Not only do Americans not spend much time thinking about death, they also do not appear to fear it. Only 23 percent of those polled said they feared death, in contrast to the three-quarters who did not. The fear of death appears to diminish with age. One-third of those 18 to 29 years old reported being afraid of death compared to only 16 percent of those 50 and older (Table 10.2).

TABLE 10.1
How often would you say you think about your death?

Very often	7%
Somewhat often	9
Every now and again	47
Almost never	36
No opinion	1
	100%

TABLE 10.2
Do you fear death, or not?

	Yes	No	No opinion
Total	23%	75%	2%
Age:			
18-29	33	66	1
30-49	25	74	1
50 & older	16	83	1

TABLE 10.3
Do you think there is a Hell, to which people who have led bad lives without being sorry are eternally damned?

Yes	60%
No	32
No opinion	8
	100%

Source of above tables: The Gallup Poll Monthly, (Princeton, NJ, 1991)

TABLE 10.4

Are You Going to Heaven, or Hell?
(November 15-18, 1990; telephone; Survey GO 122008, Q.'s 34 & 36)

QUESTION: Here is an interesting question... How would you describe your own chances of going to Heaven — excellent, good, only fair or poor? (Based on those who think there is a Heaven, 775 respondents).

How would you describe your own chances of going to Hell — excellent, good, only fair or poor? (Based on those who think there is a Hell, 590 respondents).

	Prospects for Heaven					Prospects for Hell				
	Excellent	Good	Fair	Poor	No. of interviews	Excellent	Good	Fair	Poor	No. of interviews
National	29%	48%	17%	3%	775	2%	2%	15%	77%	590
Sex										
Male	30	43	20	4	370	2	3	17	74	288
Female	28	53	14	2	405	1	2	14	80	302
Age										
18-29 years	26	51	20	2	189	1	2	24	71	156
30-49 years	32	48	15	3	326	1	2	16	78	252
50 & older	28	48	17	2	251	2	3	8	82	178
Region										
East	22	54	19	2	184	1	3	15	79	139
Midwest	26	53	18	2	214	1	2	14	80	153
South	36	44	16	3	235	1	2	17	76	204
West	32	43	16	3	140	4	1	17	73	92
Race										
White	29	50	15	3	673	1	2	15	78	506
Black	28	47	25	0	54	0	4	16	77	51
Other	34	24	34	5	39	11	0	25	61	28
Education										
College grads.	39	47	9	1	184	1	1	14	81	128
College inc.	33	51	14	1	176	1	2	17	79	140
High school grads.	25	51	19	3	299	1	3	16	76	234
Not H.S. grads.	23	44	21	5	110	3	4	14	75	85
Politics										
Republicans	35	49	12	3	251	1	2	11	83	190
Democrats	25	51	20	2	259	3	3	18	74	211
Independents	27	47	17	3	244	1	2	16	75	176
Ideology										
Liberal	31	46	20	2	202	33	3	22	71	161
Moderate	22	60	14	1	64	2	4	11	83	44
Conservative	32	48	16	2	369	1	2	14	80	282
Income										
$50,000 & over	31	52	13	1	131	0	2	12	84	97
$30,000-49,999	27	54	17	2	202	2	3	18	75	158
$20,000-29,999	37	38	17	4	148	2	1	15	77	110
Under $20,000	26	51	18	3	239	2	4	16	75	183
Religion										
Protestant	33	47	15	3	467	1	2	14	79	363
Catholic	18	58	20	1	202	2	3	18	74	142
None	30	31	23	6	37	2	7	30	61	30
"Born-again"										
Yes	42	46	9	1	318	•	2	10	86	278
No	20	52	21	3	415	3	3	22	67	284

• Less than one percent. Note: "No opinion" omitted.

Source: The Gallup Poll Monthly, (Princeton, NJ, 1991)

The "Afterlife"

One reason Americans do not generally fear death is their expectation of an after-life. Since 1944, Gallup polls have found that between 67 and 77 percent of Americans believe in an afterlife. Nearly eight out of 10 Americans believe that there is a heaven where good people are eternally rewarded. On the other hand, only 60 percent believe that there is a hell to which bad people will be eternally damned. (See Table 10.3.)

Who will go to heaven? Fully 77 percent of those who believe in heaven thought they stood an excellent chance of making it, and another 17 percent believed they have a fair chance. Only 3 percent thought they had a poor chance of going to heaven. Women were more optimistic about going to heaven, as were college graduates, Republicans, and those who live in the South and the West. Catholics were less certain about their chances for heaven — only 18 percent thought their chances were excellent, although over half thought their chances were good compared to one-third of all Protestants and 42 percent of fundamentalist Protestants. (See Table 10.4.) For the most part, all the respondents thought their chances of going to hell were no better than fair, and the majority (61 percent or more in all categories) thought they stood a poor chance of ending up in hell.

A small number of people (13 percent) claim to have had contact with an angel or a devil, and one quarter think it is possible to have contact with the dead. In fact, 17 percent of Americans claim to have done so. Twenty-three percent of respondents believe in reincarnation (being born into a another life after death) (Table 10.5).

GETTING OLDER AND DYING

The Gallup researchers found that the majority of Americans claimed that getting older does not bother them. Only 6 percent said it bothers them a great deal, 30 percent indicate somewhat, and 63 percent reported that it does not bother them at all. Slightly more younger people and women are bothered by getting older than are older people. Those who fear death are most likely to be concerned with getting older.

The Gallup Organization found that, for the most part, people wanted to die after a certain point and did not desire to prolong life. The average American would like to live to age 85, about one in five would like to make it to 90 years or more, while 37 percent said the ideal life span would be under 80 years of age. Earlier Gallup Polls have found that only 5 percent of Americans would like to live to be over 100 years old.

The Middle Age Point of View

The American Board of Family Practice (a physician's organization) conducted a study of middle age including attitudes towards death (1990, *Perspectives on Middle Age: The Vintage Years*, Lexington KY). Overall, this group of people, ages 36 to 75 years old, did not wish to die before getting too old. Only 21 percent of those polled responded affirmatively to the question, "Do you wish to die before you get too old?" Of those who did say yes, it was not surprising that the older the respondent, the older the age he or she thought was the best for death. Those who were under 46 picked age 71; those 46 to 65 chose 77, while the oldest group, 66+ said they thought a good age to die was 86 years old. The least likely to want to die were men between the ages of 46 and 65 (9 percent), while 22 percent of women in the same age category ex-

TABLE 10.5	
Do you believe in reincarnation — that is, the rebirth of the soul in a new body after death or not?	
Yes	23%
No	69
No opinion	8
	100%

Source: The Gallup Poll Monthly, (Princeton, NJ, 1991)

pressed a wish to die before getting too old. (See Tables 10.6 and 10.7.)

CONDITIONS FOR DEATH — EUTHANASIA

There are two aspects of euthanasia (mercy killing): passive euthanasia where the patient or surrogate decides to terminate treatment that is sustaining life, and active euthanasia, where the doctor or family member takes action such as a lethal injection to actually end a patient's life. (See Chapter V.)

The majority of Americans do not wish to remain alive in conditions of permanent pain or on life support systems. Two-thirds of those interviewed by Gallup in November 1990, thought a person has the moral right to commit suicide if he or she is in great pain and there is no hope for recovery. Fifty-eight percent thought the patient had a right to suicide if that person has an incurable disease. Americans did not believe in suicide, however, in cases where the person is a heavy burden on his family (only 33 percent) or if the person is otherwise healthy (16 percent). Only 11 percent of Americans feel that a terminally ill patient never has the right to end his or her life.

Older people are less likely to agree that it is morally right to commit suicide in cases of terminal illness or great pain, although they are just as likely (32 percent) to accept it if the person is a great burden. Blacks are much less likely to accept suicide than are whites (blacks have a generally lower suicide rate than whites): 36 percent of blacks versus 60 percent of whites think it is acceptable in cases of incurable disease; 40 percent

as compared to 68 percent find it acceptable for great pain; and only 19 percent of blacks approve of suicide if the patient is a heavy burden, while 34 percent of whites can accept this. For the most part, upper-income, college educated, liberal, and politically independent people are more accepting of suicide. About half of "born-again" Christians who often have strong vitalist (preserving life above all else) beliefs, support the moral right to suicide in cases of incurable illness (47 percent) and great pain (55 percent). (See Table 10.8 for details of the above data.)

TABLE 10.6
THE ASSOCIATION BETWEEN SEX, AGE AND EVER WISHING TO DIE BEFORE GETTING TOO OLD

	SEX		AGE		
	MEN	WOMEN	<46	46-65	66+
Ever wish to die before getting too old:	%	%	%	%	%
Yes	20	23	24	16	19
No	80	77	76	84	81
	(599)	(601)	(775)	(303)	(117)

IF "YES"	AGE				
Average age they wish to die:	70	75	71	77	86
	(113)	(142)	(172)	(48)	(34)

Interpretation: 24% of those less than 46 years old wish to die before getting too old, compared to only 16% and 19% of those 45-65 and 66 plus who feel the same way.

TABLE 10.7
THE ASSOCIATION BETWEEN AGE WITHIN SEX EVER WISH TO DIE

	MEN			WOMEN		
	<46	46-65	66+	<46	46-65	66+
Ever wish to die before you get too old:	%	%	%	%	%	%
Yes	23	9	26	26	22	15
No	77	91	74	74	78	85
	(421)	(136)	(42)	(354)	(167)	(75)

Interpretation: Only 9% of middle-aged men wish to die before becoming too old, compared to 23% of younger men. By contrast, 15% of older women are at least likely to wish to die before becoming too old.

Source of both tables: Perspectives on Middle Age: The Vintage Years, American Board of Family Practice Report, conudcted by New World Decisions, (Princeton, NJ, 1990)

TABLE 10.8

Moral Right to Commit Suicide

QUESTION: Do you think a person has the moral right to end his or her life under these circumstances (ROTATED): when this person has a disease that is incurable; when this person is suffering great pain and has no hope of improvement; when this person is an extremely heavy burden on his or her family; when an otherwise healthy person wants to end his or her life?

	Incurable disease		Great pain		Heavy burden		Otherwise healthy		
	Yes	No	Yes	No	Yes	No	Yes	No	No. of interviews
National	58%	36%	66%	29%	33%	61%	16%	80%	1018
Sex									
Male	58	35	67	26	36	57	19	77	507
Female	58	37	64	31	30	64	13	83	511
Age									
18-29 years	61	33	74	20	32	64	25	73	228
30-49 years	60	35	70	26	34	60	14	83	428
50 & older	53	39	55	37	32	59	12	81	349
Region									
East	57	33	68	24	34	60	16	80	249
Midwest	56	36	59	34	33	62	13	81	261
South	56	41	64	31	30	61	18	78	300
West	65	30	72	25	34	61	17	81	206
Race									
White	60	34	68	27	34	59	16	80	886
Black	36	59	40	52	19	77	16	81	62
Other	54	35	68	26	33	61	22	69	60
Education									
College grads.	62	31	73	23	38	56	19	78	272
College inc.	56	40	63	31	31	64	15	83	228
High school grads.	59	34	69	26	33	60	14	80	375
Not H.S. grads.	50	43	53	40	26	66	18	79	136
Politics									
Republicans	57	36	65	29	35	59	12	86	315
Democrats	52	41	61	32	27	66	16	79	330
Independents	64	31	73	23	36	57	19	76	344
Ideology									
Liberal	63	32	74	21	37	58	19	76	281
Moderate	62	31	76	18	36	58	16	78	91
Conservative	54	41	61	33	27	66	13	84	461
Income									
$50,000 & over	65	30	76	21	35	59	12	86	191
$30,000-49,999	61	34	69	26	39	55	18	78	275
$20,000-29,999	57	35	65	26	35	57	19	75	182
Under $20,000	52	42	62	34	27	67	16	81	291
Religion									
Protestant	57	37	64	30	30	64	14	81	564
Catholic	56	38	65	27	33	62	13	84	247
None	68	26	75	23	46	44	35	64	90
"Born-again"									
Yes	47	48	55	41	23	70	10	86	350
No	65	29	73	21	38	56	21	75	614

Note: "No opinion" omitted.

Source: The Gallup Poll Monthly, (Princeton, NJ, 1991)

TABLE 10.9

If you, yourself, were on life support systems and there was no hope of recovering, would you like to remain on the life support system or would you like treatment withheld so that you could end your life?

Kept on life support system	9%
Treatment withheld	84
No opinion	7
	100%

Source: The Gallup Poll Monthly, (Princeton, NJ, 1991)

Nonwhites, born-again Christians, people who are very religious, and those over 65 years old were slightly more likely to think the patient's life should be saved, but even within these groups, a clear majority believed that there are cases when life sustaining treatment is unnecessary.

Personal wishes for life-sustaining treatment vary according to the circumstances. More than half would want their doctor to terminate treatment if they had an incurable illness and were suffering a great deal of pain, or if they were totally dependent on another family member for daily care. If their terminal disease made it difficult to accomplish day-to-day activities, 44 percent versus 40 percent said they would like medical treatment stopped.

When Gallup asked if the individual would personally want to be kept alive on life support systems, an overwhelming 84 percent said they would want treatment withheld. Less than one in 10 reported wanting to be kept alive (Table 10.9).

The National Opinion Research Organization found that 56.5 percent of respondents in 1991 approved of suicide for cases of incurable illness, but only 12.5 percent thought it was acceptable if the person was simply tired of living and ready to die (Table 10.10).

For many, religious beliefs play an important role in reaching these decisions. About 52 percent of the very religious report they would want treatment stopped if they were in a great deal of pain. As in the Gallup poll (above), non-whites were less likely to think they would want to stop treatment than were whites.

A recent "Reflections of the Times" poll of 1,213 people nationwide (conducted for the Times Mirror Center for the People and the Press, WDC) found that 80 percent of the people interviewed thought there are circumstances when it is appropriate to let a patient die. Only 15 percent indicated that doctors and nurses should always do everything possible to save a life.

TABLE 10.10

Do you think a person has the right to end his or her own life if this person ...

Has an incurable disease?

RESPONSE	PUNCH	1972-82	1982B	1983-87	1987B	1988	1989	1990	1991	COL. 75 ALL
Yes	1	1843	77	2193	0	492	469	519	579	6,172
No	2	2545	261	2237	0	454	488	354	408	6,747
Don't know	8	170	10	160	0	37	47	54	35	513
No answer	9	10	6	13	0	5	2	1	2	39
Not applicable	BK	9058	0	2939	353	493	531	444	493	14,311

Is tired of living and ready to die?

RESPONSE	PUNCH	1972-82	1982B	1983-87	1987B	1988	1989	1990	1991	COL. 78 ALL
Yes	1	595	27	643	0	120	134	133	129	1,781
No	2	3864	311	3847	0	834	846	754	865	11,321
Don't know	8	96	9	96	0	26	21	38	27	313
No answer	9	13	7	17	0	8	5	3	3	56
Not applicable	BK	9058	0	2939	353	493	531	444	493	14,311

Source: The Roper Poll, National Opinion Research Organization, (Chicago, IL, 1992)

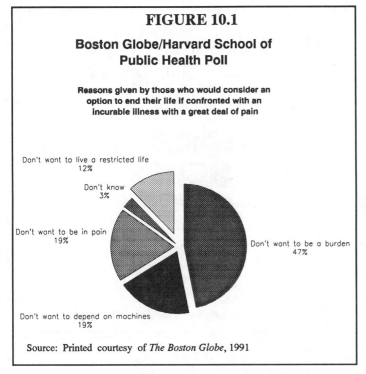

FIGURE 10.1

Boston Globe/Harvard School of Public Health Poll

Reasons given by those who would consider an option to end their life if confronted with an incurable illness with a great deal of pain

Don't want to live a restricted life 12%

Don't know 3%

Don't want to be in pain 19%

Don't want to be a burden 47%

Don't want to depend on machines 19%

Source: Printed courtesy of *The Boston Globe*, 1991

TABLE 10.11

When a person has a disease that cannot be cured, do you think doctors should be allowed by law to end the patient's life by some painless means if the patient and his family request it?

RESPONSE	PUNCH	1972-82	1982B	1983-87	1987B	1988	1989	1990	1991	COL. 73 ALL
Yes	1	2704	113	2946	0	648	657	635	719	8,422
No (ASK A)	2	1650	220	1480	0	287	300	243	255	4,435
Don't know (ASK A)	8	199	18	166	0	48	45	47	48	571
No answer	9	15	3	11	0	5	4	3	2	43
Not applicable	BK	9058	0	2939	353	493	531	444	493	14,311

Source: The Roper Poll, National Opinion Research Organization, (Chicago, IL, 1992)

Louis Harris poll to the 81 percent who agreed in this poll. In addition, 76 percent thought it was right to withdraw life support, including food and water, for permanently comatose patients if the patient had earlier requested it or if the family wanted it.

About half of those polled (52 percent) would consider ending their own life if they were faced with an incurable disease with a great deal of pain. Of those, nearly half (47 percent) gave not wanting to be a burden as their most important reason, about one in five did not want either to be in pain or to be dependent on machines, and 12 percent did not want to live a restricted life (Figure 10.1). There was some uncertainty, however, since 63 percent of respondents would consider or would probably consider whether to ask a doctor to withhold life sustaining treatment, but not food and water. Over half, 53 percent, would consider asking the doctor for a lethal drug for later personal use, and 54 percent would consider asking the doctor to give the lethal injection.

The Doctor's Role

In a 1991 National Opinion Research poll, 70 percent of those asked thought doctors should legally be permitted to terminate a life if the patient and family requested it. (See Table 10.11.) The Boston Globe poll asked Americans whether they would vote for Proposition 119 if it were on the ballot in their state. Interestingly, Catholics gave it the most support (71 percent), followed closely by 69 percent of Jews. Among all Protestants, 57 percent said they supported the bill, 61 percent of fundamentalists approved, and the smallest support came from born-again Christians with 49 percent voicing approval. (See Figure 10.2.)

Who Should Be Responsible?

In November 1991, residents of Washington State had the opportunity to vote on Resolution 119, a law which have would permitted doctors to lethally inject terminal patients under certain circumstances (see Chapter V). There was a great deal of public debate including a Boston Globe/Harvard School of Public Health poll conducted by KRC Communications. The poll found that the percentage of Americans who thought the law should support doctors in honoring patients' rights to die had increased from 65 percent in a 1982

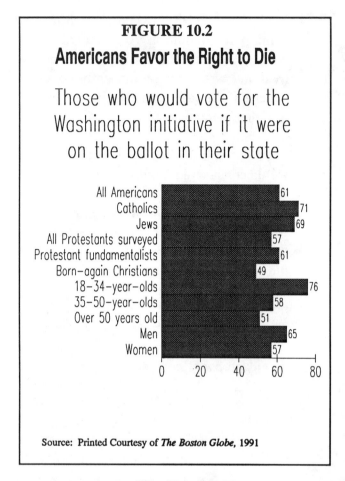

FIGURE 10.2

Americans Favor the Right to Die

Those who would vote for the Washington initiative if it were on the ballot in their state

All Americans	61
Catholics	71
Jews	69
All Protestants surveyed	57
Protestant fundamentalists	61
Born–again Christians	49
18–34–year–olds	76
35–50–year–olds	58
Over 50 years old	51
Men	65
Women	57

Source: Printed Courtesy of *The Boston Globe*, 1991

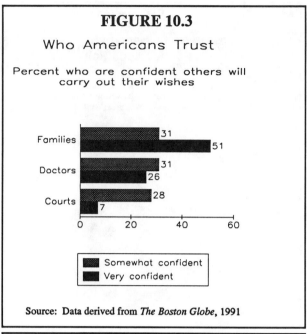

FIGURE 10.3

Who Americans Trust

Percent who are confident others will carry out their wishes

	Somewhat confident	Very confident
Families	31	51
Doctors	31	26
Courts	28	7

■ Somewhat confident
■ Very confident

Source: Data derived from *The Boston Globe*, 1991

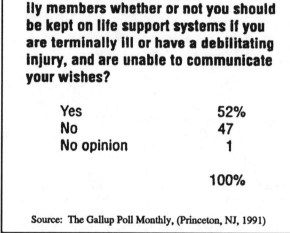

TABLE 10.11

Have you, yourself, discussed with family members whether or not you should be kept on life support systems if you are terminally ill or have a debilitating injury, and are unable to communicate your wishes?

Yes	52%
No	47
No opinion	1
	100%

Source: The Gallup Poll Monthly, (Princeton, NJ, 1991)

The Family

The *Boston Globe* poll found that 37 percent thought relatives or close friends should be allowed to assist in suicides, while 48 percent thought they should not. However, when asked if you, the respondent, were incurably ill and in great pain, only 32 percent said they would consider asking a relative or close friend to help them and only 14 percent said they would help a relative or close friend take their life.

Americans believe that others will carry out their wishes if they are in a terminal state. They have the most confidence in their families — 31 percent were somewhat confident, and 51 percent were very confident that their families will follow their requests. Thirty-one percent were also somewhat confident about doctors, but only 26 percent were very confident. The respondents were least trusting of the courts — 28 percent were somewhat confident and only 7 percent were very confident (Figure 10.3).

LIVING WILLS

About half (52 percent) of Americans polled in the Gallup "Mirror of America" survey have discussed terminating life support with their families (Table 10.11). Living wills (see Chapter VI), which are expressions of a person's interests, are intended to ensure that the patient's wishes will be carried out. Despite some mistrust of the medical profession and a great deal of it for the legal profession, only about 20 percent of Americans have a living will. Three-quarters of those who do not, however, would like to have one in the future.

CHAPTER XI

REFLECTIONS: IS ACTIVE EUTHANASIA MORALLY JUSTIFIED FOR TERMINALLY ILL PATIENTS?*

Ronald E. Cranford, M.D.

Neurologist and Medical Ethicist
Hennepin County Medical Center
Minneapolis, Minnesota

In my opinion, the extensive support for active euthanasia shown in recent polls of physicians and the general population does not relate so much to a desire for euthanasia but to the public's fear (in large part justified) that they will have no control over their own dying. People fear that they will become prisoners of an unthinking, uncaring medical technology applied by timid, fearful physicians who don't have the moral courage to do the right thing and who are much more concerned about the remote chance of legal liability than they are about doing what's best for the patient.

. . . The futile attempt by conservatives to classify the legitimate withdrawal of artificial nutrition and hydration from hopelessly ill patients, like Nancy Cruzan from Missouri, as "euthanasia by omission" only confuses issues in the long run. It does exactly the opposite of what is intended by prolife forces; it drives people toward active euthanasia by reinforcing their fears of spending the last years of their life in mindless, degrading existence. It is ironic that the two groups most opposed to active euthanasia — the medical profession and the prolife movement — are the ones most responsible for this grassroots movement toward active euthanasia.

. . . The movement of the populace toward active euthanasia cannot be countered by silence or by simple opposition to active euthanasia; it must be fought by being for something in this case, the humane care of the dying, genuine respect for patients' wishes, a commonsense approach to stopping treatment and ameliorating suffering, allowing families broad discretion in making life and death decisions for their loved ones (consider, for example, the tragic case of Rudy Linares in Chicago, who disconnected his comatose infant son from the respirator while holding the medical staff at bay with a gun) — and by relying less on legalism, vitalism, and absolutism.

. . . At the present time, my major objections to active euthanasia as a social or medical policy outweigh my support for the practice in individual circumstances. My objections to active euthanasia are many. Active euthanasia would not be necessary in most circumstances if there was more humane care of the dying. Cases of extreme and refractory suffering, if the patients were treated well, are uncommon, but they do occur. There are

---

*This was a question posed by the *Park Ridge Center for the Study of Health, Faith, and Ethics.* The responses were published in *Active Euthansia, Religion and the Public Debate* (1991, Park Ridge Center).

meaningful descriptive and moral distinctions between letting die and killing such that a line can and should be drawn between these two practices, and these lines should be more fully understood before we embark on any course of widespread active euthanasia or even physician-assisted suicide. The practice of active euthanasia would be a new role for physicians and could dramatically change — perhaps for the better, perhaps for the worse — the relationship between patients and physicians. There could also be more widespread abuse of active euthanasia, and it would be more difficult to establish procedural safeguards to minimize such abuses, especially in chronic care facilities.

I do not believe that active euthanasia or physician-assisted suicide is intrinsically immoral. I am much more concerned about abuses than I am about the practice itself.

But the sorry fact is that we are driving people toward an option that doesn't have to be except in very unusual circumstances.

James F. Bresnanhan, S.J., L.L.M., Ph.D.

Co-director, Ethics and Human Values
in Medicine Program
Northwestern University Medical School
Chicago, Illinois

. . . What I call "appropriate care of the dying," a studied, compassionate, affirmative response to the needs of a dying person by caregivers, is entirely feasible today. It does not involve initiating a new lethal process with the purpose of precipitating death. But, unhappily, such good care of the dying is still not the rule in medical care in our society . . .

It is my experience that the strongest motivation to seek assisted suicide or active euthanasia for oneself is a sadly well-founded fear that neither medical practice nor the law strongly enough favors discontinuing excessively burdensome medical treatment (so judged by each patient, one by one). A substantial minority of the medical profession does not recognize in practice the harmful impact of patently futile cure-oriented treatment of the dying. What those who fear uncontrolled use of medical technology are demanding, therefore, is authorization for a preemptive response to the dangers of cure-fanaticism and technologically elegant but humanly futile dike-plugging in modern medical practice.

At the same time, the hospice approach to a dying person is denied standing as a legitimate alternative medical treatment. This is apparent even in the language of many court cases allowing the discontinuing of unwanted or futile treatment when by silence it is supposed that the alternative to so-called life-sustaining treatment is simply no treatment at all. Hospice medicine includes not only adequate and effective pain control but also, above all, personal communication and response to the dying person's needs. It includes as well the promise not to continue any kind of treatment that merely prolongs inevitable dying. But hospice is still all too often either openly despised or tacitly ignored as "not *real* medicine."

In such proposals [to allow active euthanasia], too, we confront but another manifestation of our growing incapacity to recognize the demands of human solidarity, which can require sacrifice of individual autonomy to protect others from being brutally constrained to kill themselves or to ask others to kill them. As I see it, then, proposals to empower, legally and by moral affirmation, medically assisted suicide and doctor-effected active euthanasia can only lead to further distortion in our cultural inability to come to terms with death and dying. Far from being a reasonable response to legitimate requests for patient autonomy, such measures will make worse our disposition to take refuge from distressing human experience by seeking the deceptively easy technological "quick fix." This will be simply the ultimate triumph of technical virtuosity over humane medicine.

But what I most fear is that such proposals are being made with a kind of insouciance about the violent character of our culture and our society. Already we have returned to the barbarism of the death penalty, and we disguise infliction of death as a benign medical treatment by using "lethal injection." In such proposals if finally accepted, I fear that we shall come face to face with the specter of our deeply hidden acceptance of violence — with psychologically hidden horrors that will take shapes we have not imagined in our worst nightmares.

Ronald Otremba, M.D.

Director, Hospice HealthEast
St. Joseph's Hospital
St. Paul, Minnesota

Is active euthanasia ever morally justified for patients who are terminally ill and who request either orally or through a written directive to have their lives ended? My answer to that question would have to be an unequivocal "no." Active euthanasia is never morally justified. On what basis do I make this decision? First, there is the principle that life itself is intrinsically valuable. This value is independent of one's physical or mental state of health. It is based on the principle that God is the sole creator of life and has sovereign authority over life and death. To some, this principle may seem cruel and unsympathetic, but it is, on the contrary, very respectful of the individual's needs and dignity. No matter what the condition of a person's life, there is still value in it. Value is not predicated on physical, emotional, economic, or social status but by the mere fact that one is human.

. . . Who determines when life becomes burdensome? The individual, the physician, society? What standards would be used if the individual were to choose? They would be totally subjective and relative to whatever circumstances the person found himself in. For one it might be a state of quadriplegia or the loss of a limb; for another it might be terminal illness, for another the loss of a loved one, and for still another, just the fear of being a burden. If active euthanasia were allowed on the basis of life's being unduly burdensome, each of the above circumstances could qualify; each could be considered so burdensome that death would seem a relief.

. . . My obligation as a physician is, first and foremost, to practice within the guidelines of my faith and, second, to practice within the guidelines of my chosen profession. I am dedicated to the care of the total patient: to cure disease when possible, to alleviate pain and suffering as best I'm able, and to respect the dignity of the human person no matter how undignified his or her state of life may be.

Karen Lebacqz, Ph.D.

Professor of Christian Ethics
Pacific School of Religion
Berkeley, California

. . . I think there are circumstances in which active euthanasia is *morally* justifiable. To say it is morally justifiable is not to say that it should become social policy; that is another matter. Moreover, the situation posed here is very limited: circumstances in which patients are terminally ill and have requested that their lives be terminated, along with the further qualification that they are in enduring and intractable pain.

. . . I love life. I want my parents to live forever. I wish my grandmother had not died. I resist my own aging and movement toward death. And yet I am also a Christian. I know that death is not the last word, not the greatest evil. Failure to love, to care, to enact justice, to be in proper relationship — those are greater evils. Death can serve evil or it can serve the values of life. As a way of bringing about death, active euthanasia can serve evil or it can serve the values of life. When it serves the values of life, it can be morally justified.

Stephen Sapp, Ph.D.

Professor of Religion
University of Miami
Coral Gables, Florida

. . . Institutionalizing the practice of active euthanasia will invariably lead to reducing the need for tremendous moral struggle in each instance, for wrestling with the awesome decision to take another human being's life. This reduction can only bode ill for our moral condition.

Our society, basing its view primarily on the fundamental values of Judaism and Christianity, has always forbidden the taking of innocent life and has considered that act one of the most serious, if not the most serious, breaches of morality possible. That one requests to be killed does not eliminate the very sound basis for that prohibition (leaving aside the significant question of whether such a request is genuinely voluntary, for all the reasons well known in the literature on this topic). There are more ways to violate a person than by violating his or her will, and even actions voluntarily consented to can still be wrong. The classic example is of course the voluntary selling of oneself into slavery, which is forbidden precisely because it precludes further exercise of one's autonomy. Certainly being killed, even if one requests it, shuts off even more completely any possibility of further choice.

. . . One group of special interest to me and for whom this issue has particular relevance is the elderly. Of any identifiable group in our society, the elderly are most likely to be seen as the "beneficiaries" of a policy that makes active euthanasia acceptable and readily available. Much has been written about the recent marginalization and devaluation of older people, their loss of meaningful roles and thus a sense of contributing to society, and their rapidly increasing numbers and their proportion in the total population. All these factors have led to calls that the elderly acknowledge their obligation to "get out of the way" so that younger, more productive people can have access to the resources the elderly are currently using. It is impossible to analyze the shortcomings of this position here, but we can hardly deny that our society's current treatment of older people destroys the self-worth of many and leads to their considerable guilt about merely continuing to be alive (witness the elderly suicide rate). Thus the truly voluntary nature of active euthanasia among the elderly seems hard to guarantee. The possibility of ending their lives sooner, with moral and legal sanction, may well lead to a form of subtle coercion, with the implication that the responsible course to pursue is to utilize this option. Advocates of active euthanasia, who see it as an expansion of individual autonomy, perhaps need to give more thought to this concern.

For some time we have been trying to solve the problem of aging by removing the aged from view. Now it appears we want to resolve the problem of suffering by removing the sufferer altogether. Is it mere coincidence that the two efforts are coming together in the push for active euthanasia of the terminally ill, given that such illnesses occur in the elderly in significantly higher proportion? The genuinely human (and certainly Christian) solution to the meaninglessness and isolation of old age as well as that associated with terminal illness — is not to kill the old or ill person but to eliminate the meaninglessness and isolation through compassion and true caring. Having the option of ending a terminally ill person's life early — along with the possibly implicit coercion to do so — will not improve the quality of care given to such patients and may in fact lead to even worse care for those who do not choose euthanasia. The problems health care professionals have in dealing with dying patients are well documented. How will they feel when the patient could have "already checked out" but has chosen not to? Similarly, it troubles me that a society that does such a poor job of providing a minimum of decent health care for many of its members, and often offers only impersonal, noncompassionate care for those who receive any at all, can be seriously considering making available a vehicle for eliminating many of the people who most need genuine care and treatment.

Robert Moss, M.D.

Director of Geriatrics
Department of Family Practice
Lutheran General Hospital
Park Ridge, Illinois

During the past 25 years, significant advances in medicine have enabled physicians to extend life beyond limits previously thought possible. For many the introduction of these newer technologies offers the hope of a prolonged and productive life, while for the less fortunate they appear to do nothing more than prolong the process of dying and human suffering. In our attempts to add quality years to our lives, the distinction between what is living and what is dying has become more artificial. We have redefined what it means to die by turning it into an unnatural process, often obtainable through the withdrawal of life-supporting therapies. And it is partially because of this transformation of death that we have been forced to look at ourselves, challenge our own ethics, and redefine our moral priorities.

The past decade in medical ethics and case law has been dominated, in a way, by our attempts to recapture the essence and meaning of this so-called good death. Policies on the withholding and withdrawal of life-sustaining therapies have afforded some individuals the opportunity to "die with dignity," but for an increasingly demanding public these policies have not gone far enough.

. . . It is clear that active voluntary euthanasia takes us to the limits of both patient and physician autonomy and must be approached with great caution and respect. We cannot, however, ignore our responsibility to address growing public sentiment and the unmet needs of suffering patients who are the victims of our own interventions. To do so could further erode the trust that patients have in their doctors and even promote the proliferation of less scrupulous physicians who would be willing to perform euthanasia more indiscriminately. As physicians, we must make greater efforts to comfort and alleviate the pain and suffering of dying patients and insure [sic] that they are not abandoned. Only under exceptional circumstances, when the needs of our patients cannot be met otherwise, and in accordance with the guidelines above, should active voluntary euthanasia be considered an alternative from a public policy perspective.

Don C. Shaw

President, Hemlock of Illinois

. . . Ralph Mero, president of the Hemlock Society of Washington State and prime activist in the campaign there, has stated the issue clearly:

Death with dignity simply means the opportunity to choose a death without pain, without fear, and without physical, mental or spiritual degradation. It is the right to retain control of the final stage of one's existence, and to affirm even to the last one's self-respect. Such a choice must be without coercion, freely chosen out of one's own integrity as consistent with a dignified life. Now is the time to let a dying person determine the final step of one's own life journey, and be allowed to say goodbye before the process of dying has stolen away the quality of life, leaving behind only the empty shell of what was once a beautiful human being.

Obviously, there are those who oppose both passive and active euthanasia and for a variety of reasons. Some are opposed on philosophical and religious grounds. Their beliefs are fully respected by the proponents of euthanasia. They are most often Roman Catholic and fundamentalist Christians. Other opponents contend that legalizing euthanasia will open the door to abuse and lead to the killing of the handicapped, the elderly, and others who are a burden to society. Our response to this latter group is that every good known to humankind can be abused. It is our responsibility as a civilized society to see to it that such abuses are not permitted.

Albert R. Jonsen

Professor of Ethics in Medicine
Department of Medical History and Ethics
School of Medicine
University of Washington
Seattle, Washington

By drawing killing out of the realm of private transactions, such as the personal vendetta and the private revenge, into the harsh light of law, society attempts to restrain the inevitable tendency for abuse by forcing anyone who kills to defend the action publicly. The ancient commentators on revenge often saw little wrong in revenge itself: it was frequently seen as justified. Rather they were concerned that the anger inherent in revenge would carry the justifiable practice much further to the great detriment of a peaceful society. So today, even when a particular act of euthanasia might be morally justifiable (and hypothetically one might be), the force of the compassion that motivates it might also drive our acceptance of the practice of killing those in pain and distress beyond the careful limits we may set around it . . . In my view, the reintroduction of private killing is a step backward in our struggle to build a moral culture.

It is not enough to assert that, unlike the anger and vengeance that motivated the vendetta, this new form of private killing rests on an inherently moral motive, compassion. Compassion is indeed a moral motive, but it is not in itself a justification for all behavior. Compassion for the poor may inspire Robin Hoods, and yet society must repudiate private redistributions of property. Compassion for the oppressed may inspire terrorism, yet even those who espouse the cause of the oppressed may find terrorism an unacceptable instrument of liberation. It has been, and in some places, still is, thought to be an act of compassion to put a heretic or blasphemer out of the misery of their ignorance. Compassion, then, while noble, is not itself sufficient to render an action morally acceptable.

. . . It is clear that Initiative 119 [*] wishes to reserve this new medical procedure for the voluntary, competent patients. It is less clear that, once established, patients will be free of coercion to request it. The coercion may be subtle and unspoken, but families distressed by their relative's illness may hint at it as a way out. Patients may themselves feel that they are undue burdens on their families and so should remove themselves. It is a voluntary option that has coercive possibilities. The same may be true for the physician. While Initiative 119 does not require a physician to participate in aid in dying, it is possible that many reluctant physicians will come under pressure from patients and families to do so. It would be particularly tragic for a physician who has moral scruples about aid in dying to find himself or herself petitioned by a long-time, devoted patient and forced to refuse this last request.

It seems to me that the two considerations above make up the "slippery slope" that we worry about with proposals like Initiative 119. In itself, it attempts to make legal a very limited, carefully restricted activity. However, the limited activity is so limited that it fails to meet the needs of the people who support it. If they want relief from deterioration and future pain, 119 cannot give them that — it can only provide relief after these have come. Thus, there may be pressure to make the legalized action more liberal, allowing people to choose aid in dying before deterioration and pain appear. This is a first slip down the slope. Initiative 119 applies only to the competent, voluntary patient, but much of the pain and distress of dying comes to the incompetent and to their families. 119 cannot help them. Thus there may be an inclination to extend the scope of the legalized action to those who "would certainly have wished it, had they been able." Of course, these pressures and inclinations cannot be certainly predicted, and perhaps, if they do appear, can be resisted, but the "slippery slope" argument suggests that, given the nature of the problem, they are not improbable and that they will be difficult to resist.

---

*Initiative 119 was a proposal to legalize physician aid-in-dying that was turned down by Washington State voters in 1991. See Chapter V.

Albert W. Alschuler

Wilson-Dickinson Professor
University of Chicago Law School
Chicago, Illinois

We dread these decisions. When should we allow death to come even though we might, through ordinary or extraordinary action, preserve life? When, if ever, should we act affirmatively to bring life to an end? Rather than confront these issues, we may conclude that we should do what we can to preserve life and then leave it to fate or to God to decide.

This view might have been plausible when our medical efforts in extremis were gallant, quick, and unsuccessful — in particular, when we were unable to maintain "vegetative" patients for extended periods. Almost no one takes this view today. All of us seem agreed that we need not — and should not — take extraordinary measures to preserve life in all circumstances. Justice Scalia spoke in this year's *Cruzan* decision of "the constantly increasing power of science to keep the human body alive for longer than any reasonable person would want to inhabit it," and our best judgment is that a majority of the two million deaths that occur each year in the U.S. now follow a decision to forgo some life-sustaining treatment. "A time to be born, and a time to die." There comes a time to let go of life, to *choose* to let it pass.

This recognition of responsibility brings a rush of other decisions. To invoke the familiar metaphor, we find ourselves on a slippery slope. Once we have decided to let go of life, what sorts of support and treatment may we appropriately discontinue?

. . . The reasons suggested for distinguishing the withdrawal of a feeding tube from the withdrawal of other forms of treatment may seem strained; and once we allow the withdrawal of nutrition and hydration, it becomes almost equally difficult to maintain the next line. The next line, moreover, is the one upon which we have insisted most vigorously — the line between permitting a person to die, on the one hand, and killing or aiding suicide, on the other.

What is to be said in favor of a patient's slow, certain death by starvation when an infection could bring the same result more quickly and perhaps with less pain? What is to be said in favor of preserving the old line between . . . action and inaction?

. . . In this situation, the strongest argument for the action-inaction line is that, despite its indeterminacy and imprecision, we need it. We have no other line, and without it we sense no limits. Shall we impose an affirmative obligation to reach out to save a drowning child? What, then, of the mother who refuses to approve the donation of some of her child's bone marrow to save the life of the child's half-brother? What of the physician who refuses to fly to Calcutta (or to walk across the hall) to perform a lifesaving operation that she alone can perform? What of the person who purchases a stereo rather than send $1,000 to the famine relief fund?

Even as we recognize the artificiality of the action-inaction line, we hesitate to impose new affirmative duties. Similarly, we hesitate to authorize traditionally prohibited acts that, we realize, cannot be neatly distinguished from permissible omissions. We may forbid assisted suicide and active euthanasia while recognizing that the alternative is likely to be the withdrawal of medication or nutrition — and a death that may be equally chosen but that will be accompanied by greater suffering. We have no very strong conviction that the line to which we cling is the correct one; but once we cross this line, where will we stop? Where does the slippery slope hit bottom?

. . . In a sense, it is every person for herself. In an equally significant sense, however, it is all of us together. We must struggle as a community to resolve these issues, recognizing that our own answers are fallible and that others' are worthy of respect. In *Cruzan*, the Supreme Court wisely declined to take these issues from us.

I doubt that Providence works in quite this way, but it is almost as though God had led us to face these issues. God once permitted us to believe that none of these decisions were ours to make. It is much more difficult to take that view today.

English legal history offers something of a parallel. Eight hundred years ago, people believed that judging criminal guilt was too terrifying a task to entrust to mere mortals. These people sought the judgment of God through forms of trial like the ordeal, which left the outcome largely to fate or chance. In 1215, the Fourth Lateran Council under Pope Innocent III forbade the ordeal; and for a century thereafter, our English forbears struggled uncomfortably toward an alternative. They even-tually settled on trial by jury, a somewhat less mystical institution. As the Fourth Lateran Council recognized, God does not judge criminal guilt, at least not for us. After blessing us with reason and the power to choose, God may have given us responsibility for other awesome decisions as well — choices that we would rather leave to God but cannot.

We speak of rationing resources and think of scarcity. Our new responsibility for choice has arisen, however, not because the resource of life has grown rarer but because it has grown more plentiful. A gift for which we can only be grateful has brought with it a new obligation to confront a very old issue.

APPENDIX I

THE NATIONAL HEMLOCK SOCIETY

GENERAL PRINCIPLES

1. HEMLOCK seeks to provide a climate of public opinion which is tolerant of the rights of people who are terminally ill to end their own lives in a planned manner.

2. HEMLOCK does not encourage suicide for any primary emotional, traumatic, or financial reasons in the absence of terminal illness. It approves of the work of those involved in suicide prevention.

3. The final decision to terminate life is ultimately one's own. HEMLOCK believes this action, and most of all its timing, to be an extremely personal decision, wherever possible taken in concert with family, close friends, and personal physician.

4. HEMLOCK speaks only to those people who have mutual sympathy with its goals. Views contrary to its own which are held by other religions and philosophies are respected.

OBJECTIVES

• Continuing a dialogue to raise public consciousness of active voluntary euthanasia through the news media, public meetings and with the medical and legal professions, and others.

• Supporting the right of a dying person to lawfully request a physician to help them die (*The Death With Dignity Act*).

• Publishing informational materials to help members decide the manner and means of their death. *Let Me Die Before I Wake* and *Final Exit* are the only guides to self deliverance for the dying in the USA.

• Issuing a quarterly newsletter to members providing up-to-date information on issues of death and dying.

• Providing members upon joining a free Living Will and Durable Power of Attorney for Health Care, plus a medical treatment card for purse or wallet.

APPENDIX II

NATIONAL RIGHT TO LIFE COMMITTEE, INC.

Official Version

RESOLUTION ON EUTHANASIA

WHEREAS, incompetent patients of all ages are increasingly being deprived of appropriate medical care and treatment, nutrition, and hydration;

WHEREAS, certain courts have allowed third parties to refuse nutrition and hydration to incompetent patients whose death is not imminent, and who are not in the final stages of terminal illness;

WHEREAS, the denial of appropriate medical treatment, nutrition, and hydration for incompetent patients is being done for the sole purpose of hastening their death;

WHEREAS, competent patients have a right to consent to, request, or refuse medical treatment and care, and incompetent patients have the right to receive medical treatment and care;

WHEREAS, certain states have adopted legislation which facilitates the denial of medical treatment nutrition, and hydration;

WHEREAS, current law does not provide a sufficient mechanism for a competent person to direct that he/she will receive medical treatment, care, nutrition, and hydration when incompetent;

WHEREAS, disabled persons have been intentionally killed or encouraged, coerced, and/or assisted to commit suicide; therefore be it

RESOLVED: that the National Right to Life Committee, Inc., urges the adoption of legislation to protect the right of competent and incompetent persons to receive medical treatment and care, nutrition, and hydration; be it further

RESOLVED: that such protective legislation must incorporate principles and policies including, but not limited to, the following:

(1) With limited exceptions, competent persons have the right to consent to, request, or refuse medical treatment.

(2) A competent person's decision to request or refuse medical treatment should be operative after that person becomes incompetent.

(3) Nutrition, hydration, warmth, and nursing care are not forms of medical treatment and must be provided to patients.

(4) Adequate safeguards must be provided to ensure that a person's directive to refuse medical treatment is not a result of duress, coercion, or undue influence, and has been made after receiving sufficient information in order to give full and informed consent.

(5) A third-party decision-maker must be subject to appropriate standards and procedures that recognize the limited power of a third party to refuse appropriate medical treatment for an incompetent patient.

(6) Appropriate medical treatment shall not be withheld or withdrawn from an incompetent patient who is not in the final stage of a terminal illness or injury.

(7) Incompetent patients who while competent, had not made a medical treatment directive should receive appropriate medical treatment.

(8) No person should be permitted to cause or assist the death of another person through mercy-killing or assisted suicide.

and be it further

RESOLVED: that the National Right to Life Committee, Inc., urges opposition to the "Uniform Rights of the Terminally Ill Act."

Adopted by the National Right to Life Committee Board of Directors
September 29, 1985.

APPENDIX III

RESOLUTION
APPROVED BY THE DELEGATES
OF THE NATIONAL HOSPICE ORGANIZATION
ANNUAL MEETING — NOVEMBER 8,1990
DETROIT, MICHIGAN

WHEREAS, The National Hospice Organization is considered the voice of the nation's hospice community; and,

WHEREAS, The National Hospice Organization is often requested to provide comment to the Congress, the Administration, the Courts, the media and the general public: and,

WHEREAS, The National Hospice Organization is on record supporting a patient's right to palliative care, a patient's right to refuse unwanted medical intervention including the provision of artificially supplied hydration and nutrition; and,

WHEREAS, There has been increased public attention and focus on the issue of voluntary euthanasia and assisted suicide; and,

WHEREAS, We believe hospice care is an alternative to voluntary euthanasia and assisted suicide; therefore,

RESOLVED, That the National Hospice Organization reaffirms the hospice philosophy that hospice care neither hastens nor postpones death.

RESOLVED, That the National Hospice Organization rejects the practice of voluntary euthanasia and assisted suicide in the care of the terminally ill.

APPENDIX IV

ADVANCE DIRECTIVES

LIVING WILL

TO MY FAMILY, MY PHYSICIAN, AND OTHERS CONCERNED FOR MY WELFARE: If the time comes when I cease to be able to participate in decisions for my own future, let this statement stand as evidence of my wishes: If there is no reasonable expectation of my recovery from physical or mental disability, I _____ request that I be allowed to die and not be kept alive by either artificial means or heroic measures. I fear death less than I fear the indignity of deterioration, dependence or hopeless pain. Accordingly, I request that medication be mercifully administered to me for terminal suffering even if it hastens the time of death. This request is made after careful reflection and consideration. I hope that those who care for me will feel morally bound to follow its mandate. I recognize that it places a heavy burden of responsibility upon you, and it is with the intention of sharing that responsibility and of alleviating or mitigating any feelings of guilt or indecision on your part that I make this statement.

_____

Date:_____

ADVANCE DIRECTIVE TO MY PHYSICIANS, HEALTH CARE PROVIDERS, AND FAMILY

I, _____, being of sound mind, willfully and voluntarily execute this directive to express my wish concerning medical treatment of I am no longer able to make decisions concerning such treatment, have an incurable condition caused by injury, disease or illness that will cause me to die within a relatively short time and the use of life-sustaining procedures will serve only to prolong artificially the process of dying. In these circumstances, I direct my attending physician to withhold or withdraw all life-sustaining procedures, including artificial feeding, not necessary to my comfort or to alleviate pain, and to allow me to die naturally. I ask that my attending physician and those concerned with my care honor this directive as an exercise under the circumstances described of my constitutional and common law right to refuse life-sustaining medical treatment. I am mentally and emotionally competent to understand the meaning of this directive.

Dated:
Signed:
Witness:
Witness:

HEALTH CARE PROXY APPOINTMENT

In the event that I am no longer able to make decisions concerning my medical treatment, I hereby appoint _____ as my health care proxy to decide whether life-sustaining medical treatment, including artificial feeding, should be withheld or withdrawn. The proxy I have named has been chosen by me as familiar with my beliefs, wishes and attitudes and I direct my attending physician and health care providers to follow this proxy's instructions. If the person whom I have appointed proxy is mentally or physically unable to make medical decisions, I appoint _____ as my health care proxy.

Dated:
Signed:
Witness:
Witness:

DURABLE POWER OF ATTORNEY

KNOW ALL MEN that I, _____residing at _____,do hereby appoint_____, residing at _____, my true and lawful attorney, and in my name and stead and for my benefit, to have full power and authority to execute and perform acts and do things of every kind and nature that should be executed, performed or done in the management or my personal, life or business affairs, or that, in the opinion of my said attorney, should be executed, performed or done, as fully as I might execute, perform or do them if personally present; and I hereby ratify and confirm all that my said attorney shall execute, perform or do, or cause to be executed, performed or done, by virtue thereof.

This power includes the power and authority to make decisions concerning my medical treatment if I am unable to do so and to direct my attending physician.

WILL TO LIVE

GENERAL PRESUMPTION FOR LIFE

I direct my health care provider(s) and health care agent to make health care decisions consistent with my general desire for the use of medical treatment that would preserve my life, as well as for the use of medical treatment that can cure, improve, or reduce or prevent deterioration in, any physical or mental condition.

Food and water are not medical treatment, but basic necessities. I direct my health care provider(s) and health care agent to provide me with food and fluids orally, intravenously, by tube, or by other means to the full extent necessary both to preserve my life and to assure me the optimal health possible.

I direct that medication to alleviate my pain be provided, as long as the medication is not used in order to cause my death.

I direct that the following be provided:

· the administration of medication;

· cardiopulmonary resuscitation (CPR); and

· the performance of all other medical procedures, techniques, and technologies, including surgery — all to the full extent necessary to correct, reverse, or alleviate life-threatening or health - impairing conditions, or complications arising from those conditions.

I also direct that I be provided basic nursing care and procedures to provide comfort care.

I reject, however, any treatments that use an unborn or newborn child, or any tissue or organ of an unborn or newborn child, who has been subject to an induced abortion. This rejection does not apply to the use of tissues or organs obtained in the course of the removal of an ectopic pregnancy.

I also reject any treatments that use an organ or tissue of another person obtained in a manner that causes, contributes to, or hastens that person's death.

The instructions in this document are intended to be followed even if suicide is alleged to be attempted at some point after it is signed.

I request and direct that medical treatment and care be provided to me to preserve my life without discrimination based on my age or physical or mental disability or the "quality" of my life. I reject any action or omission that is intended to cause or hasten my death.

I direct my health care provider(s) and health care agent to follow the above policy, even if I am judged to be incompetent.

During the time I am incompetent, my agent, as named below, is authorized to make medical decisions on my behalf, consistent with the above policy, after consultation with my health care provider(s), utilizing the most current diagnoses and/or prognosis of my medical condition, in the following situations with the written special conditions.

WHEN MY DEATH IS IMMINENT

A. If I have an incurable terminal illness or injury, and I will die imminently — meaning that a reasonably prudent physician, knowledgeable about the case and the treatment possibilities with respect to the medical conditions involved, would judge that I will live only a week or less even if lifesaving treatment or care is provided to me — the following may be withheld or withdrawn:

WHEN I AM TERMINALLY ILL

B. <u>Final Stage of Terminal Condition</u>. If I have an incurable terminal illness or injury and even though death is not imminent I am in the final stage of that terminal condition — meaning that a reasonably prudent physician, knowledgeable about the case and the treatment possibilities with respect to the medical conditions involved, would judge that I will live only three months or less, even if lifesaving treatment or care is provided to me — the following may be withheld or withdrawn:

IF I AM PREGNANT

D. <u>Special Instructions for Pregnancy</u>. If I am pregnant, I direct my health care provider(s) and health care agent to use all lifesaving procedures for myself with none of the above special conditions applying if there is a chance that prolonging my life might allow my child to be born alive. I also direct that lifesaving procedures be used even if I am legally determined to be brain dead if there is a chance that doing so might allow my child to be born alive. Except as I specify by writing my signature in the box below, no one is authorized to consent to any procedure for me that would result in the death of my unborn child.

If I am pregnant, and I am not in the final stage of a terminal condition as defined above, medical procedures required to prevent my death are authorized even if they may result in the death of my unborn child provided every possible effort is made to preserve both my life and the life of my unborn child.

Notice: *Although this is the content of the Will to Live, it is not itself a legal document. Different forms exist for each state. Do not attempt to sign this version. Instead, to obtain the Will to Live valid in your state, send a self-addressed, stamped business (9 1/2" wide) envelope to Will to Live Project, Suite 500, 419 Seventh St, N.W. Washington, DC 20004*

APPENDIX V

ORGANIZATIONS CONCERNED WITH THE RIGHT TO DIE

American Association of Retired Persons
(AARP)
601 E Street NW
Washington, D.C. 20049
(202) 434-2277

Choice in Dying
200 Varick Street
New York, NY 10014
(212) 366-5540

Hastings Center
255 Elm Road
Briarcliff Manor, NY 10510
(914) 762-8500

National Conference of Catholic Bishops
(NCCB)
Committee for Pro-Life Activities
1312 Massachusetts Ave., NW
Washington, D.C. 20005
(202) 659-6673

National Hemlock Society
P.O. Box 11830
Eugene, OR 97440
(503) 342-5748

National Hospice Organization (NHO)
1901 North Moore Street
Suite 901
Arlington, VA 22209
(703) 243-5900

Older Women's League (OWL)
730 Eleventh Street NW
Suite 300
Washington, D.C. 20001
(202) 783-6686

Park Ridge Center
676 North St. Clair Street
Suite 450
Chicago, IL 60611
(312) 266-2222